SHEET METAL
SHAPING
TOOLS, SKILLS, AND PROJECTS

By Ed Barr

motorbooks

Quarto.com

First published in 2019 by Motorbooks, an imprint of The Quarto Group,
100 Cummings Center, Suite 265D, Beverly, MA 01915 USA.
T (978) 282-9590 F (978) 283-2742

Motorbooks titles are also available at discount for retail, wholesale, promotional,
and bulk purchase. For details, contact the Special Sales Manager by email at
specialsales@quarto.com or by mail at The Quarto Group, Attn: Special Sales
Manager, 100 Cummings Center, Suite 265D, Beverly, MA 01915 USA.

ISBN: 978-0-7603-6574-8

Library of Congress Control Number: 2018967547

Acquisitions Editor: Dennis Pernu
Project Manager: Alyssa Bluhm
Art Director: Cindy Samargia Laun
Layout: Danielle Smith-Boldt

Contents

Introduction

My favorite color is bare metal. I love the tactile sensations that come with working with metal, and I adore the sweet bouquet it gives off when it's cut. Most of all, I love the challenge of turning flat sheets of steel and aluminum into car and motorcycle shapes. If you are exploring metal shaping for the first time, you are in for a great adventure. Offering some guidance via this book will be my privilege. If you've shaped metal before, your fire has most likely already been lit. I will gladly pour on more fuel. Take heart in knowing that you are not the only person who ruminates over sheet metal problems when you are supposed to be sleeping.

If you are new to metal shaping or your past experience with this discipline has been frustrating, do not worry. I have included a series of exercises designed to acquaint readers with the fundamentals of this challenging craft. As with drawing or playing a musical instrument, each of us has a different aptitude for performing this activity. Nevertheless, I am convinced that anyone can learn enough to be able to realize some success working with sheet metal.

As you read through this book, I hope you will be pleasantly surprised by how closely the do-it-yourself exercises mirror problems you have struggled with in the past or that you know lie ahead on your project vehicle. I also hope that you find my explanations and proposed solutions clear and easy to follow. As you work through the exercises, think about the results in light of what you have read. What could be improved? Repeat each exercise until you have mastered the concepts. Repetition, coupled with thoughtful analysis, will keep you moving forward. One day you will look back with surprise and satisfaction at what you have accomplished and what you have figured out on your own. You may even find yourself lying awake at night, ruminating on your next sheet metal challenge.

Chapter 1
The Peasant's Toolkit

One afternoon while waiting in line to pay for medications at the vet's office, I searched the internet to see what car I could buy for the amount I spend on dog meds each month. I burst out laughing when I saw a used Maserati. It was even red. Of course, I'd rather have giant, aged mastiffs lumbering around the house than a Maserati. The latter doesn't salivate or leave the house smelling like moldy Parmesan cheese (traits you just can't buy), but living costs money, usually a lot of it. If you, like me, are interested in making the most of every penny, here are some tips to help you have fun shaping metal as inexpensively as possible.

In my previous book, *Professional Sheet Metal Fabrication* (2013), I discussed tool choices for metal shaping and automotive restoration. At home, my interests lean much more toward shaping and coachbuilding than pure restoration, so I have refined my selection to squeeze more metal-shaping exhilaration into each day. Moreover, while the exhilaration can spill over into both sides of a two-car garage, the tools that make it happen need to be collapsible into one side of our home garage. My wife has sacrificed too much to indulge my appetite for old cars to park out in the cold. I've built most of an aluminum sports car body using a paltry

Don't let a dearth of space and tools keep you from realizing your sheet metal dreams. Make the most of what you have. You will be surprised by what you can achieve.

The two tools I use the most are a stump and a wheeling machine. I have included a chapter on building your own wheeling machine if you desire, so I will not elaborate on that tool here, other than to say it is a great value for the money and a good choice for the home enthusiast because it is quiet, doesn't require power, and does not have to take up a lot of space.

THE STUMP

Although I have a freestanding stump that I got for free, a smaller block of wood could be substituted. In the classroom, I use large rectangular blocks made from tree trunks that can be easily moved around. Wood blocks are also more versatile than a freestanding stump because you have more surfaces to modify. The freestanding stump I use at home has many purposes, not all of them strictly related to shaping. It serves as a welding table, worktable, lunch table, and iPhone stand. Dean Martin's voice sounds even more mellifluous when it is projected out of a hollow in a metal-shaping stump.

If, like me, you have almost no workbench space, a freestanding stump might be a better choice than a block of wood that sits on a table. I built a base on the bottom of my stump to keep the top surface stable and level. I also mounted two casters vertically on the back and a handle on the front. I simply tilt the stump back on the casters to roll it about the shop.

In my experience, large blocks of wood tend to dry out over time. When they do, I turn them into firewood and replace them. Because my freestanding stump is a piece of furniture, however, I have gone to the trouble to wrap a steel strap around it that can be cinched tighter with a turnbuckle. In a stroke of environmentally friendly zeal, I recycled a used serpentine belt from my wife's minivan for use as a hammer retention strap.

TUCKING TOOL

The next tool I frequently use in my home shop is a tucking tool for shrinking metal. I discussed the tucking tool at length in *Professional Sheet Metal Fabrication*, but I neglected to give directions for making one. Take two of the longest grade eight bolts you can find and cut their heads off. If you have access to a lathe, taper the shafts. If you do not have access to a lathe, spin each bolt in a drill press or drill while you apply a handheld grinding tool to the shaft of each bolt. Tapering the bolts removes the threads so they won't mark the metal and optimizes the tool shape for creating wrinkles or tucks along the edge of a piece of sheet metal. Make the small ends of each tong about as big as the diameter of your pinky

A wooden block will perform most of the shaping duties of a stump, but a freestanding stump might still make sense if you can use it for other purposes, such as a welding table or breakdance platform. The casters mounted vertically on the back and the handle on the front make this one easy to move.

assortment of tools, so I know it can be done, and not because I'm a metal genius. On the contrary, my gifts are enthusiasm and perseverance. Fortunately, those gifts have been enough to keep me gainfully employed. There will always be haters who raise their noses at you for what they perceive you to lack. Ignore them. If you are covered in mastiff slobber and reek like moldy Parmesan, as I do, then they won't come close enough to be critical.

Ironically, being completely spoiled by an embarrassment of riches at my workplace—two power hammers, a Pullmax machine, five wheeling machines, sundry other delights—has made me absolutely comfortable with few tools at home. Using aluminum as my chosen material helps. Shaping aluminum with hand tools is much easier than shaping steel, but I would still use the same selection of tools at home if I were working with steel.

A tucking tool is an indispensable part of any peasant's metal-shrinking toolkit. This selection illustrates several designs. The horizontal handles are more useful for hanging the tools on a tool board than for twisting metal.

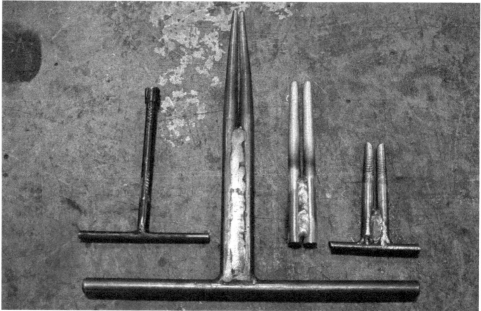

To make a tucking tool, grind or cut the threads off two 6-inch grade-eight bolts, preferably at a taper, and weld them together with enough of a gap between to fit sheet metal.

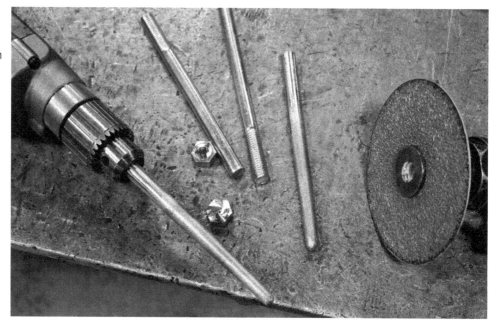

finger for your first tucking tool. This size will be sturdy enough for annealed 14-gauge aluminum or 20-gauge steel. You will not be tuck shrinking anything heavier than that unless you are a superhero, and in that case you'll be too busy to shape any metal anyway. When you come across an area that needs to be shrunk but the panel will not fit in your Lancaster-style shrinker, a tuck might save the day. If the access is so restricted that the tucking tool will not fit, use a pair of 90-degree pliers to fold a tuck into a panel's edge.

WIRE-EDGING TOOL

Another homemade tool that sees frequent use in my shop is a wire-edging tool. I use this for wrapping sheet metal around a wire for stiffness, as was commonly done on antique cars. My tool was previously either a dentist's tongs from the 1800s or a farrier's tool, maybe both. I illustrated the first iteration of this tool in *Professional Sheet Metal Fabrication* and described its use in detail. Since then, I have modified the tool for better performance. I enlarged the bottom jaw to make it less likely to leave marks on the sheet metal receiving the wire.

To make a wire-wrapped edge with this tool, thin the metal on the bend line with the bead roller. The width of the metal beyond the bend line should be equal to three times the diameter of the wire you intend to wrap. With hand tools or a wheeling machine, bend the metal over into a U shape on the side that will receive the wire. Make one pass down the panel edge with the wiring tool to trap the wire. The wide bottom jaw rests against the exterior flat side of the panel. The narrow jaw squeezes the U shape around the wire. Rotate the metal slightly in the tool to make sure the squeezing happens in the right place, and make a second pass down the edge to crimp the metal tightly around the wire. Cleanly wrapping a wire is all about squeezing the unsupported metal in the right place. Never grip the metal around the wire tightly and attempt to rotate the tool. Rotating the tool scratches the metal. Clamping with the tool does not.

SPOON

A spoon deserves a place in any peasant's toolkit because it is handy for stretching out welds and planishing (flattening) surfaces. Although I sometimes use it for sorting through food other people have foolishly and prematurely thrown away, in sheet metal the spoon spreads out the force of your blows and does not leave marks. If you lack a power hammer, wheeling machine, or planishing hammer for finishing shaped panels, a spoon is certainly the best hand tool for that job.

Although you can purchase spoons, I have to wonder how some of them came into being; their design is bizarre. The angle of the striking face is sometimes nonsensical and the balance bad, or the face is covered with sharp teeth that mark the metal. Nowadays, a person seldom has a chance to hold a specialized tool like this before buying. Because shipping an online order costs about as much as the tool, most of us are not likely to return such a purchase. Instead, we use it anyway and feel bitter about it every time we do.

Life is too short and car time is too valuable to put oneself through needless suffering. If you are an old-car enthusiast, you probably have countless sets of used leaf springs that could be called into service. Old files are serviceable too, as long as the file has enough mass to accomplish some work, but you should expect to spend some time grinding the teeth off the striking surface of a spoon made from the file. Even if you have a spoon, consider making one like that demonstrated here. You may become aware of characteristics you prefer. Through trial and error, I have determined that

If you anticipate wrapping wire into the edges of panels, make your own wire-wrapping tool from a pair of nippers. One tool can wrap more than one size of wire.

I like a spoon that balances in the middle and has a fairly flat striking surface. I hold this type of spoon with my index finger falling over the bend in the middle. The combination of this spoon and this grip transmit surface information to your brain as if by telepathy.

At McPherson College, our metals lab has one Porter-Ferguson spoon with a 2-inch convex striking surface that I like for hitting concave surfaces, though I usually try to avoid putting welds in such places because they are harder to finish out. Thus, you will find yourself more often planishing welds on flat or convex surfaces where a flatter spoon provides a larger contact patch.

For a second spoon, copy the spoon demonstrated here, but grind the flat face to a 2-inch radius.

Having personally never thrown away a piece of metal, I found a good spoon candidate for this demonstration on the first shelf I explored. I chose an old leaf spring about 2¼ inches wide and ¼ inch thick. If I had wanted a spoon for prying, I could have used the end of the leaf as I found it; the tip tapered out to about ¹⁄₁₆ inch thick. Because I wanted a slapping spoon, however, I backed off about an inch from the end and cut a 15-inch section of the leaf with a plasma cutter. A plasma cutter is the best

A slapping spoon is an inexpensive but effective tool for planishing welds, smoothing surfaces, and prying unmentionable things from the floor of a house inhabited by mastiffs. I like a spoon like this, which balances between the handle and the contact patch.

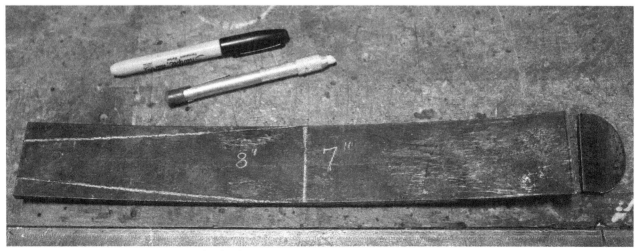

I drew out my spoon blank on a 15-inch length of leaf spring and tapered one end for a handle.

I bent my spoon blank twice: first at 45 degrees, then back again at 35 degrees 2¼ inches behind the first bend. The shallower second bend helps your hand clear the work surface or a hot griddle. You are going to like this spoon so much that you will certainly find other ways to incorporate it into daily life.

tool for quickly cutting out a spoon blank because it does not heat up the metal very much. My next choice would be a cutoff wheel. My last choice would be an oxyacetylene cutting torch. Depending on how much you needed to trim your spring, the oxyacetylene torch might come close to annealing the piece and removing the temper. Steel can, of course, be re-tempered by heating it red-hot, quenching it, and then reheating it to a straw color before quenching again, but that is more work. The telepathic quality of the spring is enhanced by its springiness, so strive to retain this as much as possible.

I left my blank a little longer than necessary to enable me to trim it as needed for balancing. I drew a taper onto the 8-inch end with a piece of soapstone so that the extreme end of the handle was 1 inch wide. After grinding the edges of the blank smooth, I inserted the 7-inch end of the spring in a vise, quickly heated

it dull red along the bend line with a large welding tip, and bent it 45 degrees from its position at rest. I removed the spring from the vise and allowed the piece to cool. Using the same technique as before, I installed a 35-degree bend 2¼ inches behind the first bend. Although a 45-degree bend would have made the handle parallel to the contact surface, the lesser bend provides more hand clearance for optimum spanking action. Whatever your proclivities outside the workshop, you are going to like using this spoon.

Using the first bend in the contact side of the spoon as my fulcrum, I determined that the handle end of the spoon was a little heavier than the work end. I lopped about ¾ inch off the end of the handle and ground it until the spoon balanced on the first bend. I finished the spoon by cleaning up the work surfaces and edges with a belt sander. The spoon is now ready for years of metal-shaping enjoyment.

Fellow peasants will recognize the world's least expensive bead roller. Although it certainly has its limitations, adding a sturdy stand and bolstering the main body make it sturdier. Mine bolts to anchors set in the floor so I can roll it out of the way when a minivan full of cold groceries needs the garage.

OTHER USEFUL TOOLS

I'll be the first to admit that a bead roller cannot match the awesome power of the 2,000-pound Pullmax machine I have access to at work. The Pullmax is easily my favorite Swedish-made pleasure-inducing appliance. Nevertheless, for the cost of eating out with a family of four, you can acquire something that will put joggles and a few beads in your projects at home. Come up with an excuse for a "healthy" evening of fasting, and you'll free up some extra funds for a purchase. Each year new products give you more options for spending what you can afford, sometimes on features you may not need.

Although not essential for everyone, if you plan to build a wood buck, a Kreg pocket-screw jig will earn its keep in the first hour of work. Intended for folks who want to build shelves with concealed fasteners quickly, the Kreg jig is a huge help for buck building because it allows you to affix stations in line with each other instantly and eliminates the need for predrilling holes to prevent splitting. Craig Williams from Reno, Nevada, gave me the idea to try the Kreg and the time saved was incalculable, in my opinion.

As I have gotten older, I've come to realize how important light is to old eyes. In the garage I can usually open several doors for plenty of natural light, which is by far the best for reading the surface of metal; it's absolutely transformational if you are accustomed to artificial light. However, depending on what the mastiffs have been up to and where, I sometimes leave the door to the backyard closed. In those cases, and other times when I need more light, I don a pair of 3M illuminated safety glasses. Although not necessarily dirt cheap, these glasses fall into the same category as good beer and parachutes—they are well worth their cost.

If you want to build a wood buck in a hurry—like before your spouse gets back to town so she can have back her side of the garage, which you promised you would never use—get a Kreg pocket jig and some coarse Kreg screws.

Tony Urich turned me on to 3M's illuminated safety glasses. For thinning a line in the bead roller, keeping both hands free during nocturnal jaunts, and other precise tasks, these glasses are a lifesaver.

Chapter 2
Building Your Own English Wheel

For value per dollar, the English wheel, or wheeling machine, is tough to beat. The wheel is easy to learn because it moves metal at a slow, controllable rate compared to a power hammer. The wheel has a larger tool face than a planishing hammer, so perfect surface finishes are easy to achieve. In addition, the wheel is a highly effective small-dent removal tool if you carefully monitor your progress and don't stretch the metal.

While there are many commercially available wheels and wheel kits, I have designed a wheel that I think is very well suited to just about anybody wanting to get into metal shaping and auto restoration. My wheel is rugged, easy to build, easy to customize to different dimensions, and inexpensive. Apart from the wheels themselves, the total materials cost about $150.

Admittedly, I am spoiled by the tools at my disposal at work. At home, however, I am just like everybody else: underequipped and always wanting more. As many readers may already know, the barter system is a superb way to acquire essential tools without diverting funds from the family budget. Just make sure that any livestock you acquire through the barter system is tolerant of your car hobby.

THE DESIGN

A few years ago, I traded some sheet metal work for a small tabletop English wheel with a 25-inch throat. Before I owned one, I would have never considered purchasing a small wheel for no other reason than I was accustomed to full-size wheels. Now that I've logged some hours on a small wheel, I can see how narrow-minded I was. If your spouse has patiently surrendered one half of the garage to make room for your tools and non-running old car or cars, consider building a small to medium-size wheel. As long as the upper and lower wheels can be easily rotated 90 degrees, you will be able to shape any panel that can be supported by one person. A small wheel becomes a limitation when you have welded multiple panels together and you want to stretch out the welds. If space is not a problem in your

The wheeling machine described in this chapter can easily be adapted to any size that meets your needs. Follow along as I build two wheels.

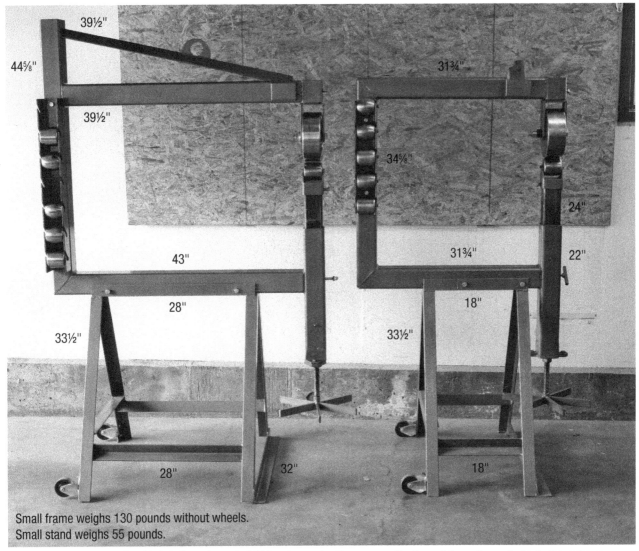

39½"

44⅝"

39½"

31¾"

34⅝"

24"

43"

31¾"

22"

28"

18"

33½"

33½"

28"

32"

18"

18"

Small frame weighs 130 pounds without wheels.
Small stand weighs 55 pounds.

Here are the two wheels I built, with their dimensions noted. While a larger wheel is more versatile, the usefulness of a small wheel will surprise you, as long as the wheels can be rotated 90 degrees, as on these.

workshop, then by all means build a larger wheel. I have built a larger wheel as well, and you will see how the essential design elements that follow can be translated into other sizes.

My English wheel design is based on commonly available hot-rolled ¼-inch-wall square steel tubing in two sizes: 3 inches and 3½ inches outside dimension. I chose this material for several reasons: (1) it provides excellent stiffness without the need for additional gussets; (2) maintaining alignment during fit-up and welding is a snap; (3) with a little work, these two tubing sizes can be made to telescope, thus eliminating all slop from the movable lower anvil wheel assembly; (4) square tubing allows for the rotation of the upper and lower wheel assemblies to 90 degrees for more versatility; and (5) with very little work, ¼-inch-wall 3½-inch square tubing makes a terrific anvil wheel yoke for a standard 3-inch-wide anvil wheel.

I've incorporated a sealed roller bearing into the Acme thread attached to the kickwheel to make adjusting the tension between the upper and lower wheels deliciously smooth. Furthermore, because the Acme thread is positively locked to the underside of the anvil wheel support, the anvil wheel raises and lowers only in relation to the kickwheel. Relying solely on gravity, wheels that lack this feature have an annoying lag when friction from the tension screw on the lower anvil wheel keeps it from descending. Last, this wheel design can be bolted to the wall and pivoted out when needed. It can also be bolted to a table, or you can mount it on a movable frame.

Whether you choose to buy or build a wheeling machine, consider several things. Can the wheels be turned 90 degrees? How deep is the throat? Is the tension applied with a kickwheel below or a handwheel either above or below the work? How high is the panel during wheeling? What size and radius are the wheels? What are the edges of the upper wheel like?

Being able to rotate the wheels 90 degrees is not a deal breaker, but it does add flexibility. The depth of the throat is easily evaluated in light of the space at your disposal and type of work you anticipate doing. Good work is achievable regardless of how the tension between the wheels is applied, but a kickwheel allows you to make very small pressure adjustments *while the wheels are in motion*. In addition, a kickwheel gives you one more point of contact between your body and the work to receive feedback as you wheel. The height of the workpiece during wheeling is important because you need to be able to evaluate the stretching that is taking place. For me, 52 inches from the floor is just right. As I was building the wheels described in this chapter, I experimented with small adjustments up and down, and mid-chest height is optimum.

Lower anvil wheels are available with a true radius or with a flat contact patch combined with a radius out past the contact patch. Keep in mind that larger tool surfaces give more even stretching and better surface finishes, but if you wheel with too much pressure, any anvil wheel will leave marks. Sharply radiused wheels are particularly prone to marking because of their small contact surfaces. Sharply radiused wheels are best used when a flatter wheel will not fit due to the curvature of the panel. The large upper wheels are always flat, but I have noticed that the edge radius of the upper wheel can leave marks if it is too crisp. The wheels I discuss in this chapter rely on commonly available 3-inch-wide upper and lower wheels. Wider wheels are terrific, but be prepared to modify your design to accommodate them. As for the diameter and weight of the upper wheel, I have not observed an overwhelming benefit of larger and heavier wheels. It might seem a larger-diameter, heavier wheel would be easier to roll, but I personally have never noticed this in practice, even though I regularly use 8 × 2-inch, 9 × 3-inch, and 6 × 3-inch upper wheels; some are solid and some are relieved to reduce weight. Like playing guitars, you focus on the music and the instrument fades into the background.

LIST OF MATERIALS

2 – Cart-King casters, rigid 3" × 1¼" phenolic wheel, 350-pound capacity (McMaster-Carr part 2370T59, $11.50 each, $23.00 total)

1 – 1-4 Acme thread 12" (McMaster-Carr part 93410A952, $34.83)

1 – 1-4 Acme nut (McMaster-Carr part 94815A037, $6.65)

1 – 1" double-sealed roller bearing for 1" shaft, 2" OD, ½" wide (McMaster-Carr part 60355K708, $13.42)

1 – Clamping two-piece shaft collar for 2"-diameter shaft, 3" OD (McMaster-Carr part 6436K27, $15.26)

1 – 8"- or 9"-diameter upper wheel, 3" wide

Assorted lower anvil wheels, 3" wide

2' of 3" × ¼"-wall square tubing

16' of 3½" × ¼"-wall square tubing (12' for small wheel)

32' of 2" leg ³⁄₁₆"- or ¼"-thick angle iron

16" of ⅜"-thick steel 3" wide

42" of ¼"- or ⅜"-thick steel at least 1½" wide (kickwheel spokes)

2' of 1"-diameter ⅛"-wall steel pipe

1 – 4" × ½" square steel bar

1 – 6" × 5½" piece of 16g steel (receptacle for sandpaper)

1 – ½-13 × ¾" bolt (anvil wheel yoke)

1 – ½-13 × 1½" bolt (for applying tension to tube assembly beneath anvil wheel)

1 – ½-13 × 1" bolt (upper wheel yoke)

4 – ½-13 × 1" bolts (for securing wheel frame to base)

2 – ½-13 × 1" bolts (cap at bottom of lower tube assembly)

4 – ⁵⁄₁₆-18 × ¾" bolts with nuts and lockwashers (for securing casters)

1 – 2" OD steel washer

2 – ¼"-28 grease fittings

Finally, consider a couple of features found on manufactured wheels: the anvil wheel with adjustable sides and the quick-release. Some manufactured wheels have a threaded adjuster under each side of the lower anvil wheel to allow you to dial in even contact between the upper and lower wheels. I see the benefit of this feature and I do not disparage the toolmakers who incorporate it into their wheels. However, there is an easier low-tech way. John Glover's proven method is to insert a small scrap of sandpaper under one side of an uneven anvil wheel to even out the contact patch. I have used Glover's method for years and it works great. There is much to be said for simplicity.

As for the quick-release, this mechanism allows the user to swap out anvil wheels instantly without changing the pressure between the wheels. Similarly, the quick-release facilitates panel insertion between the wheels without changing pressure. Frankly, I do not see the benefit of this feature. Changing anvil wheels changes the size of the contact patch, which ought to involve a pressure change if the user is paying attention. Likewise, you should always be aware of where you are on the squeezing spectrum during wheeling. Fixating on recapturing the magical pressure of a few moments ago is an unnecessary distraction. Where are you *now*? Tune in to the panel and make it sing. I suspect the quick-release feature is left over from the early days of wheeling when the machines were used assembly-line fashion to stretch out torch-weld seams. In a volume production setting, I can see the benefit of consistent pressure as you quickly run widgets through one after another, possibly relying on output for a paid bonus.

THE BUILD: STAGE 1

I began my wheel build with the anvil wheel yoke. I started with a long piece of $3\frac{1}{2} \times \frac{1}{4}$-inch-wall tubing that I drilled with a $^{31}/_{64}$-inch-diameter hole for the anvil wheel axle approximately $\frac{1}{2}$ inch from one end. Leaving the tubing long makes the work easier to clamp during drilling and cutting. A drill press will do a better job of drilling a straight hole through the tubing, but you can get by with a hand drill. Even if the holes do not end up even, you can file them as needed to even them up later.

I drilled a $^{27}/_{64}$-inch-diameter hole 1 inch below the axle hole on one side of the tube and tapped it for a $\frac{1}{2}$-13 bolt. This bolt will lock the anvil wheel yoke in place but will be easy to loosen and allow the yoke to be rotated 90 degrees. I was tempted to weld a lever onto the head of this bolt but thought better of it when I weighed the possible interference a lever might cause against the infrequent need to pivot the wheel 90 degrees. In practice I have noticed that tightening this bolt too much tends to tilt the anvil wheel yoke slightly. You could counteract this by adding a second bolt on the opposite side. Because I noticed the phenomenon, I know to watch for it and have not had a problem.

A small but key obstacle to overcome with my wheel design is the weld seam on the inside of the square tubing I have chosen. If you decide to price telescoping square tubing, you will see the benefit of this route. The bead on the inside of the $3\frac{1}{2}$-inch square tubing prevents the 3-inch square tubing from sliding inside it. The easiest and fastest way I have found for removing the proud excrescence along the seam is to shear it off with an air chisel. Once I removed the weld bead from the inside of the anvil wheel yoke, I trimmed the extra metal off the top of the piece and filed the axle-mounting holes slightly until I could slide an anvil wheel in position without binding. I cut a 3-inch square of $\frac{3}{8}$-inch flat steel and tacked it in place inside the yoke to limit the distance it could slide down over

To ensure that the hole for the anvil wheel was even from side to side, I drilled the hole in a drill press prior to cutting away any material. Leaving the section of tube untrimmed made it much easier to secure in the drill press.

the 3-inch tubing. In addition, the ⅜-inch flat steel will ensure that the anvil wheel stays flat and doesn't move when tension is applied to it. I didn't weld 360 degrees around the perimeter of the flat steel for fear that the tubing might shrink and refuse to slide easily on and off the smaller tubing inside it. A couple of taps from a rubber mallet are needed to free the yoke from its perch on the end of the 3-inch tubing. The finished anvil wheel yoke is 2½ inches high, deep enough to be held securely in place on the 3-inch tubing that nests inside it, but it is not so big that it will become an obstruction during wheeling. I then cut upper and lower arms, a rear vertical arm, and a front vertical arm from my 3½-inch square tubing.

Time for this stage: 3½ hours.

STAGE 2

Although the weight of the upper wheel will make it more of a hassle to rotate 90 degrees than the anvil wheel, the combination of 3-inch square tubing nested inside 3½-inch tubing is nevertheless a sound design choice. On the smaller wheel I used a solid 50-pound wheel obtained via the barter system. For the larger wheel I used a 17-pound 9 × 3-inch wheel from Hoosier Profiles. As one would expect, the heavier upper wheel is significantly more difficult to rotate than the lighter wheel. I cut one 3½-inch-tall piece of 3½ × ¼-inch-wall square tubing and a 3-inch-tall piece of 3 × ¼-inch-wall square tubing to support the upper wheel. I drilled and tapped one side of the 3½-inch tubing for a ½-13 × 1-inch bolt to hold the upper wheel assembly in place.

Time for this stage: 1 hour. Total time so far: 4½ hours.

STAGE 3

This wheel design is very flexible in terms of how it can be mounted: on a stand with casters, on a bench top, or on the wall. I chose to mount these wheels on frames of an identical design, but different dimensions. I cut all the frame pieces from 2-inch angle iron 3⁄16 inch thick. The wheel frame is cradled between two pieces facing each other and drilled with 27⁄64-inch holes. The holes in the main tube were tapped for ½-13 bolts. The holes in the angle iron were drilled out to 7⁄16 inch to allow the bolts to pass through and secure the stand to the wheel frame. Depending on how you decide to mount the smaller wheel, you could turn the angles out so they easily bolt on a table.

Time for this stage: 1 hour. Total time so far: 5½ hours.

I capped the upper end of the anvil wheel yoke with a section of steel plate. I did not run a weld bead around the perimeter of the plate for fear that the tubing would shrink and no longer fit on top of the 3-inch tubing beneath it.

I fashioned this stand for the small wheel while on break from a therapy session for anal-retentiveness. The wheel frame rests in a cradle made of two pieces of angle iron facing each other. The cradle allows the frame to slide forward or backward for optimum placement.

STAGE 4

I made the upper wheel bracket out of ⅜-inch flat steel. I cut two sides 3 inches wide and 6 inches long, and a top at 3 × 4 inches. To make sure my upper axle hole was even between the sides, I tack-welded the sides together and drilled one ¾-inch-diameter hole through both of them simultaneously. I placed a single thin flat washer on both sides of the upper wheel, sandwiched them between the side pieces using a bolt through the axle, and tacked the pieces of the upper wheel bracket together. It is critical that you protect the upper wheel from weld spatter during tacking. I shielded my wheel with a scrap of 20-gauge steel each time I placed a tack. I centered and tacked the 3-inch square section I cut out earlier on top of the upper wheel bracket.

RIGHT: To keep the sides of the upper wheel holder in alignment during drilling, I tack-welded them together before I drilled the hole. I tacked them to the rest of the support with the upper wheel installed and protected from weld spatter.

BELOW: Keeping your frame pieces flat and in alignment during fit-up and welding is easier if you have a flat steel table free of weld spatter and a C-clamp for every hair on your head. I believe I have six or eight of both.

Happy with the upper wheel holder, I turned my attention to the wheel frame. First I laid the wheel frame members flat on a sturdy steel table, aligned the corners at 90 degrees with a carpenter's square, and C-clamped everything in place. I gradually worked my way around the frame, tack-welding the joints without disturbing the fit. I did not put any tacks on the side resting against the table because I wanted to make sure I could maintain one flat surface in case I needed it. I checked the 3½-inch square top wheel holder in two planes and tacked it in place at the end of the upper beam.

Time for this stage: 3 hours. Total time so far: 8½ hours.

STAGE 5

Easily the most arduous task of this wheel build was removing the weld bead from the inside of the 22-inch-long 3½ × ¼-inch-wall square tube through which the 3-inch square tube beneath the anvil wheel slides. An air chisel works like a dream for about the first 4 inches in from the end. An extra-long cold chisel will get you to about 7 inches deep. At that point, the small opening prevents you from getting enough angle on your chisel to be able to peel back the weld.

I welded an old file to a large 2-inch-diameter solid steel bar weighing about 20 pounds and slid this contrivance over the weld until the 3-inch tube passed freely through the 3½-inch tube. Of the two tubes that I reamed out, one took only about half an hour while the other took over two hours. I have included the time for the longer version.

Time for this stage: 2¼ hours. Total time so far: 10¾ hours.

STAGE 6

With the 3- and 3½-inch tubing now telescoping as planned, I drilled and tapped a hole in the outer tubing for a ½-13 bolt. In practice I have not needed to tighten this bolt to keep the anvil wheel from dropping during use, but that is the bolt's purpose. I slid my 3-inch tubing down through the upper wheel holder and the lower wheel holder to make sure they stayed aligned during welding. I clamped the assembly down to a table and tacked the 3½-inch square tubing in place. The top

Filing out the weld seam to allow the 3-inch tubing to slide into the 3½-inch tubing is a chore, but the money you save will go a long way toward the purchase of your wheels. A heavy steel bar with an old file welded to it did the trick. I can't imagine how well a file with teeth would perform.

The best way to ensure that the upper wheel mount and lower wheel perch are in perfect alignment is to run a length of 3-inch tubing through both entities prior to tack-welding. As I can expect about one good idea per year, I was thankful this one came along when it did.

of the 3½-inch tubing is 7 inches above the bottom horizontal beam of the wheel. I mocked up the top and lower wheels in their respective yokes and spent quite a bit of time checking to make sure that everything was level. Minor adjustments were possible with a sharp rap from a hammer. I added a few tack welds to keep everything secure.

Time for this stage: 3 hours. Total time so far: 13¾ hours.

STAGE 7

Pleased with the alignment of the wheels, I removed the 3-inch square tubing from beneath the anvil wheel

and began working on the Acme thread and kickwheel adjuster. I welded a 2½-inch square piece of ⅜-inch plate just inside the bottom of the 3-inch square tubing for the Acme thread to push against. I beveled the edges of the plate for good weld penetration and ground the welds flat. Then I welded a bearing retainer in the center of the 2½-inch square plate. The purpose of the bearing retainer is threefold: (1) it keeps the Acme thread of the kickwheel stable and centered inside the tubing; (2) it holds a roller bearing in place on the Acme thread; and (3) it gives the end of the Acme thread something to pull against when the anvil wheel is lowered. Next, I welded a 2-inch-diameter washer on the end of the Acme thread,

On one wheel I used a bearing retainer with a single opening on the side. On the second wheel I used a two-part bearing retainer. Both worked well. The bearing prevents the end of the Acme thread from moving side to side as the inner tube is raised and lowered. The washer is welded to the end of the Acme thread to enable pulling against the trapped bearing to lower the bottom wheel.

inserted an appropriately sized roller bearing onto the threaded shaft, and checked for binding as I slid the 3-inch tubing inside the 3½-inch tubing.

Time for this stage: 2¼ hours. Total time so far: 16 hours.

STAGE 8

I capped the end of the 3½-inch square tubing assembly with a piece of ⅜-inch-thick plate with a hole cut in the middle for the Acme thread to pass through. I welded two short ears of angle iron to the main tube for attaching the cap, and I drilled and tapped the ⅜-inch steel cap for ½-13 bolts and tack-welded an Acme nut over the 1-inch hole. Use care when welding this or any fastener—overzealous welding will shrink the fastener to the point that its threads bind up.

Sensing completion of this phase, I drilled two ⁷⁄₃₂-inch holes for grease fittings in the outer 3½-inch tubing: one in the lower third and another in the upper third of the piece. I tapped these holes and installed ¼-28 grease fittings. To test the Acme thread assembly, I attached a Vise-Grip to the bottom of the shaft to make sure the anvil wheel moved up and down as anticipated.

The steel plate through which the Acme shaft passes bolts to the bottom of the 3½-inch tubing at the front of the machine. It is simple, compact, and functional.

Through trial and error, I decided that 7 inches seemed a good length for the spokes or legs of the kickwheel. Using a 12-inch-diameter shot bag stand as a jig, I laid out six pieces of steel approximately $7 \times 1\frac{1}{2} \times \frac{3}{8}$ inch evenly spaced around the perimeter of the stand. I bolted a length of 1-inch-diameter steel pipe in the center and welded the spokes to the pipe. After welding the kickwheel to the bottom of the Acme thread, I tested the wheel with the frame bolted upright on a table. All moving parts worked smoothly.

Time for this stage: 5 hours. Total time so far: 21 hours.

STAGE 9

Next, I laid out the pieces for the stand that supports the wheel on a table and welded them together. Knowing where I was headed, the second stand I built took only about a quarter of the time as the first one. I filled in the upper end of the 3-inch square tubing that helps secure the upper wheel with a piece of $\frac{3}{8}$-inch steel and welded all the remaining joints.

Time for this stage: $2\frac{1}{4}$ hours. Total time so far: $23\frac{1}{4}$ hours.

STAGE 10

Using 16-gauge steel, I fabricated a small box, $4 \times 3 \times 1\frac{1}{2}$ inches, for holding scraps of sandpaper to use as anvil wheel shims and tack-welded it in place on the upper arm. Needing a place to store my anvil wheels, I drilled five pairs of $\frac{1}{2}$-inch holes spaced 4 inches apart along an 18-inch-long piece of $3\frac{1}{2}$-inch square tubing. I cut one side of the tubing off and made a series of 45-degree cuts from the $\frac{1}{2}$-inch holes out to the open edge to serve as slots for housing the wheels.

I temporarily converted this shot bag stand into a welding fixture for my kick wheels. Depending on who will be using your wheel, excessively long legs may provide too much leverage for overzealous users. You don't need to worry about breaking anything, but remember that the magical part of the squeezing spectrum that generates nice panels is at the light end.

To house extra anvil wheels, I built a rack for each wheeling machine from 3½-inch tubing that I cross-drilled. Include a few extra slots in case you expand your arsenal of anvil wheels in the future.

To ensure proper placement, I clamped the casters, tack-welded them, drilled them each for two ⁵⁄₁₆-inch bolts, and then cut the tack welds. Finally, I added a 4-inch-long piece of ½-inch square stock to the 1½-inch-long ½-13 bolt that applies tension to the tubing beneath the anvil wheel. Having this bolt a little long allows you to use it as a handle when you want to tip the wheel up on its casters to move it around. I placed the bolt far enough down the shaft that it won't get in the way during wheeling.

Time for this stage: 1 hour. Total time: 26¾ hours.

I have logged quite a bit of time on the smaller of these wheels and have been very happy with its performance. I feel the larger wheel could benefit from the addition of one triangular gusset where the lower frame joins the 3½-inch vertical member beneath the anvil wheel. There is a miniscule amount of flex at that union, which most people would not notice, but I do. Because of its weight, I added a loop for lifting the larger wheel with an engine hoist. I found the center of gravity by placing a block between the bottom of the frame and its stand. I moved this block back and forth until I could balance the frame on the block, and placed the lifting loop in line with this point. The larger wheel is still easy to tilt back and move on its casters, but it would be difficult and awkward to load into the bed of a pickup truck, for example.

I located the wheel rack vertically on the main beam, tack-welded it in place, drilled and tapped holes for ½-13 bolts, then ground off the tack welds.

Time for this stage: 2½ hours. Total time so far: 25¾ hours.

STAGE 11

In the last phase of the build I added casters to the rear legs of the wheel frame. Dissatisfied with the first set of locking casters I purchased, I mounted nonswiveling casters vertically. To get the alignment spot-on, I cut about ½ inch off the flange nearest the ground when the wheels are tilted vertically. Removing the extra material allowed me to seat the flange flat against the leg *and* have the wheel touching the ground. Without trimming, the mounting flange was so long that it would have left the wheel ¼ inch off the ground. This wouldn't have given me the silky-smooth tilting action I wanted. As it stands now, the wheeling machine rests solidly on all four legs during use without the slightest jiggle, and yet it is easily tilted back and relocated as needed.

Past experience with locking casters led me in a new direction. I trimmed the mounting pads from some fixed casters and mounted them vertically on the rear legs of my wheeling machines. This simple fix gave me exactly the rigidity I had hoped for.

Chapter 3
Building a Power Hammer from a Kit

In the United States during the peak of the custom coachbuilding era of the 1920s and early '30s, the Yoder and Pettingell brands of power hammers were the tools of choice for quickly and efficiently producing sheet metal panels for highly specialized, and often unique, custom cars of the day. Later, these hammers were used to build race cars, movie cars, prototypes, and "kustoms" by many of the same craftsmen who had been coachbuilders years before.

The rarity, size, and cost of these old hammers make them unlikely to appeal to the average sheet metal enthusiast. They are also, sadly, too loud for use in residential areas without extraordinary sound insulation. A handful of companies sell new versions of power hammers, but these too are quite expensive. If you know that these tools are beyond your means, or perhaps you just want to learn more about power hammers, there is a less expensive version available. Mittler Brothers sells a power hammer in kit form that grants the dedicated enthusiast access to this glorious, life-enhancing tool. I have built two of these kits and started a third. In my opinion, the Mittler kit delivers exactly the power hammer experience that curious enthusiasts are hoping for. If your desire justifies the cost, or if you need the tool for your business, you will not be disappointed.

In case you are wondering what a power hammer does and what it is like to use, I will do my best to describe it. The power hammer slings a heavy, ordinarily flat top die against a radiused bottom die. The user controls the speed of the strikes with a foot pedal. The strike is similar to a dead blow hammer in that peak force is delivered over a short lapse of time rather than all at once. The dead blow quality of the power hammer is different from the fixed stroke of the Pullmax reciprocating machine. The dead blow stroke leaves a nice finish when stretching and shrinking by compression between steel dies. With the Pullmax, shrinking is possible with smaller thumbnail shrinking dies, but stretching between steel dies should be avoided because you can break the machine. The Pullmax can be used for shearing, for making louvers, and for forming operations such as beading, but the dies do not contact face to face.

The chief benefits of the power hammer are the large contact surfaces of its tooling and its ability to shrink and stretch with ease any gauge of sheet metal found on an automobile body. These benefits lead to high-quality work produced quickly. Just as important, using the power hammer is great fun—perhaps the most fun a person can have fully clothed. For the sake of not embarrassing my children, I won't elaborate on the joys of hammering in the nude other than to say it is time well spent. With experience, the user develops an uncanny tactile sensitivity for what is happening to a piece of metal being worked between the dies. I don't believe new users will be aware of this right away, but over time one's feel for "just right" develops like a musician's ear for pitch. Watching the metal stretch completely under your control at arm's length is like inflating a balloon: if you need more shape, softly hit the metal a few more times and you will see the shape develop before your eyes. The sensation is better than magic—it is real, concrete, and measurable.

How does the Mittler Brothers hammer perform? Although this tool is not perfect, it is close. The feel of the two kits I built is superb, though not because of any excellence I contributed. The mechanism is a simple slipping belt system, but it works great. I feel I could harmlessly pet butterflies between the dies or smash walnuts to dust if the need arose. I would not change anything about the way the foot pedal controls the speed of the machine. The only flaw on the hammer kits I built has to do with how the dies are secured with bolts and set screws. In the time since I built these hammers, Mittler Brothers has improved this die-retention system. I have not evaluated the new design personally, but one of my former students told me that he was very happy with one of the newer designs about a year after he began using it.

The glorious power hammer gets you about as close as possible to experiencing coachbuilding as it was practiced in the United States in the days when the finest cars were handmade.

As delivered from Mittler Brothers, the kit contains drawings, the power hammer mechanism, the upper and lower die holders, and two dies. There are no instructions, but presumably anyone willing to undertake such a task will be handy enough to complete the build without any drama. Our hammers depart from the plans slightly because of the addition of supports recommended to me by Fay Butler. Also, knowing that I was planning for two hammers from the start, my base and central column were perhaps larger than necessary for a single hammer. Because I do not wish to infringe on the copyrighted material contained in the drawings, I will not be overly specific regarding dimensions of the various components during my description of this build. My purpose is to show exactly what is involved in building one of these kits, not to provide a substitute for the plans.

PREPARING FOR THE BUILD

The drawings from Mittler Brothers make specific recommendations regarding a substantial column and base, but I opted for some free salvaged materials. I used a mammoth steel pipe cap for the base and welded two 7 × 13 × ⅜-inch I-beams together for the column. I boxed in the open sides of the I-beams with ⅜-inch plate and filled the entire unit with 700 pounds of sand. While this was surely overkill for a single hammer, I wanted the base assembly sturdy enough for a second hammer. If I were building one for home use, I would be strongly tempted to use a single ⅜-inch-thick I-beam for the column. I think the kit could be built in less than 40 hours using the column and base Mittler recommends. Our first hammer took a while longer because of my elaborate column and various supports.

To build the power hammer successfully, you need a welder capable of fusing up to ¼-inch steel in a single pass. This will most certainly be at least a 220V machine. A MIG (GMAW), TIG (GTAW), or SMAW (arc or stick) would be the best choice. An oxyacetylene torch is not recommended because of the tremendous heat and distortion that would result. I used a Millermatic metal inert gas (MIG) welder that is probably almost as old as me and it worked perfectly.

Other tools you will need include C-clamps, a level, a carpenter's square, a framing square, a measuring tape, and a grinder for cleaning off firescale and shaping the ends of the tubing prior to welding. For cutting I used a plasma cutter and an oxyacetylene torch. The thickest steel called for by the kit is ⅝-inch-thick plate, which seemed to be a little beyond the capabilities of our plasma cutter. A band saw or chop saw might work for some of the tubing, but these tools were too slow for my tastes on ¼-inch-wall material. You will also need a hefty flat steel table to clamp workpieces to during welding.

To avoid wasting any material, take a few minutes to study the drawings that come with the kit and write on your material which metal will be used for what purpose. Once you have successfully cut and welded a few pieces together with jaw-dropping accuracy, it is easy to become giddy with visions of using the power

hammer. Before you realize your mistake, you may inadvertently cut the wrong material to the perfect size. This will only happen late at night or on a weekend. In either case, you'll be forced to ruminate on your foolishness for a day or more until you have a chance to purchase more material.

Next, make some test cuts with your equipment to find out how much of an allowance you need to make for the width of your cut (the kerf) and for accurate cutting-guide placement. By dragging the tip of our plasma cutter's torch along a scrap piece of aluminum angle, I found that I could cut exactly ³⁄₁₆ inch from

Building the Mittler Brothers hammer kit requires a lot of accurate cutting. Find your chosen cutting tool and dial it in. Since our plasma cutter cuts exactly ³⁄₁₆ inches from a guide, I adjusted a pair of dividers to that dimension and ran it along every proposed seam to speed cutting.

LIST OF MATERIALS

8' of 3" × 4" × ¼"-wall tubing

5' of 2" × 2" × ⅛"-wall tubing

4' of 2" × 4" × ³⁄₁₆"-wall tubing (optional for gussets not specified in Mittler drawings)

6' of 1" OD threaded steel rod (optional for lower arm supports not specified in Mittler drawings)

4' of ⅝"-thick plate 12' wide (double that for second hammer)

1 – 12" × 12" × ¼"-thick plate

2 – 3" × 6½" × ¾"-thick plates

All steel was hot-rolled. For purposes of comparison, this list of materials totaled $238.91 in May 2013. The same materials were $355.40 in April 2016.

the edge of my guide. Therefore, each time I needed to make a perfectly accurate cut, I scribed a line with a divider 3/16 inch back from the finished edge. Although surely not accurate to the thousandth of an inch, this method was equal to the demands made of it by any measuring tape. On the finished hammer you will be able to move the lower die mount in relation to the top die, so this degree of accuracy will suffice, provided the main arms are parallel. Execute some sample welds to find the optimum machine settings and technique for each new thickness of material. Write these settings down on the material itself. Don't forget to grind off all firescale before welding.

THE BUILD: STAGE 1

I recommend beginning with the small L-shaped arms that support the upper half of the hammer. These arms involve a small amount of measuring, cutting, and welding. They are a perfect introduction to the power hammer kit for refining your skills and building your confidence to tackle the rest of the build. Again, study the drawings and think through the various cuts at least twice. The arms are *not* interchangeable, so try to avoid making two perfect left arms, for example.

The L-shaped supports are composed of two lengths of 1/8-inch-wall 2 × 2-inch tubing with a 45-degree angle cut at one end and a small section of the same tubing welded at 90 degrees at the opposite end. Make sure your worktable is level and free of weld spatter or other foreign material that might prevent your pieces from lying flat, and clamp the necessary sections of tubing to the table at 90 degrees. Check both the inside and the outside of the angles with a carpenter's square for accuracy beforehand. Always tack your joints in an alternating fashion to limit distortion. These pieces should look easy to make because they are, but your success here, thanks to a little attention to detail, will set the tone for the rest of the build. The left arm needs to be drilled for attaching the belt brake assembly. Drilling this arm now in a drill press is easier because the through holes are sure to be perpendicular. Nevertheless, if you forget, the holes can be drilled later when the unit is fully assembled.

Time for this stage: 1 hour.

STAGE 2

I cut three sections of (1/4-inch-wall) 3 × 4-inch rectangular tubing: one at 3 inches and two at 3 5/16 inches. The 3-inch block will go under the lower die holder. The two 3 5/16-inch blocks go under the two pillow block bearings that support the crankshaft at the top of the machine. After cutting, write the final destination of each block in soapstone, paint marker, or silver Sharpie on the pieces to avoid confusion later.

Time for this stage: 3/4 hour. Total time so far: 1 3/4 hours.

The power hammer's upper arm supports are a perfect place to start your build. You can test your cutting and welding techniques and build confidence at the same time. Next, cut out the three blocks of 3 × 4-inch tubing that comprise the lower die support and the two bearing supports on the upper arm.

The electric motor base is made of ¼-inch plate. Although I welded the first one completely, such thorough welding was overkill that required more grinding for clearance between the upper arm supports. Alternating stitch welds would have sufficed.

STAGE 3

Next, I cut from ¼-inch plate the base and two sides for the electric motor mount that resides at the top of the column. I drilled the base for four holes for the electric mount and welded the sides to the mount. On the first motor mount I welded the sides completely. On the next two bases I alternated my welds every few inches. In practice this was perfectly adequate. The electric motor spins quietly, so there is no need to over-weld these mounts.

Time for this stage: 2 hours. Total time so far: 3¾ hours.

STAGE 4

I tapped four ½-13 holes in two ⅝-inch-thick plates for mounting the pillow block bearings. I bought these plates precut to size and was glad I did. Fortunately, the bearing mount holes that line up with these tapped holes are slotted, so you'll have a little wiggle room to get everything lined up later.

Time for this stage: 1 hour. Total time so far: 4¾ hours.

STAGE 5

I cut out four ⅝-inch-thick plates for mounting the power hammer arms to the column. I drilled four ⁹⁄₁₆-inch holes in each plate using a paper template for bolts at the corners to secure the plates to the main column. I also cut one 6 × 6 × ¾-inch-thick lower die plate with the oxyacetylene torch and used a 4½-inch grinder to clean up the edges of all the plates cut in this stage.

Time for this stage: 3½ hours. Total time so far: 8¼ hours.

STAGE 6

I drilled two ⁹⁄₁₆-inch-diameter holes in the lower die-mounting plate. The plans call for two holes per side in close proximity to make a slot to secure the die holder and make it movable. I didn't do the slot on any of the

The scale and simplicity of the lower arm, once welded, is sure to bring a surge of satisfaction and forward momentum. The 3-inch-tall block of 3 × 4-inch tubing welded to the end of the horizontal arm serves as a lower die support.

sets of arms I built and had no trouble lining up dies. In addition, the plans call for four holes at the corners of this plate. Omit them—they are superfluous. I called Mittler Brothers and they seemed as puzzled as I was regarding the corner bolt holes.

Time for this stage: ½ hour. Total time so far: 8¾ hours.

STAGE 7

For the machine's lower arm, I cut two lengths of rectangular tubing to the specifications in the drawing. The forward end of the lower arm main beam is cut at 45 degrees. The support beam beneath it is cut at 45 degrees on both ends. I welded the 3-inch-long block of rectangular 3 × 4-inch tubing I cut earlier to the end of the lower arm main beam. Because the end of the main tube is cut at 45 degrees, a handy lower tool post is thus formed that leaves room for deeply crowned or curved pieces to fit between the dies without hitting the front of the machine. The support arm beneath

the main beam needs to be attached at 45 degrees. Although its end is already trimmed at the appropriate angle, checking the angle where the tubing comes together with a framing square is a good idea. I clamped the assembly to the table to keep it all flat, ground off all firescale, and welded together the lower arm pieces.

Time for this stage: 1¼ hours. Total time so far: 10 hours.

STAGE 8

In preparation for welding the cast-steel dovetail provided with the kit to the forward end of the machine's upper arm, I ground all weld spatter off the tabletop and beveled the end of the upper arm main beam where it joins the dovetail for maximum penetration. There are two ways the dovetail needs to be square: (1) the dovetail block must be at 90 degrees vertically to the main beam; and (2) the machined surface needs to be at 90 degrees horizontally to the main beam. In addition, the brass jib needs to go on the right side as you stand in front of the assembled hammer. A series of small threaded holes identifies the jib side.

Look over the unmachined sides of the dovetail block to see whether one side looks flatter than the other. You can determine whether the block is flat by laying it on one side and using a carpenter's square to check whether the machined side is perpendicular to the table. If neither side is perfectly flat, grind one side flat. When you are satisfied with the fit of the block against the main beam, C-clamp everything in place, protect the machined surfaces from weld spatter, and tack-weld the block to the main beam. Recheck the block for squareness afterward. Weld the dovetail block to the beam.

With the dovetail block secure, I turned the upper arm main beam over so that it was parallel to the table and leveled it. This is its normal orientation during use. I located the two $3 \times 4 \times 3\frac{5}{16}$-inch-tall bearing support blocks on the beam and leveled them as well. Place a long level across their tops and grind them as needed.

These bearing supports *must* be perpendicular to the dovetail and parallel with the electric motor mount.

Time for this stage: 1½ hours. Total time so far: 11½ hours.

STAGE 9

To prepare for welding the power hammer arms to their backing plates, I drew a line on the table and lined up everything in relation to that centerline. Unless your plates are milled to perfection, aligning everything from the centerline is more reliable than working from the edges. I placed a punch mark on the centerline of each backing plate near the edge to make lining up everything easier. I beveled the ends of the tubing where it gets welded to the backing plates to enhance weld penetration.

Next, I tack-welded the electric motor mount to its backing plate and placed the unit in position on the centerline the appropriate distance from the dovetail assembly. I lined up the L-shaped support arms that I

Take your time getting the steel dovetail lined up with the main beam of the upper arm. To ensure even contact between the dies and avoid uneven wear of moving parts, the dovetail needs to be accurately placed in the X, Y, and Z axes.

The blocks supporting the pillow block bearings need to be parallel with the upper arm main beam. Time spent checking to make sure each surface is plumb or level is time well spent.

Using a centerline drawn on the table, I lined up the upper and lower arms in preparation for welding to their backing plates.

had welded together earlier and tacked them in place at a 45-degree angle to the table. With the upper arms resting vertically on the tabletop, checking the alignment of all pieces was a breeze. In the event you need to make a change, a 4½-inch electric grinder with a cutoff wheel gives you the best access for cutting tack welds. On the first hammer I built, I welded the upper

arm components completely except for the backing plates, which were only tacked to the arm in case changes were needed. On the second and third sets of arms I built, I welded the arms to the backing plates at this stage.

Time for this stage: 1 hour. Total time so far: 12½ hours.

I made sure the lower die holder support plate was level and parallel with the lower arm main beam before tack-welding. I welded the plate completely only after I had assembled and tested the hammer.

STAGE 10

As I was building my column out of an assemblage of recycled I-beams and plate steel, I had to make some progress on the column before I could finish welding the mounting plates to the hammer arms. I laid two I-beams next to each other on the floor, leveled them on their X and Y axes, and welded them together. Had I not anticipated filling the column with sand, I could have welded alternating stretches and saved a lot of time. Because I did not want students to get distracted by spontaneous matches of beach volleyball in the metals lab, I welded the I-beams completely where they met. The I-beam situation is unique to this build and can be avoided by using the column Mittler recommends, but I am not including the time involved in this portion of the build.

Basing all of my alignment on a centerline that I drew down the middle of the column, I placed the power hammer arms in their anticipated positions and tack-welded the backing plates to the column to keep them from shifting. I drilled and tapped all of the holes at the corners of the backing plates for ½-13 bolts. Because I had extra 3 × 4-inch tubing left over with one end cut at 45 degrees, I cut a piece 11 inches long and welded it in place between the lower arms as an additional support. After checking everything yet again, I welded the lower arms to the backing plates.

Time for this stage: 3½ hours. Total time so far: 16 hours.

STAGE 11

Next, I filled the open end of the lower arm main beam with a rectangle cut from ¼-inch plate. Because the most important feature of the entire hammer assembly is even contact between the dies, accurate placement of the 6 × 6 × ½-inch-thick lower die support plate is critical. I beveled the top edge of the 3 × 4-inch lower block that supports this plate and tack-welded the die support plate on top of it. Ensuring that the plate was level in every dimension was a tedious process that required several minute adjustments achieved by grinding the top of the 3 × 4-inch block. I did not weld this plate completely because I wanted to check the fit on the assembled hammer first, but these tack welds were quite solid.

Time for this stage: 1½ hours. Total time so far: 17½ hours.

STAGE 12

Although not called for in Mittler's drawing, I added several extra gussets to the hammers I built according to Fay Butler's recommendations. First, I added a support made of 2 × 4-inch tubing behind the dovetail. The hypotenuse was 7 inches on this 30/60/90 triangle. Then I added four side gussets to the lower arms and one set of gussets to the upper arms made from 2 × 2 × ⅛-inch-wall tubing. These are 45/45/90 triangles with 2½-inch sides and 3½-inch hypotenuses. I also added pipe plugs to the main cavities in anticipation of filling them with oil or sand. (I used oil in the first hammer. Play sand would have been a better choice, however, as a miniscule leak developed that was impossible to weld closed due to the presence of the oil.) I added two 1-inch-diameter threaded rods to stabilize the lower arm assembly, as well as a length of 2 × 4 × ³⁄₁₆-inch-wall tubing connecting the lower arm to the base. Because none of these additions is part of the Mittler drawing, I am not including them in the time involved in building their kit.

On the first power hammer I built, I had the luxury of getting both upper and lower arm sets lined up perfectly while my column was lying flat on the ground. I was also able to assemble all the moving parts to check their alignment before permanently erecting the column. Working on a horizontal column is easier for a first build, though it won't be the end of the world if you are forced to build the arms on a table and swing them into position on an existing column or beam.

Time for final assembly stage: 1½ hours.
Total time for the build: 19 hours.

Following the recommendation of Fay Butler, I added extra supports to the upper and lower power hammer arms. As I have added these gussets to each set of arms I have built, I cannot attest to the arms' rigidity without them, but with them the arms do not move at all.

The support I fabricated beneath the lower arm on the first hammer I built was made of ½-inch plate and a length of ³⁄₁₆-inch-wall tubing. After approximately a year of use, I added a piece of ¾-inch plywood under the lower die holder to help absorb vibration from the dies' impact.

TIPS FOR ADDING A SECOND SET OF ARMS

Knowing that I would be exposing legions of young enthusiasts to the indescribable ecstasy of metal shaping with power, at least two hammers were in my plans from the beginning. While two hammers allow more people to shape simultaneously, the main benefit is that you can more easily avoid die changes. Normal shaping typically involves lots of shrinking and stretching. More than likely, every time you do any shrinking, you will follow that shrinking with stretching. Changing the dies with the bolts and set screw system on these hammers is tedious. Original power hammers use tapered wedges that can be driven in and out rather quickly. Thus, if you see yourself shaping metal all day every day, plan on two hammers. Two Mittler kit hammers are still far less expensive than any other option I am aware of.

If you later add a second hammer to a single column, you can drill and tap mounting holes for both hammers while the column is lying on the ground. Unfortunately, I can't speak to the flow characteristics of sand through $\frac{9}{16}$-inch-diameter holes, so if you go this route you are on your own. I filled the column on our hammer to cut down on vibration and to minimize the echo. The monstrous column I built performs these tasks admirably. If I were to do another hammer for home use, I would hang it on a single I-beam and see how it performed. I could box in the I-beam later and fill it with sand if needed.

Because I did not want to drill and tap holes in a column filled with sand, I came up with a system of $\frac{5}{8}$-inch plates sandwiched together. One set, to be welded to the column, was drilled and tapped for studs. The second set, to be welded to the power hammer arms, was drilled slightly larger to slide over the studs in the first set of plates. This method worked great.

First, I tack-welded eight $10 \times 12 \times \frac{3}{4}$-inch-thick backing plates in sandwiches of two. Then I drilled four $\frac{27}{64}$-inch holes at the corners of each pair of plates. I tapped these holes for $\frac{1}{2}$-13 studs 2 inches long and marked each pair of plates so that all plates would be kept with their companions. After completing the first set of holes, I cut the tack welds and drilled out the holes in the outermost plates to $\frac{9}{16}$ inch so they would slide over the studs and stay aligned. Although the drawings call for four $\frac{3}{4}$-inch-thick backing plates at a smaller size than these, I used larger plates because the strip of $\frac{1}{2}$-inch plate I bought was already 12 inches wide. Leaving the piece at this dimension allowed me to make fewer cuts. I chose the large size out of convenience, not necessity.

Adding four $10 \times 12 \times \frac{3}{4}$-inch backing plates to these already heavy arms makes manually hoisting them into position out of the question. I chained the upper arm assembly to a single forklift fork and swung it into position against the column. I made sure the upper arm was centered and level and then tack-welded

Because I was adding a second set of arms to a vertical column filled with sand, I decided that mounting a set of plates with threaded studs at the corners would be the easiest way of securing the arms to the column.

I lifted the welded upper arm into its final position with a forklift. After making sure it was level, I partially welded it and placed the lower arm in relation to the upper arm.

it in place. At this point, the weight of the arm was still supported by the forklift. I manually hefted the lower arm assembly into place, centered it, leveled it, and tacked it in place as well. I checked the alignment of the machined dovetail with the 6 × 6 × ¾-inch lower die-support plate directly beneath it. These surfaces must be level and exactly perpendicular to each other. This took a couple of tries to get spot-on, but once I was satisfied with the fit, I welded both sets of arms well enough to hold them in place without additional support (but still not completely welded). I removed the forklift and installed the power hammer mechanism, electric motor, lower die holder, and belt-brake assembly.

I inserted the brass jib in the dovetail and greased all the bearing surfaces. If the brass jib is too tight, the upper die holder will not move. If it is too loose, it will slide up and down with the die holder. I oiled a piece of steel, turned on the hammer, and tested the contact patch by pulling down the belt-tensioning lever by hand. Fortunately, the quarter-size contact patch left in the oil assured me that the dies met perfectly. I unbolted

and removed the lower arm assembly and completely welded the lower die-holder support plate. I welded this piece with the arm upside down on a table because I knew I would do a better job than if I tried welding from underneath.

Although the first hammer came with a pedal as part of the kit, the second hammer did not. I fabricated a pedal according to the drawings out of a scrap of conduit and 16-gauge steel identical to the first pedal. If you build your own hammer, the cable lengths will have to be customized to work with your belt tension and brake adjustment. I attached a mount for a belt tension return spring high on the column according to the drawings.

In testing, the belt tension proved too tight, giving the user the choice of either high speed or no speed. I added washers beneath the pillow block bearings on the crankshaft to reduce the belt tension until the pedal feel of this hammer matched the buttery smooth feel of the first hammer. Take a little time to dial in the belt tension just right because it is critical to the feel of your hammer.

Once I had tested the hammer and determined that I needed more slack in the belt, I inserted washers beneath the bearing mounts. Raising the bearings in relation to the motor loosened the belt and made the pedal controlling the hammer's speed less sensitive.

In case I ever need to drain the sand from the power hammer column, I placed a few enormous pipe plugs near the base of the column. When the time came to add the second power hammer to the column, one of these plugs prevented me from replicating the triangular plate steel support under the opposite arm. However, the newer support is simpler, uses less material, and allows an additional plywood cushion beneath the lower arm.

Previously I installed several large pipe plugs in the bottom of the column to drain out the sand if needed. One of these plugs prevented me from supporting the bottom arm of the second hammer as I had the first. An additional support under the lower arms is not included in the Mittler drawings; I have added them to all the arms I have built following Fay Butler's recommendations. For the second hammer, I designed a different mounting point for the lower arm support

and added a piece of ¾-inch plywood to help absorb vibration. Both hammers have a piece of plywood under the lower die holder as well. Without the wood, the first hammer I built started to develop cracks in the 3 × 4-inch rectangular block under the lower die holder after about a year of use. Since adding the wood I have not had any cracking on either hammer.

The lower arm support for the first hammer was composed of a length of 2 × 4 × ³⁄₁₆-inch-wall tubing bolted to a large triangle of ½-inch plate. For the second hammer I used the same tubing for the main beam and mounted the beam to a short ramp constructed of ½-inch plate welded to the hammer base. To determine the appropriate angle at which to cut the long piece of tubing under the second hammer arm, I made a poster board template from the first hammer. I added pipe plugs to all the large hollow cavities in the second hammer just like I did on the first hammer. I finished the second hammer the day before another round of classes was to begin. After unsuccessfully attempting to fill the arms with clumpy swimming pool filter sand (the best I could find locally on a Sunday), I gave up and left the second set of arms empty. The second hammer is more "clacky" than the first hammer, which is "thumpy," but it is not any louder. I did not have time to add the large 1-inch-diameter outrigger arms to the second hammer either, but their absence has not been noticeable. I placed two 1-inch-thick rubber horse stall mats side-by-side between the column base and the concrete floor. Without the rubber mats the hammers' presence could be felt through the floor at quite a distance.

The finished second hammer looks right at home opposite its predecessor. Much to my delight and surprise, mounting two hammers on a single column did not present any vibration or shaking problems.

Chapter 4
Introduction to Shape and Form

In my first book, *Professional Sheet Metal Fabrication* (2013), I introduced two terms that are indispensable to understanding old-car sheet metal: *shape* and *form*. As I described in that book, I learned these terms from my personal metal hero, Fay Butler, who inherited them from Scott Knight and Arvid "Red" Tweit, of the now-defunct California Metal Shaping, which was the epicenter of professional automotive sheet metal work in the United States in the last half of the twentieth century.

I use these terms for three reasons: (1) I respect the tradition begun by these giants; it is our link to the coachbuilders of the 1920s and '30s; (2) I think it is important to have standardized terminology in the sheet metal trade; and (3) understanding the difference between these two concepts will go a long way toward demystifying the behavior of sheet metal. Over the next few chapters, I will reintroduce the terms of *shape* and *form*, demonstrate how they apply to real-life situations, and provide concrete examples of the three main shapes

you are likely to come across in old-car sheet metal work so that you practice forming and shaping on your own.

DISTINGUISHING BETWEEN SHAPE AND FORM

Form refers to any change in sheet metal that does not alter the thickness of the metal. Bending sheet metal in a brake and folding it over your knee are two examples of forming metal. If you can lay a straightedge along a panel on one axis, that panel is form. A typical 1920s car hood, for instance, is pure form. Form is easy to change.

Shape, in contrast, refers to any change in sheet metal that alters the thickness of the metal. When metal is squeezed thinner (or "stretched"), or when it is drawn together and made thicker ("shrunk"), the metal has been shaped. Shape is more difficult to change than form. To change the shape of a piece of metal, stretched metal must be shrunk and shrunk metal must be stretched.

A characteristic of sheet metal that often befuddles beginners is its uniform appearance. Whether metal has

You don't always need to have an example of the thing you want in order to build the thing you want. My former student Michael Cosby didn't have a Ferrari. He built one anyway and now works on them every day at his job. What follow are some exercises anyone can do at home to learn the skills to build what they want.

been bent, stretched, or shrunk, the surface always looks the same—beautiful, but the same. In introducing students to the wonders of old-car sheet metal, I often tell them to try to imagine how a given shape deviates from a flat panel. For example, does the panel rise from the middle? How do the edges relate to the middle? Are there any curves involved? If so, the flat panel might have to move into a tighter or larger radius as it departs from a flat plane.

To illustrate the concepts of form and shape, I have chosen to re-create a seat shape. I am using this shape because I feel confident that it is sufficiently embedded in our collective conscience that every reader will be familiar with it. We've all owned or seen a toy car, tricycle, riding mower, tractor, or barstool with this shape. Even viewed from the floor beneath the barstool, the shape looks familiar. How does this shape deviate from a flat panel?

Imagine a hologram of a flat plane passing horizontally through the middle of the seat. The rear of the seat curves up, the front curves down, and the narrow portion that roughly corresponds with the rider's crotch is slightly higher than the area just behind it. Because the rear of the seat curves along its perimeter, to raise the outer edge in relation to the inboard part of the seat, the outermost edge must necessarily take up a shorter radius than when the metal is flat. My favorite analogy to describe this phenomenon is a running track. If a broken-down old geezer such as myself wanted

to "run" a mile, naturally I would shuffle around the inside lane for four grueling laps, clutching my jitterbug phone the entire way just in case of an emergency. I'm not sure that really adds up to a mile, but most people would feel sorry for me and would be too polite to argue with the old guy blocking the inside lane. If one of my college students wanted to run a mile, however, he or she would be annoyed by an old geezer plodding along on the inside lane and would likely swing out wide, perhaps as far as the outside lane out of deference for the doddering codger a few lanes away. Being older and wiser, I know that the outer lane is a lot farther around, so I'd stick to the inside and bask in the satisfaction of having completed a mile, sort of.

Similarly, in the case of the seat, we are asking the metal along the outer edge to assume a tighter radius—perhaps one lane in on the running track—than the radius it assumes when it is flat. Bunching that metal together—or "shrinking" it, as the process is usually called—gives us the bun-friendly curve along the rear edge of the seat. Not only is the curve ergonomically beneficial, but it might also help keep you upright for an extra cocktail or two! Anyway, whether the curve goes up or down in relation to the seat base is merely a question of form. I could push it up, down, or change it back and forth.

Because I wanted the rear of the seat to go up in relation to the middle of the seat, as this is most conducive to bun-cradling comfort, I made sure as I

Learning opportunities for developing your metal-shaping skills are everywhere. I chose this mechanic's stool to introduce readers to shaping because it is a shape everyone instinctively knows.

Making a paper template is a reliable first step in any metal-shaping project. Here the spread-open slits around the perimeter tell me that the metal will need to stretch to assume the larger circumference or radius of the outside of the stool. Shrinking will be required where the slits overlap in the crotch area.

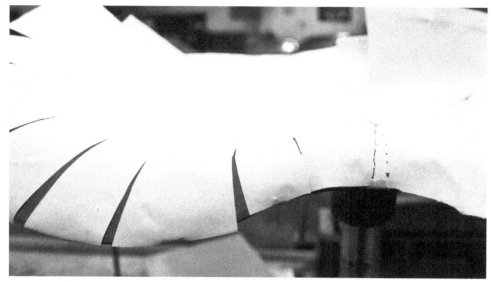

Long hours in the metals lab have left instructor and student pallid and eager for exercise. The instructor—dapper, wise, and sporting a full head of hair—takes the inner lane around the stool seat because that's the shortest route. The naïve college student, eager to make his way around the doddering old codger, takes the longer outside lane at a brisk pace.

After shrinking the metal in a few places around the outside of the seat, the metal is pulled into a smaller-circumference circle like a drawstring snugs up a hoodie.

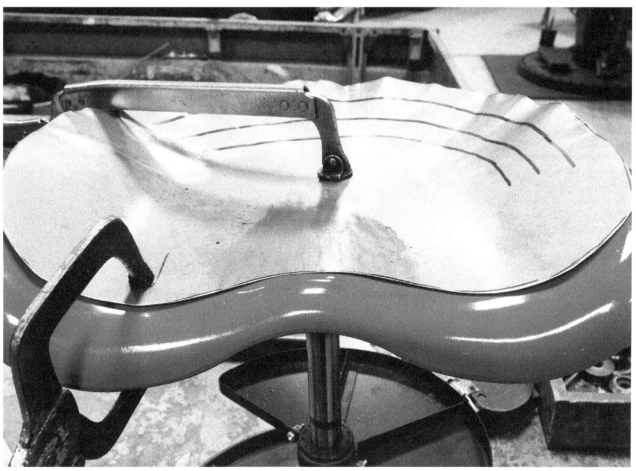

The deepest part of the seat has been hammered and stretched down in relation to an imaginary horizontal plane passing through the middle of the seat. Meanwhile, the metal in the crotch area has been hammered and stretched up in relation to the same plane.

shrunk the metal that I directed it where to go (up), thus defining its form. I will discuss these ideas further later in the book. For now, I want you to become accustomed to the terminology and to start thinking of sheet metal shapes in terms of planes and radii.

As a sheet metal problem, the front of the seat is more squared off than the rear, but it varies in height quite a bit from the flattest part of the seat. Not surprisingly, these changes in height will mean that our flat plane will have to get longer—or be "stretched"—in order to follow the undulations across the front of the seat. In addition, the metal will travel through more than one radius as we go from flat, up over the bump in the crotch area, and then down over the front of the seat. The areas on either side of the central bump roll forward as dramatically as Mick Jagger's lips. As is commonly done in sheet metal work, I made a paper pattern to illustrate the changes that must take place in the metal to enable it to follow the contour of the seat.

Seeing the central bump as an obstacle to further progress, I stretched the metal to allow it to drape over the protrusion at the front of the seat. This scenario raises another constantly recurring phenomenon: whenever you add length or surface area through stretching or reduce it through shrinking, the surrounding metal will always be affected. In this case, stretching the metal over the center rise helped send the metal down on either side.

With my metal blank clamped in place on the chair, I flipped it over to check the fit through the holes in the underside. The metal was tight across the rear curve of the seat and the front bump, but there was a small gap in the central part of the seat between the metal and the chair. Again, how does this vary from the flat plane I started with? As viewed from the underside, the metal needs to be stretched to close the gap. After stretching, the metal blank nestled down into the seat.

I'd like to bend (form) the sides of the seat down to match the front, but the metal is too tight. If we return to the analogy of the running track, this situation will make perfect sense. Where the curved rear of the seat meets the sides of the seat, there is a short expanse of material where the curve reverses from an outside curve to an inside curve. The metal is tight because it is too short. We are asking the metal to assume a slightly larger radius on the inside curve, hence we need to stretch it.

Like a wood buck commonly used in metal shaping, the stool's perforated surface makes checking the fit of the metal on top easy. After shrinking around the outside perimeter and stretching the middle of the blank, the contour of my steel matches that of the stool.

The steel blank fits the stool everywhere except where the top edge curls back toward the ground. Here, the metal must be stretched to flow out into the greater circumference of the curl.

The student, intent upon circumambulating the stool, does not realize he has taken the longest path—a path that takes him dangerously close to a precipice—nor does he see the malevolent instructor sneaking up behind him.

This 12-inch length of welding rod, sandwiched between two clamps, rose approximately ¼ inch when a mere 0.035-inch strip of metal was inserted between the end of the rod and one of the clamps. The dramatic rise illustrates the profound effect small changes to the thickness of metal can have. Compressing sheet metal between a hammer and dolly or other tools turns material thickness into length or surface area.

We are almost finished. The only work remaining to be done is to create some transitions and raise the flat spots where the shrinking stops. We'll do this by stretching. From this exercise, hopefully we can take away the idea of the difference between shape and form and the idea of how the thickness of metal must change as it travels through different radii. This process will work no matter what panel you need to make. How does it deviate from a flat plane? Are we asking the metal to travel through a changing radius? If so, shrinking or stretching will be needed.

A LITTLE THICKNESS CHANGE MEANS A LOT

Having reviewed the terms *shape* and *form* and discussed their application, I want to explain a phenomenon that sometimes befuddles beginners. My students often exclaim, "I just did this little thing here and the whole thing went crazy!"

Even small changes in the thickness of sheet metal can have drastic ramifications. I remember seeing a brilliant demonstration in Robert L. Sargent's *Chilton Mechanics' Handbook, Vol. 3: Auto Body Sheet Metal Repair*, that dramatically illustrates this idea. Sargent rested a flat length of sheet metal between two clamps on a table. The metal was not clamped in any way, but there was no extra space between the ends of the metal and the clamps either. Sargent slipped a 0.005-inch feeler gauge between one end of the sheet metal and the clamp. The sheet metal rose almost 0.025 inch in an arc between the clamps. The lessons to take away from this demonstration are how important thickness is and just how exacting this discipline can be. Every atom is related to every other atom. When one atom is out of place, a misfit will be painfully apparent, or at least it seems that way. You should not get discouraged, therefore, when you hear your inner voice exclaiming, "I just did this little thing here, and the whole thing went crazy!" Of course it did. A few atoms are out of place. The more you work in this field, the better you will get at finding the errant atoms and squeezing them back into place. I wish this process were easier, but if you realize that this is the nature of the material and not a result of your own shortcomings, you can enjoy the challenge rather than be discouraged by it.

Chapter 5
The Low Crown Panel

Of the many lessons I have learned from Fay Butler, one of the most valuable is the condensation of compound-curve sheet metal work into three basic types of shapes: (1) the low crown panel, (2) the high crown panel, and (3) the reverse curve panel. According to Fay, practically all classic car sheet metal falls into one of these types of shapes, or the panel is pure form and does not need any thickness change at all.

The low crown panel does not have much shape. The middle of the panel is higher than the edges, as one would expect to find on a door skin, for example. The low crown panel is made by stretching the middle in relation to the edges. Consequently, the middle receives more work than the edges, which are worked only to the extent needed to blend the transition from the area with the most shape to the area with the least shape.

A high crown panel, such as one half of a motorcycle gas tank, is made by shrinking the sides and stretching the middle.

A reverse curve panel, such as the back half of a swoopy front fender on a 1930s car, is made by stretching just the edges.

To explore these three shapes in more detail, I have designed a series of exercises to provide some hands-on experience in this and the next two chapters. These exercises do not require that you have a certain fender, for example, nor do they require certain tools. Instead, they can be replicated by anyone with a minimum of tooling. To encourage readers to see past the tools, I have chosen to demonstrate these exercises with a range of equipment. The principles behind shaping metal into low crown, high crown, and reverse curve panels are universal. If you understand what needs to happen to the metal to get the required shape, then you will be able to get there with whatever tools you happen to have at hand. Granted, some tools will dramatically improve speed, accuracy, and the surface finish of the part created, but that doesn't mean you cannot get good results by other methods or that your life will be incomplete until you buy such-and-such tool.

SWEEP EXPLAINED

I call the low crown panel in this chapter the "Luxury Lovechild" because it is based on the actual crown of the doors from a 1938 Cadillac and a later Jaguar saloon. The crown of these doors, as well as the compound curve surfaces of all automobile bodies following the Detroit model of automotive design, have been defined

A carpenter's square placed across this 1938 Cadillac door reveals the gradual horizontal rise of the low crown panel. The vertical curvature is more prominent.

A combination of the surface topography of two classic car doors, my "Luxury Lovechild" buck can be easily replicated by anyone who wants to learn how to make a low crown panel. An arc rising to 3 inches over 30 inches gives you the horizontal sweep. An arc rising to 5¼ inches over 30 inches gives you the vertical sweep. The metal piece is my homemade 24 sweep.

by standardized templates called *sweeps* since the late 1920s. Sweeps measure the rise of a true radius in eighths of an inch relative to a line 60 inches long. This sounds much more complicated than it is.

A sweep represents a small piece of a circle. Because describing an arc in terms of its radius would get really cumbersome quickly, especially when the dimension is carried out to three decimal places, the sweep number simplifies and clarifies communication for parties in the know. For example, a number 1 sweep rises ⅛ inch over a 60-inch span. A number 2 sweep rises ⅜ inch over 60 inches, and so on. The horizontal curvature of the sample door is a 24 sweep. The vertical curvature is a 42 sweep. Thus, the 24 sweep of the Luxury Lovechild rises ²⁴⁄₈ inch (3 inches) over a 60-inch span. The 42 sweep of the Luxury Lovechild rises ⁴²⁄₈ inch (5¼ inches) over a 60-inch span.

Note that the span is consistent. The length of the arc varies, of course, according to the amount of rise and is not calculated because you don't need to know it to describe the arc. For the mathematically sadomasochistic, a 24 sweep represents a circle with a radius of 151.5 inches; a 42 sweep represents a circle with a radius of 88.339 inches. Before you run out in search of a 152-inch rod to load into your beam compass, you can consult a sweep chart like the one in Fred Hoadley's *Automobile Design Techniques and Design Modeling*, plot out the appropriate rise at various points across a 30-inch span—one half of a

full sweep—on a piece of poster board, and trace the arcs using a welding rod as a flexible ruler. You now have poster board templates for 24 and 42 sweeps. For people in possession of that elusive phantasm money, you can purchase full sets of sweeps. If you aren't overly concerned with accuracy, just trace a welding rod in a clean arc that rises from a straight line to 3 inches in 30 inches. Hold one end to a straight line drawn on poster board. Bend the rod so that the other end rises to 3 inches above the straight line and have an assistant trace the resulting line. Make a second tracing that rises 5¼ inches. Because this template is for onetime use, the accuracy isn't as important as the concept.

BUILDING A SIMPLE BUCK FOR THE LOW CROWN PANEL

For the Luxury Lovechild, we're going to build a wood buck, or shaping model, based on some doors I have at hand. To make the buck's vertical stations, screw together three pieces of ¾-inch-thick plywood, each measuring approximately 4 × 24 inches, trace out your 42 sweep template, and saw away the negative space. Trace your 24 sweep template onto a piece of sheet metal and cut it out. Separate the three plywood stations and saw ¼ inch off the flat side of two of them; these will be the outer stations. Removing ¼ inch from the flat side of the two outer stations establishes the ½-inch rise you need across the horizontal span of the door. Screw the three stations parallel to each other to a plywood base

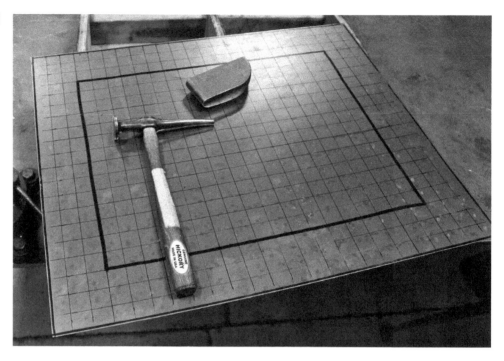

The low crown panel lesson could be learned on a much smaller panel, but here I demonstrate it on a large panel to show that the principles are the same at any scale. I drew a grid on the metal to make it easy to measure the amount and location of stretching put into the panel.

measuring 22 × 24 inches. Predrill your screw holes to keep the plywood from splitting. Check the horizontal sweep with your 24 sweep template. You can sand the stations to remove high spots, build up low spots with plastic body filler, or simply cut new stations as needed. You should be able to drag the horizontal sweep from the top of the door to the bottom without discrepancies between the template and the stations. You are ready to start shaping.

MAKING A LOW CROWN PANEL WITH HAND TOOLS

The first technique I want to demonstrate is the least tool-intensive, but the most labor-intensive. Observing it may be enough for all but the most ardent enthusiast. This method was used by coachbuilders before wheeling machines and power hammers became prominent. It is still used from time to time today, and you could use it effectively in the event your tool budget lags behind your enthusiasm. I have used it to put a crown in small patch panels when the only tools I had available were hammers and dollies. I am using a 20 × 24-inch piece of 0.036-inch 20-gauge steel, but aluminum in the 0.050- to 0.063-inch range would be easier to shape, albeit at about twice the cost. If you choose aluminum, annealing the material will make it too soft. A half-hard condition is ideal for helping a low crown panel hold its shape without over-crowning.

Draw a border with a permanent marker around the perimeter of the panel approximately ⅛ inch from the edge. Draw a grid of 1-inch squares over the surface of one side of the panel. I am certain coachbuilders back in the day did not take the time to draw a grid on their panels. For teaching purposes, however, the grid mandates consistency and reinforces the idea of how much work goes into which zone to make a low crown panel such as this. Using a hammer with a flat or low-crowned face, strike your panel twice in each square of the grid against a clean steel surface. Strive to have the hammer face land flush to minimize tool marks. Leave the small edge border untouched. As you hammer the squares, the metal is made thinner, its surface area is increased, and yet the border remains the same. You need not hammer with extreme force—a firm blow will suffice. The added surface area will manifest itself as a crown in the panel. I was surprised how many passes I needed to make to generate much crown on a panel of this size. In a typical class, I have students do this exercise on an 8 × 10-inch panel and it does not take long. On the 20 × 24-inch piece I made six passes with two strikes per square over the large grid.

If you compare the panel to the buck, you will likely find that more shape is needed. Draw a dark border three squares in from the edge and repeat the hammering process with two blows to each square within the confines of the entire second border. Check the shape against the buck. If still more shape is needed, draw yet another border three squares in from the last one. Repeat the hammering process with two blows per square within the new border. By now your panel will certainly have gained some crown. From the exterior, the panel will look like it has smallpox, just like all the hand-built Ferraris of the 1950s, but it *will* have a crown.

After the first batch of stretching over the largest grid, I struck each square in the second grid approximately six times and the innermost grid another six times. These passes were all completed with two strikes per pass to keep from creating unsightly tumors. With any piece you make, changing the form is always permissible to get the best fit with the shape that you have. Thus, if two sides seem low and two sides seem high, push down on the high sides to raise the low sides. Try to average out the shape in comparison to the buck by bending the sides as just described. If more shape is needed in the middle, stretch it by hammering to raise it. You will know if more shape is needed because the panel will touch the buck only in the middle and will teeter around the point of contact. Conversely, if too much shape has developed, choose a path of stretching around the outer two or three squares and leave the middle undisturbed. Too much shape will be indicated by a gap between the middle of the panel and the buck. The panel

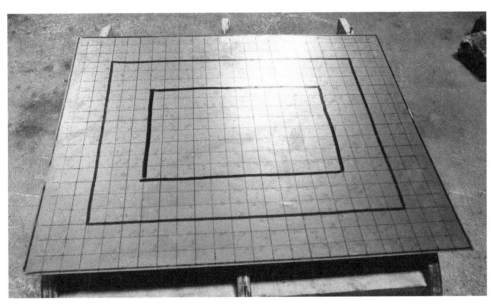

The dark borders indicate zones with progressively more stretching toward the center of the panel. Try to keep your hammer face hitting flush to obtain even stretching with fewer hammer marks. On a large scale, accuracy will vary with waning mental capacity.

Once my panel draped comfortably over the buck, I made a single pass of shrinks around the edge. The surface finish was better than I expected, but would require work with a vixen file to be smooth.

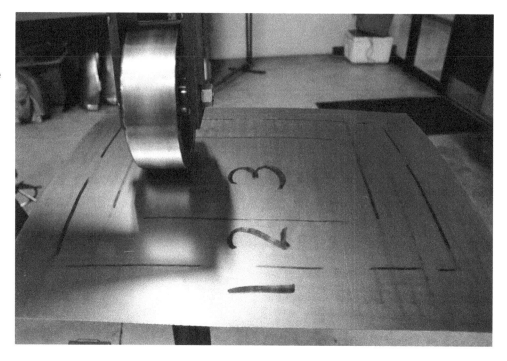

Like the hand-hammered panel, I drew three different zones on the wheeled panel. Using a 12-inch-radius lower wheel with a flat contact area, I stretched the center of the panel in relation to the edges.

will rest against the buck only around its perimeter; the crown in the center of the panel will be too high. After about an hour and a half of hammering and checking, I had enough shape in the middle, but my edges were a little flabby. I made one pass around the perimeter with Lancaster-style shrinking jaws and the panel sat evenly on the buck. I was grateful to be finished.

MAKING A LOW CROWN PANEL WITH A WHEELING MACHINE

For the second demonstration, I will use an English wheel. A 20 × 24-inch panel is the perfect size for learning the process without the panel becoming too cumbersome to handle alone. As panels get larger, their weight exacerbates the stretching that takes place between the wheels unless an assistant is available to provide support.

First, draw three zones on your panel. You may measure them if you wish, but do not be too persnickety about wheeling within the borders. If you are, your panel will look like an eroded ziggurat. If your anvil wheels have a flat contact area ground into them, a 12-inch-radius anvil wheel will work beautifully. If your anvil wheels are ground on a true radius, you will want something much larger, such as a 24-, 36-, or 42-inch radius. Using John Glover's long-long-short-short tracking pattern I described in *Professional Sheet Metal Fabrication*, I traversed the panel twice from side

to side, wheeling vertically. I executed two more passes across zones two and three and checked the panel on the buck. When viewed from behind the buck, the sliver of light I noticed between the outermost stations and the panel indicated that more shape was needed in the center. Because the grain of my metal was oriented top to bottom, and because until now I had only wheeled in that direction, my panel naturally was starting to curl or form in that direction. To counteract this curl, I wheeled horizontally across the panel through zones two and three twice, followed by a single pass through only zone three (the innermost zone). I wheeled diagonally across the panel twice to even out the tension in the panel. At this point, the panel had enough shape to lie comfortably on the buck without gaps.

MAKING A LOW CROWN PANEL WITH A POWER HAMMER

For the third example of shaping a low crown panel, let's turn to the power hammer. My student David will make a piece to fit a Cadillac door in order to convince you that you can do just about any low crown panel if you can successfully complete the Luxury Lovechild exercise. Obviously, pieces get more difficult to manage as they get larger, but the shape of the Luxury Lovechild is very similar to the center of this door. Furthermore, if a person had to make the entire Cadillac door, the upper portion with the window opening would certainly be a

Do not obsess about the direction of your wheeling. What direction allows the largest radius wheel to fit? The panel will naturally try to form itself to the curvature of the lower wheel. This is not the same as shape. Wheeling from a new direction counteracts the panel's tendency to form one way.

Lay your panel on the buck from time to time to assess your progress. Stretch the middle in relation to the edges until the metal drapes over the buck.

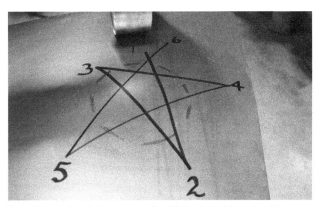

I'm not suggesting that anyone reading this book would create a flat spot by leaving one area inadequately stretched, but if you need to help someone suffering from this malady, wheel the flat area in a star shape. Think of it as a star for good behavior for helping your fellow enthusiast. The star allows you to sneak in more localized stretching where it's needed without creating a tumor. A star is *not* the same as an asterisk, by the way.

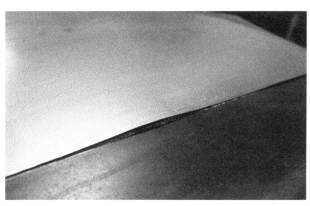

By now you know how much fun this metal stuff is. It is easy to get carried away. Wheeling too much along an edge excessively stretches the metal, which manifests itself as flabby lettuce. Shrink it with a Lancaster-style shrinker. The flab is at left. The cure is at right.

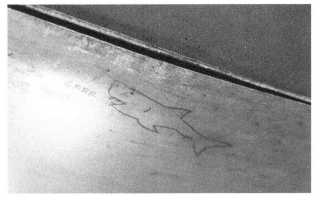

A cartoon image of an angry shark along the edge of your panel is a sure sign that you've shrunk the panel too much. The tight edge bunches up the metal like a sock garter on a chubby calf. For your benefit, I'll keep that image to myself. I'll wheel out the tight spot along the panel edge and consider going on a diet.

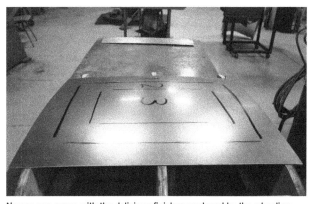

No one can argue with the delicious finishes produced by the wheeling machine. Should you feel inspired to dine from a low crown panel's gleaming surface, choose highly adhesive foods such as peanut butter and jelly or pizza served facedown. Soup, meatballs, and green peas can be elusive prey.

separate piece anyway, so even a vastly more experienced shaper would make the same low crown panel that you have.

To create the low crown panel with the power hammer, David has installed a 24-inch-radius die on the bottom and a flat die on the top. If you are new to metal shaping, do not be persuaded by an ambitious salesperson that you need every radius under the sun for all your tooling. With power hammers, planishing hammers, and anvil wheels for the wheeling machine, different radii give you more options for maximizing contact between the tool and the work, but you certainly don't need to match the radius of the tool to the piece in every case. In fact, better surface finishes and more even stretching are achieved by using a large-radius tool and changing the form of the piece as you hold it to fit the tool. This is a Fay Butler principle that I will come back to when I discuss deep shrinking on the power hammer.

David liberally coated the panel with a mixture of automatic transmission fluid thinned with mineral spirits. This helps the panel slide easily between the dies, helps you see your hammer blows, facilitates reading the play of light across the surface, and acts as a cushion, which students appreciate when getting a feel for the force of the hammer blows.

For students' benefit, I often compare the power hammer to an electric guitar. Sadly, though fewer and fewer young folks have heard of Jimi Hendrix these days, those who have can readily grasp the similarities

As with the previous two panels, David's low crown panel has been marked off into three general zones of stretching. The oily film on the surface provides a cushion for David's hammering and helps him see where his blows land for consistency.

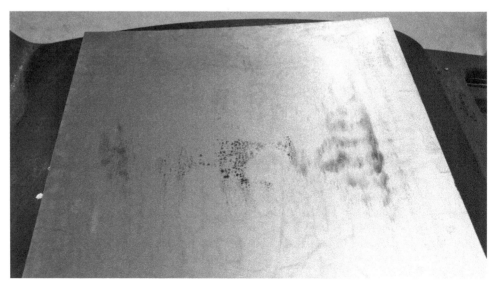

By scrubbing his panel back and forth in place on the Cadillac door, David identified areas in need of more stretching. Raising the scratched areas creates clearance for the panel to drape over the door. Always wipe off grit left from these rubbing sessions so that it does not abrade your tools.

between an amplified Fender Stratocaster played at full volume and the power hammer. At full power in untrained hands, both cease to become musical instruments—cacophony ensues and nothing of any value is produced, only deafness. On the contrary, a lot of magic is contained in the bottom 10 to 20 percent of these two instruments' power bands.

David made two full passes across the first bordered area of his panel, stopping midway across to rotate his panel 180 degrees. David turned his panel because its weight tends to unsettle the panel if too much material hangs over on the machine side of the dies. The key to consistent, controllable, and blemish-free stretching on a low crown panel in the power hammer is to maintain flush solid contact between the dies and the metal. As panel size increases, the weight and floppiness of the piece conspire to unsettle the panel. Maintaining control is a little like slaloming your car between spinning motorists on an icy highway—focus on your path, ease off the accelerator, and you can maintain control. Keep the panel flat between the dies and control the power. Anything else is a distraction.

David made another couple of passes through the second bordered area and checked the fit of the panel on the Cadillac door. By rubbing the panel back and forth in place on the door and creating scratches, David confirmed that the top and bottom of the panel needed more shape. To complete the panel, David stretched the areas of interference and blended them into the surrounding metal with light strokes.

Although this is not David's panel, stretched metal from overzealous hammering can be shrunk with a shrinking disc. The disc generates friction that heats up the panel. When quenched at its hottest point, the panel shrinks very slightly.

David stretched the two inner zones of his panel until it could be superimposed over the door without rocking. He wrapped up the piece with a few nibbles at various points along the edge with a Lancaster-style shrinking tool.

Chapter 6
The High Crown Panel

For the high crown panel example in my survey of sheet metal shapes, I have chosen to illustrate the fabrication of a large automobile cycle fender. Like the other hands-on sample pieces in this book, its creation does not require that you have a specific fender or certain tools.

This project arose out of a custom body-building project several of my students completed for a Pierce Arrow chassis. Coye Savell designed and built the fender buck based on the Pierce Arrow's 31-inch-tall tires, but it could easily be adapted to any custom car, motorcycle, unicycle, or wheeled flying machine. Coye's first step was to establish how much clearance the proposed fender ought to have over the tire. He made a small section of a sample fender, placed it on top of the tire resting on blocks of wood, and decided that a 1-inch gap looked good. He added this measurement to the diameter of the tire and built his buck around that dimension. A poster board fender could very easily be taped together to get an idea of the overall size as well.

Similarly, for the width of the fender, Coye looked at the front of the tire and estimated a 6-inch radius horizontally across the buck's stations above the tire, dropping to a 3-inch radius where the fender curves down over the tire sidewalls. To adapt these dimensions to a different tire, start with the outer circumference as Coye did. Cut out a few cross-sectional poster board templates of the negative space above the tire to test different radii. Consider choosing radii that correspond with tooling you already own. For example, if you have 3-inch-radius anvil wheel for your wheeling machine and a 6-inch-radius die for your planishing hammer, those would be logical choices over 2- and 7-inch radii. You need not have tooling that matches exactly, of course (you can always change the form of the panel during shaping to fit other tooling), but having tooling that is close will facilitate final finishing of the part.

Depending on the tools one has available, this fender could be made in several different configurations. Aluminum is infinitely easier to shape than steel, but

Coye Savell's buck is solid and easy to modify or replicate for other applications. The buck is made of two identical halves that are screwed together down the center spine. I cut away some sections from the top center of the buck to facilitate viewing panels shaped on the power hammer.

This detail of Coye's buck illustrates how the radii evolve from a flat vertical side to a 3-inch-radius highlight, then to a 6-inch radius horizontally across the top.

BUCK-BUILDING TIP

Fabricating a buck from scratch based on a set of dimensions is not as difficult as it may seem if you are a newcomer to working with sheet metal. You have complete control over the dimensions and the accuracy of the buck, which you can check by laying a ⅛-inch welding rod along the stations. If the welding rod will not lie in a continuous arc without gaps, one or more stations are off; sand as needed or build up low stations with a slathering of plastic body filler. The finished fender will only be as good as the guide, so take as much time as needed to get the buck right.

slightly harder for the novice to weld in the event that is needed. I will illustrate a number of different shaping techniques in both aluminum and steel and make the fender out of one piece to avoid welding altogether. The most significant difference in the choice of materials is the ability to shrink aluminum easily with hand tools. With a one-piece fender, shrinking becomes a factor to the extent that you want the fender's perimeter to lie perpendicular to the rest of the panel. I included some images of a classic coachbuilt Bentley to illustrate this point. Shrinking a curved piece of sheet metal to almost 90 degrees is a slow and laborious process with hand tools. Depending on the design you have in mind, welding on additional pieces might be easier than shrinking. The coachbuilders who built the Bentley did not have power hammers with shrinking dies, so they welded on separate strips of metal to create the vertical lip around the fender's perimeter. The car is beautiful and no one thinks any less of them for having done so.

GETTING TO WORK

A cycle fender is a perfect project for a newcomer for other reasons as well. Because the cross profile is continuous over the length of the fender, buck stations can be gang-sawed (see Chapter 5) to ensure symmetry and a shorter build time. In addition, you can space stations out as you see fit, with less space between stations for beginners, or more space for experienced shapers. Coye's 6-inch spacing has worked well for countless students who have shaped metal to this buck, but you are free to go your own direction. I have illustrated an even simpler version of a buck for a Stutz spare-tire well that could easily be copied too.

Because I knew the dimensions and various radii of the buck, I did not need a paper pattern to establish the size of my metal blank or to identify shape changes. Starting with a 12 × 44-inch strip of 20-gauge steel, I drew a centerline and marked off the top of the highlight lines—the areas having the

Without access to power hammers with shrinking dies, the coachbuilders who crafted the fenders for this Bentley made the sides from separate pieces to avoid having to shrink deeply in from an edge.

tightest radius—on both sides of the centerline. Then I rounded the ends of the blank to a 6-inch radius. With a more complicated shape, I could tack my pattern to the buck and assess how the paper fit: wrinkles of extra paper along the sides would indicate that shrinking is needed. However, because the dimensions of this fender are very straightforward, I started shaping immediately by shrinking outside the highlight lines and stretching inside them. With the steel fender, I worked one end with hand tools and a wheeling machine, then used the power hammer for the rest of the piece.

I shrank in to the tops of the highlight lines from the edges with the tucking tool on one end and with thumbnail shrinking dies everywhere else. As I described in *Professional Sheet Metal Fabrication*, tuck shrinking involves creating a wrinkle along the edge of a panel and hammering the wrinkle down in such a way that the metal is trapped and forced into itself. The metal becomes thicker and shorter from a longitudinal standpoint in the process. Without the use of heat, the tucking tool was probably only about 20 percent efficient on steel. Meanwhile, the thumbnail dies gobbled up the extra material below the highlight line like it was made of cookie dough. To generate greater depth down the center of the panel, I pummeled the hand-tool end with a large hammer and smoothed the worked area in the wheeling machine. I stretched the other end of the panel with a 6-inch-radius die in the power hammer and

The weld seam on these Bentley fenders is directly along the juncture between the top of the panel and the edge border.

This is the simplest buck design I have come up with. On this Stutz spare-tire-well buck, all the stations are the same and laid out to follow the panel's longitudinal curve. When kept perpendicular to the panel, stations need not be sanded or shaped. In addition, leaving the stations extra long allows them to be screwed together from the side onto a flat base, thus avoiding awkward additional trimming and fastening woes.

I began this demonstration with a 12 × 44-inch metal blank. I scribed an upper border for my highlight line 2½ inches from the edge and 3½ inches from the center, which corresponded to the surface changes on the buck. The end marked off with a black line will be worked using a tucking tool and wheeling machine instead of the power hammer.

smoothed out the evidence of my earlier edge shrinking with the same die.

By now my fender had the right overall shape, but it was not draping sufficiently over the buck. Even with access to a power hammer, my favorite way to generate maximum shape quickly is by pounding into a soft surface with a Viking marauder hammer. Although bludgeoning is no longer considered a legitimate way of attracting a bride or accumulating wealth, it works wonders for redirecting recalcitrant sheet metal in meaningful ways. (It also feels really good.) I pummeled the entire center of the blank with a large hammer to increase the drape of the metal over the buck. I

smoothed the hand-tool end with the wheel and the rest with the power hammer.

Up to now I had shrunk once up to the top of the highlight lines and a second time almost to the same spot. With all the shrinks to practically the same depth, I needed more radius all the way around the piece from the top of the highlight lines down. On the finished piece the highlight areas are a 3-inch radius. Shrinking halfway to the highlight started the metal moving in the right direction. I then smoothed the shrunken area with a 4-inch-radius die and blended the shrunken highlight into the main body of the fender on the power-hammer end.

I installed a row of tucks around the rear end of the panel by twisting the metal in a tucking tool held in a vise. I was careful to make the wrinkles rise on the inside of the panel instead of the outside to make them easier to trap in a stump.

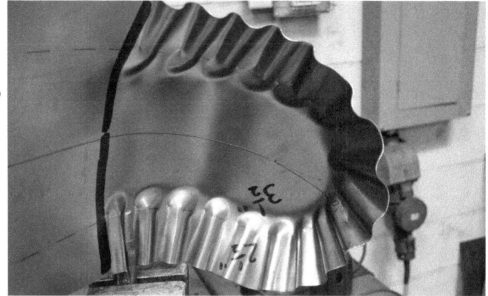

In my experience, the better you can trap a wrinkle in a depression in a stump, the more efficiently it will shrink. I hammer down the tucks starting on the outer edge, then move from the deepest point out.

A wrinkle created with thumbnail dies in the power hammer resembles a manual tuck. The process of power hammer shrinking is very similar to tuck shrinking in that metal is gathered, trapped, and thickened, but the efficiency of the mechanized version is, not surprisingly, vastly superior.

Temporarily avoiding the struggle awaiting me at the opposite end of the fender, I had been enjoying the easy success made possible by the power hammer. To draw the rear end of the fender closer to the buck with only hand tools, I carried out a series of heated tuck shrinks along the sides. Heated tuck shrinks are probably two or three times as effective as cold tuck shrinks on steel, but there is a trade-off: heated tuck shrinks leave behind surface oxides and stubborn wrinkles that are difficult to remove. To avoid the oxides marking up tools like your English wheel, scuff them off with a wire brush spinning in a heavy-duty tool. We have an ancient handheld pneumatic grinder from an age when tools were made of metal. It feels like it has about 10 horsepower and is capable of whizzing surface oxides from steel in minutes. Be sure to shrink out all unwanted wrinkles first or you may find yourself removing oxides multiple times. Heat shrinking definitely pulled the sides of the stubborn panel end closer to the buck, but it was slow work. I smoothed the shrunken area in the wheel and called the piece finished, even though in my heart of hearts I know it's only about 87 percent there.

A STROLL DOWN EASY STREET: THE ALUMINUM CYCLE FENDER

With the struggle of the hand-worked end of the fender still fresh on my mind, I was really looking forward to building the piece again with user-friendly aluminum.

The left side of this fender was shrunk around its edge by hand with a tucking tool and stretched above the highlight with a hammer on a shot bag. The right side of the panel was shrunk around its edge using the power hammer.

The rear end of the fender, worked with hand tools, lagged behind the rest of the fender. After my first round of shrinking and smoothing, I added more tucks to the rear.

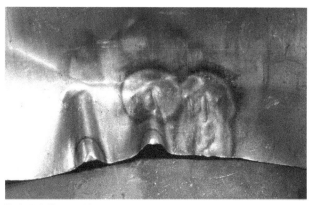

Tuck shrinking steel is not very efficient without heat. I followed the same hammering sequence as I had previously done cold, only this time I heated each spot red-hot before hammering.

I stretched the rear of the fender with a big hammer and wheeled out the many lumps from my previous shrinking and stretching efforts. In this image, the left side of the panel has been wheeled and the right side power hammered.

I stretched the main center portion of the forward end of the fender with a 6-inch-radius die in the power hammer. I used the same die with less power for smoothing the shrunken edges. During all stretching and smoothing, I averaged out the radii of the part and held it as photographed for maximum die contact.

Although the rear end of the fender could use a touch more shrinking to pull the panel down against the buck, I'm not going to express that thought out loud and will instead move on to an aluminum version of this panel.

Working with aluminum was liberating compared to steel. I made a row of tuck shrinks around the perimeter and pummeled the middle of the blank with a big hammer into a shot bag. After a few minutes of wheeling to smooth out the worst lumps, the fender looked reasonably close.

Following my initial wave of bashing, I annealed only the outer edge of the panel beyond the top of the highlight line and completed another round of shrinks along the long sides. I then smoothed the panel again on the wheel.

Additional wheeling ironed out most, but not all, of the nasty marks left by the tucking tool. The panel fits the buck, and I'm moving on to the next exciting metal-shaping adventure.

Although the material thickness of this blank is considerably more than the steel I used (0.063 inch versus 0.036 inch), the annealed aluminum felt like overcooked pasta compared to steel.

While the order of operations in this project probably does not make a big difference, I first made a lap of tuck shrinks around the perimeter of the aluminum blank coming in to the top of the highlight lines. I believe, but cannot confirm, that establishing a ring of shrunken, work-hardened metal around the perimeter of the piece directs more of the force from subsequent bashing in the middle to stretch more effectively.

Due to the wrinkles, the piece looks bizarre right away, but eventually looks better after stretching. If bashing comes first, wrinkles naturally form around the edge. Some of the stretching energy has been used to create them. Hammering down the wrinkles shrinks them, but they are not as prominent as wrinkles made by a tucking tool. My hunch is that you make more headway on an aluminum high crown piece when the shrinks come first, but the progress is immediately easier to observe when the stretching comes first. (I also spend a lot of time thinking about things that probably don't need to be thought about, like where does my crippled old mastiff go when he runs in his sleep?)

I followed the first round of shrinks by bludgeoning the main body of the piece with a big hammer. By now the blank was as misshapen as a pillowcase full of golf balls, but a few minutes of wheeling made the surface beautiful again. After checking the fit of the piece on the buck, I decided I needed a few more shrinks along the outer 2 inches down the sides of the piece. I annealed just the outer edges, shrunk them, and wheeled out most of the marks. I left the rear end of the blank unfinished, as I have a devious but educational plan to reuse it in a later chapter.

Chapter 7
The Reverse Curve Panel

Having now learned about, and perhaps experienced firsthand, the low crown and high crown panel, you are ready for the most formidable foe in sheet metal: the reverse curve panel.

What is a reverse curve? According to Fay Butler's definition, on a reverse curve panel a straightedge will rock in one dimension and span a hollow in the other. Although reverse curves shouldn't be any more

This reverse curve panel started as a 12-inch square with lines across the diagonals. The middle of each side was stretched in relation to the marker separations.

These two sample panels illustrate reverse curves. On the left, even stretching in bands along the length of the piece produced a panel resembling the inner edge of a donut hole. On the right, when stretching took place in a triangular zone midway along the length of the panel, a more relaxed curve resulted. All reverse curves require stretching one or more edges in relation to an area that isn't touched.

difficult to make than any other shape, I think they *are* more difficult to make because your shaping progress is more difficult to assess. Consider, for example, the low crown door-skin project in Chapter 5. A new metal shaper could lay his or her low crown project down on the buck and feel what needs to be raised. When the center is raised adequately, the piece drapes perfectly over the model. "*Voilà!*" the student remarks. On a reverse curve, all the work takes place on the edges and the panel fits starting from the center out. As extra length is added to the edges, the piece tends to curl up like a banana along its longitudinal axis if left to its own devices. The piece must constantly be re-formed horizontally across a curved surface to lower the sides into the hollow. A person needs X-ray vision to assess how well the panel fits. Fortunately, your eye will improve over time until you acquire X-ray vision and other superpowers, but there will likely be a difficult growth period.

BUILDING A SIMPLE BUCK
FOR THE REVERSE CURVE PANEL

For this project, I designed a shaping buck that provides, I hope, a relatively painless introduction to the reverse curve panel. The three stations of my buck, though they vary in height, are each a consistent radius across their horizontal surfaces. Such consistency throughout a reverse curve will seldom be found on a classic car, but it distills the essential principle of every reverse curve panel: stretch the edges in relation to the middle. On

a classic car, the radii of the end stations vary from the middle and thus add complexity.

Let's get the principles down and you can move on when ready. Shaping a reverse curve to a buck will be easier than shaping it on top of a fender because you can check your fit by peaking underneath. X-ray vision will not be needed.

Made entirely of ¾-inch plywood, the base of my buck measures 12 × 20 inches. The end stations are 12 inches tall and the center station is 10 inches tall. The radius across the top of each station is 24 inches. I will demonstrate the piece with a 12 × 21-inch sheet of aluminum, but a smaller piece would work just as well. You could also downsize the length as needed. The greater the height difference between the center station and the end stations, the more stretching will be needed along the panel's edges. I drew lines across the diagonals to separate the areas that need stretching from the areas that do not. Unfortunately, not all reverse curve panels will correspond to this easy formula, but this example will help you see how the thickness of the edges must change in relation to the middle of the panel.

Regardless of the tools used, the placement and quantity of stretching you put into the panel will not vary for a particular panel. There is one correct equation for this piece and every other: the right amount of shape formed into the right place will give you the panel you want. It sounds much easier than it is because you now know that a couple of misplaced atoms result in

If you do not have a classic car fender with a reverse curve handy, this simple buck will give you a chance to tackle this shape. The greater the difference in height between the center and end stations, the more stretching will be needed.

Crisscrossing the panel with a permanent marker makes knowing where to stretch easy. Pummel the long sides into a shot bag with a hammer. Pummel more near the edge because that metal must go farther to meet the buck.

Just like hammering, wheeling a long side stretches the edge and gives you the length you need to meet the buck. Pulling up against the upper wheel sends the metal down in relation to the panel's longitudinal centerline.

If you've chosen to stretch by hammering, planish the lumps against a smooth surface to flatten them out. A spoon spreads out the force of the blows, but a hammer or wood slapper also work well.

a panel that just looks *wrong*. Identifying the wayward atoms and shepherding them safely to their true home takes experience.

One more challenging characteristic of the reverse curve panel is the obvious dependency of the metal inboard of the edge on the behavior of the metal along the edge. In other words, unless the metal along the edge is moved out of the way, attempts at stretching the metal in from the edge will only result in "tumors" (up) or "hollows" (down). Whether the metal makes a tumor or a hollow is purely a question of form, but when these blemishes appear it is because you, the victim, have failed to stretch the edge sufficiently in relation to the metal inboard. When done correctly, you will feel the metal inboard squish out toward the edge like a paste. The sensation is immediately and obviously apparent with a set of linear stretching dies in the power hammer. These are the long skinny dies that strike the metal like a karate chop. I often cycle students through a session with these dies just to allow them to feel the metal flowing from inside the panel to the edge. Without that experience, you have to take my word for it, but part of the difficulty of making a reverse curve is because the inboard metal can move only as much as the outboard metal moves to make a place for it.

With only a hammer and sandbag or shot bag, you can make this panel by lightly bashing the long triangular zones at the sides of your panel. Hammer more near the edges than deeper in the panel because the metal nearer the center does not have as far to go to get to the buck. Leave the very center and the end zones undisturbed. It will be lumpy, but you will have experienced the general approach to making reverse curve panels. With a wooden mallet or steel spoon, planish your panel smooth against a round stump, a large piece of pipe, or a curved dolly resting on a shot bag. Planishing your piece evens out all the lumps and enables you to check it on the buck. Bend the piece against a large object like a trash can or welding gas cylinder to counteract its tendency to curve like a banana along its longitudinal axis. With the appropriate amount of stretching along the sides, the panel will most likely curve as I have described and look close, but be wrong, so anticipate this—it is just part of finding the proper relationship between shape and form.

You should not need to stretch the center of the panel at all. In fact, the reverse curve relies on the thickness difference between the untouched middle and the thinner, longer sides. If gaps exist between the buck and the outer long edges of the panel, more stretching is needed along the edges. Look for where the gap begins inboard and commence light bashing from that point out to the edges of the long sides. If the long edges touch first, thereby creating a gap inboard, the edges have been stretched too much. Anneal the edges by burning off some Sharpie marks and tuck shrink the extra edge length back into submission.

By stretching only the long sides with a hammer, you can make this panel fit the buck, but it will probably have a slight amount of tension that will cause the panel to spring up about $\frac{1}{16}$ to $\frac{1}{8}$ inch at the ends. You'll be able to push it down against the buck with light hand pressure, but when you remove your hand it will rise a little. Don't worry. It is the nature of sheet metal to

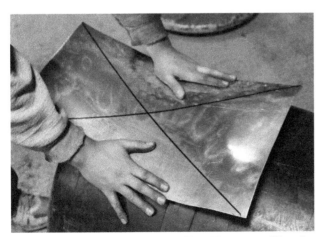

As you stretch the panel sides, the piece will want to curve up at its ends. Simply push it against the nearest large cylindrical object to reestablish the proper form.

After some smoothing and forming against a malodorous 50-gallon plastic bending die, my sample panel sat on the buck, though the surface was still bumpy and clearly needed work.

confuse, confound, and cause you to confabulate. You have done nothing wrong and truly are on the right path. Gently form the previously untouched areas over a round surface with a spoon or wooden mallet. Your panel will fit on the buck like a 12-inch-wide strip of duct tape and you'll feel like a hero.

CONQUERING THE REVERSE CURVE WITH AN ENGLISH WHEEL

With a wheeling machine, follow the same plan of attack I just described. The only difference here is that you will need to tell the metal where to go as you stretch it between the wheels.

Normally during wheeling the metal wants to arc up as you work the panel back and forth. This makes sense because the lower wheel is smaller in diameter. As the metal gets squished between the wheels, it is anxious to find a way out and squirts out through the shortest route possible: across the radius of the lower wheel. The squeezing creates shape. The direction of up or down is just form. You can change the form part of the equation by pulling up against the upper wheel during wheeling. Using this method, the squeezed metal will try to conform to the larger upper wheel. Once you have told it which direction to go, the metal will tend to keep going in that direction as you stretch

Stretched material manifests itself as a wave along an edge or as a tumor inboard of the edge. Shrink the edge with a Lancaster-style machine to tighten a loose edge; an inboard tumor can be shrunk or the edge can be stretched depending on whether the metal needs to go back up toward flat (shrink) or down toward the buck (stretch).

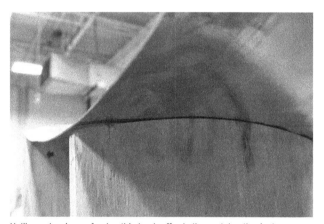

Unlike a classic car fender, this buck affords the metal enthusiast easy viewing from below to assess his or her progress. A gap between the panel and the buck, as here, indicates a need for stretching from the beginning of the gap out to the edge.

I wheeled out the lumps caused by hammering along one edge and deemed the panel complete.

Finding the tightest radius along the fender edge was the first step in making this section of a Model A Ford front fender. The highlight line is where the panel abruptly changes direction. I applied a piece of thin masking tape along the top of the highlight line to facilitate transferring this line to my paper pattern.

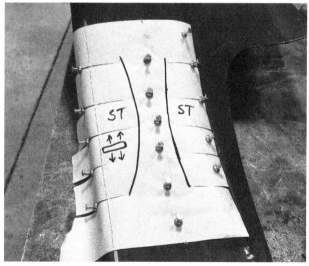

Slitting my paper pattern was necessary to get the paper to lay flat against the fender with magnets. I pressed against the tape line along the highlight to find its exact origin and drew the line on my pattern.

it. If you get sloppy and fail to tell the metal where to go—meaning you forget to exert upward pressure—the metal will once again try to conform to the lower wheel and you will end up with a tumor rising in the opposite direction of the rest of the panel. No worries. Resume wheeling and pull up against the upper wheel to remind the metal where it is supposed to go. As I have already described, the inboard metal will move only in relation to the metal alongside it, so start each series of passes from the edge, stretch as needed, then work your way back out to the edge. Don't forget to form the panel as needed against a trash can or piece of pipe to manage the relationship between shape and form.

I cannot resist pointing out another learning opportunity this panel presents. Once the shape is correct, you can wheel the panel with light pressure in any direction you choose to bring the surface to a high degree of finish—provided you do not orient the piece in such a way that the sides of the upper wheel dig into the metal. From the metal's point of view, there is no up or down, only the one true surface represented by the correct finished piece. Thus, you can wheel across the middle with the panel flipped over, or longitudinally all the way across the piece. Because shape relies on thickness change in one area relative to another area, if you treat the entire panel the same, the shape will not change. Placing pressure between the wheels adds stretching, however, so don't get carried away.

WHEN TOO MUCH IS JUST RIGHT: THE POWER HAMMER REVERSE CURVE

On the power hammer, a reverse curve is usually made using linear stretching dies. These stretch the metal much more to the sides, whereas a round die stretches equally in 360 degrees. I have chosen part of a Ford Model A front fender to demonstrate these tools. I began this demonstration with a paper pattern to identify how much stretching would be needed along the edge of the fender and where it would be needed. As on the other reverse curve examples, I have marked off three general zones of stretching. Unlike the sample reverse curve buck, however, the horizontal radius of this fender varies at every point along its length. I've included the extra metal along the outer edge to show how the reverse curve fits in the context of the rest of the fender.

Like the other reverse curve panels, I began stretching from the edges and worked my way toward the center. Although this shape could be made by working the panel from either side, I usually have new students start from the back of the panel on a reverse curve because the metal will normally tend to form up with these dies if the user applies downward pressure to keep the panel from bouncing. Working from the back, a rising panel coincides more closely with the finished piece in this example, so the metal starts out headed in the right direction. In addition, teaching students to

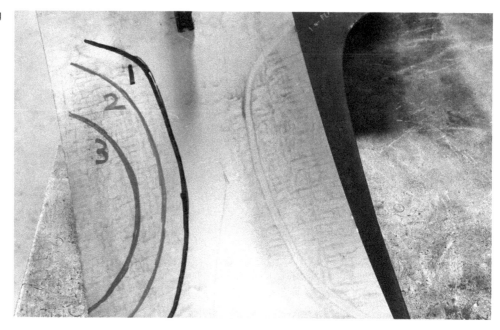

I performed most of my stretching with the linear stretching dies in the power hammer oriented perpendicular to the panel edge. I stretched both long sides of the panel in roughly three zones. The third zone in the center received the most stretching.

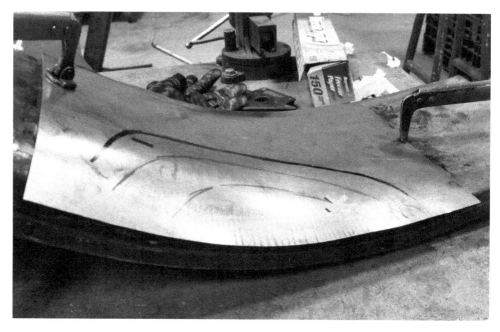

As material thickness is transformed into length along the panel sides, bending the sides to match the original fender becomes easier.

control the flow of the metal over the stationary lower die is simple. Once a student has a feel for the flow of the metal, I encourage freestyling to achieve the best fit of the dies on the piece. To work a panel from the topside on a reverse curve like this, the user needs to curve the panel edges upward in relation to the dies and the metal will tend to form down. This makes perfect sense because the metal seeks out a larger radius as it is stretched between the dies.

With the linear dies, progress comes quickly. Just like with the wheel, all inboard stretching is accompanied by outboard stretching so the metal will have a place to go. Several light passes are better than one dramatic pummeling. As with the previous two reverse curve demonstrations, the amount of stretching in zone three is about twice as much as in zone two. The stretching in zone two is about twice that of zone one. Between the dies of the power hammer, the

Once I had sufficiently stretched the long sides of the panel, I bent the outer side of the piece along the highlight to match the fender.

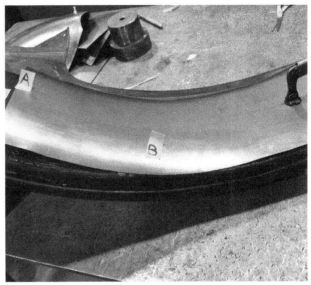

This example, separate from the demonstration piece, illustrates the problem of overstretching. Too much stretching down the long sides of this panel has made the end (marked "A") reach for the sky.

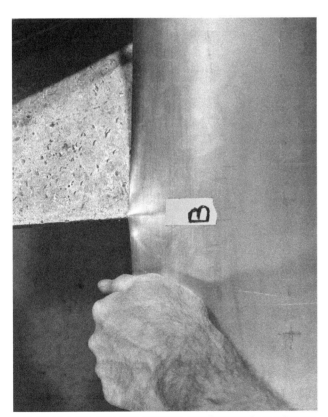

To find the location of the extra stretching, identify where the panel seems to rock back and forth—point "B" on this panel—and push it against a table edge to force the extra material into a wrinkle. Check the piece on the fender or buck. If the fit has improved, shrink the extra material in the wrinkle.

After shrinking the material at point "B" with a kick-shrinker, point "A" no longer sits high on the fender.

metal feels like thick, easily directed paste. This is a pleasurable sensation comparable to an all-expenses-paid weekend in Amsterdam, but without any negative consequences. After a few passes through the power hammer, the panel lies firmly against the original fender. Having stretched the extreme outer edge only as much as needed to get the rest of the fender into shape, I installed the bend along the highlight line against a piece of pipe.

Chapter 8
Scratch-Built Fender

If you have participated in the previous learning examples and are yearning for more, or if you are just reading ahead, the following sheet metal adventure allows you to make a fender from two of the smaller panels described in the last two chapters.

This fender is reminiscent of something you might see on a coachbuilt Bentley from about 1930. Even if you finished off both ends of the high crown cycle fender from Chapter 6, there is plenty of material to square off one end and add an additional panel. Furthermore, although the reverse curve panel I described was built to a consistent 24-inch radius across the panel, altering this contour to fit the high crown panel is not a big deal. In fact, changing this panel is part of my larger plot to demystify the process of turning sheet metal into car shapes. If you have already made the high crown and reverse curve panels from flat sheets, congratulations: both are significant milestones. Now you will combine them into a larger shape, another milestone. I hope in the process you see that even the most difficult sheet

metal challenge can be met by analyzing the shape, thinking about how the metal must depart from a flat plane to get there, and then formulating a plan of attack based on smaller achievable goals that together will give the results you want.

TURNING TWO PANELS INTO ONE

Because I left my aluminum high crown panel from two chapters ago squared off on the rear end, I turned my attention to altering the 24-inch-radius reverse curve panel from the end of Chapter 7 to match it. I could have formed the reverse curve over a pipe or cylinder to match the high crown fender, but in doing so I would have lost much of the swoopiness that makes the reverse curve shape so appealing. In fabricating this panel or any other reverse curve you have attempted, you may have noticed that pushing the long sides down straightens out the panel longitudinally. To maintain the desirable relaxed S-shape of the curve, more stretching is needed on the long sides of the panel. I redrew the diagonal

This fender combines skills and concepts learned on the two panels in the last chapter. You need neither a buck nor a model to acquire valuable new skills finishing this piece.

Sharpie lines that had by now worn off across my corners and wheeled the sides of the panel near where the lines intersect. Without an original fender to match, the amount of curve you decide to put into this panel is up to you. As long as you treat each side the same, the panel will stay even. By pulling up against the upper wheel as you wheel toward the corners on the forward end of the reverse curve panel, you can both stretch and form the metal to align more closely with the rear edge of the panel it will join. Wheeling with pressure is stretching; pulling up is forming. At any point you can bend the leading edge of the reverse curve against a pipe or a rubber mallet secured in a vise to match the rear of the high crown panel. If your reverse curve deflates too much during forming, or if the panels' sides seem too tight to bend where you want, stretch the sides more. When you are satisfied with the fit, lap one panel over the other and clamp them. Scribe a trim line and include a few registration marks across the seam to help you get the trimmed panel back where it belongs for welding.

To adapt the aluminum reverse curve panel to the aluminum high crown panel made previously, I stretched the panel's long sides and formed the body of the panel against the nearest chubby thigh.

Once I was satisfied with the shape of my reverse curve panel in relation to the high crown panel, I traced a trim line on the rear end of the reverse curve panel and lopped off the extra. I adjusted the compass to a 12-inch radius and placed it along each edge in line with the longitudinal center of the panel.

Next, I clamped the reverse curve panel in position behind the high crown panel on the buck, clamped them together with Vise-Grips, and scribed a trim line on the high crown panel.

The high crown and reverse curve panel may be welded by any means at your disposal. For tungsten inert gas (TIG) welding, set the machine to AC polarity and 110 amperes. Use between 15 and 20 cubic feet of gas per hour (CFH) of argon on your regulator. Select a ¹⁄₁₆-inch-diameter pure tungsten electrode with a ball on the tip. For 0.063-inch-thick 3003 aluminum, I like 0.040-inch-diameter 1100 filler rod for a small weld, but a ¹⁄₁₆-inch-diameter rod is a little easier to handle. Scrub both sides of the metal with a stainless-steel brush and wipe off any residue with acetone prior to tack-welding and then again after tacking. For maximum weld quality, I run a strip of fiberglass backing tape behind the length of the seam after I have wire brushed and cleaned the tacks, but before I do the weld. The tape is available from www.Arc-Zone.com.

ADDING A CREASE

Hopefully by now you have a full-size fender, ready for any kind of edge treatment you desire. One last detail you might consider is a crease down the center of the panel. The least tool-intensive way to create this detail is with a homemade hardwood chisel, or "bonking tool"

as I refer to them. If you wish to make the crease fade out at either or both ends, cut the end of your tool to a shallow angle and lightly install the detail with the fender facedown against a shot bag. Then cut the tool to a slightly deeper angle and make another pass through the center two-thirds of the piece. You will be able to feel the tool seat against the metal as you strike it. If still more depth is needed, cut the tool again and work the center one-third of the detail to deepen it. If artistic blending is needed, rub the bonking tool under pressure back and forth across the areas that need attention with the panel still facedown on a shot bag. Depending on your weight and/or strength, this absurdly easy technique works surprisingly well. The wood bonking tool will give you a soft but presentable crease. If you desire a sharper crease, support the detail from behind with a steel dolly or stake made for the purpose and planish on either side of the peak with a spoon that has a convex surface. Do *not* hit the apex of the crease. Planishing with hand tools will leave tool marks, however, so be prepared to remove hammer marks with a file.

To crease the panel in the wheeling machine, you have a couple of options. For a very crisp crease, you need to make the fender in longitudinal halves and place a weld seam about ⅜ to ½ inch to one side of the crease. Shape the panel that will receive the crease normally, then bend the crease between the flat wheels. Shrink the metal on the short side of the crease as much as is needed to bring it down to the level of the buck. On the sample fender I chose not to use this method because it would have involved a weld seam running the length of the fender.

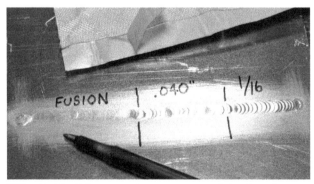

I TIG welded the high crown and reverse curve panels together using a 0.040-inch filler rod and a strip of Arc-Zone fiberglass-backed welding tape on the back of the weld. This image compares the relative weld sizes of three different filler rods. A fusion weld is tempting, but in my experience can result in low areas that require additional work.

The simplest way of adding a crease down the center of this fender was to lay out a tape line, trace its edges for reference, remove the tape, and hammer the panel over a shot bag with a custom wooden tool.

To enhance the crispness of the central crease, I supported the line I wanted to keep and planished both sides of it with a curved spoon.

ground to prevent gouging. As with the wheel, fasten a temporary guide between the power hammer arms to help you keep the panel straight during creasing. Trace a piece of tape laid down over the proposed centerline with a permanent marker. Peel away the tape. When I use this technique on the power hammer, I start at the far end of the panel and push the panel through with very soft blows between the dies. This first pass allows me to check that all is well without making any huge mistakes. Once I have pushed the panel as far as it needs to go, I pull it back toward me with as much pressure as I need to install the detail. Dragging the panel against the lower die and the guide at the same time gives you a surprising amount of control and helps steady the panel. The detail will appear like a mouse crawling under a carpet.

I used a rubber insert top die and a curved steel bottom die to crease the steel cycle fender in the power hammer. The rubber insert forms the panel over the shape of the bottom die.

The other option for adding the crease with the wheel incorporates a semisoft top wheel and a sharper-radius bottom wheel than used for normal wheeling. Metal shapers have come up with all kinds of clever wheel combinations to create this effect, from replacing the upper wheel with a rubber tire or rubber caster to Lazze Jansson's strip of inner tube installed on the upper wheel. Moving the panel between a steel lower anvil and a rubber top allows the crease to form. In my experience, a single pass does the cleanest job with this method, but guiding the panel can be tricky. It helps to clamp a piece of angle iron vertically alongside the work to serve as a fence.

To crease the panel on the power hammer, you need a rubber-faced top die and a fabricated lower die. I made a lower die out of a length of ⅜-inch-diameter steel rod bent on a slight curve. The ends of the rod are

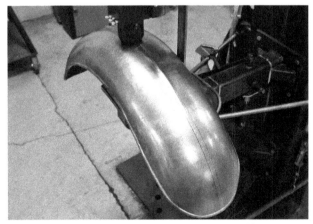

I made a temporary fence against which to steady my panel by clamping a length of aluminum angle vertically between the arms of the power hammer.

Chapter 9
Patch Panelpalooza

Although I devoted quite a few pages of *Professional Sheet Metal Fabrication* to the ins and outs of patch panel repair, I want to supplement those comments with a few observations and a checklist that I hope readers will find useful for any patch panel project.

Although I personally love the challenge of making a new fender or patch panel, not everyone needs to go to that much trouble. If original pieces can be salvaged from another car, or if high-quality replacement panels are available, then of course either option is preferable to installing a patch repair. Component replacement ensures that all vestiges of rust are addressed, both on the car and on the replacement piece. Cutting into and welding on an existing panel increases the energy in the panel and actually encourages the panel to rust in the area of the repair, just like a freshly media-blasted piece rusts more quickly than an untouched original. If you have had professional metalwork done on a car and

the shop insisted on replacing the panel, it was most likely because they were concerned about corrosion rearing its ugly head down the road; they weren't just trying to gouge you for money. Moreover, component replacement eliminates the time, hassle, and potential pitfalls involved in smoothly welding two shaped metal pieces so that they appear as one.

In the real world, however, few of us have the limitless resources needed to avoid patch panels altogether. Thus, in this chapter, I will share some tips for installing patch panels successfully. I have designed a couple of exercises for developing the essential fitment, welding, and finishing skills on harmless scrap metal, *not* your prized project car. My first patch panel exercise removes metal shaping from the equation, so the exercise is easy to repeat as many times as necessary to build your confidence. The second exercise lays out a strategy you can use to secure a new patch in the optimum spot for welding.

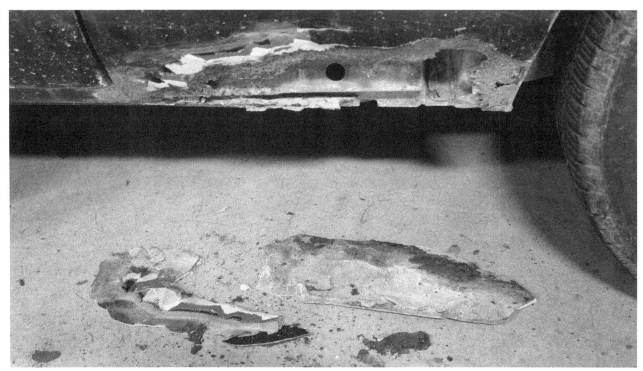

Zachary's cancerous El Camino, though horrifying, is typical of what we lovers of old cars can expect to encounter on our projects. Luckily, there are strategies for dealing with these situations.

The first critical step to any patch panel replacement is to achieve a perfect fit between the patch and the target panel. Start by bending a 12 × 12-inch panel like the one in this example.

RISK-FREE PRACTICE

Unless they are to be held in by adhesives, duct tape, telekinesis, or magic, patch panels need to be welded. As a restorer, your goal with all welded repairs is to leave no evidence of your work. Unfortunately, getting your welding and metal-finishing skills to that level takes hours of practice. Most hobbyists do not practice, per se; rather, they start with small projects on vehicles they own and gain skills as they take on greater challenges. This makes sense. Besides carrying out projects that you need to get done and running a few welds, what more can a person do?

After several years of teaching this discipline, I have come to believe that learning metal shaping and welding is a lot like learning to play a fretless musical instrument. These disciplines are certainly both an art and a science, the enigmatic blending of mathematical exactitude and intuition. Just as no one would dare call him- or herself a "violinist" without having logged hundreds of hours of practice, so should the aspiring metal enthusiast embrace practice as a key element of his or her training. These patch panel exercises, whether you are successful right away or not, are valuable, intentional practice. Moreover, the emotional scars brought on by failure tend to sear lessons into the mind.

The following stepped panel exercise is one of my favorite drills for improving students' welding of patch panels. Working with a stepped panel has several advantages: (1) it is easy to make and remake with minimal tools; (2) it reliably delivers the fitment, welding, and finishing challenges that you will face on *every* patch panel without worrying about shape; (3) the piece can be clamped rigidly to a table, which makes it easy to work with; and (4) dealing with flat surfaces is demanding; stretched or shrunken metal will be impossible to ignore. If you can do this exercise successfully without crazy distortion, tumors, or overground welds, you will have mastered the fitment, welding, and weld-finishing part of every patch panel you will ever come across. Aside from shaping, this is all there is to it.

The dimensions of the panel are not particularly important as long as the piece is not too small—say less than 10 × 10 inches. On a smaller panel there will be nowhere for the heat to go. The panel will distort more and be difficult to control. Pick lengths for the legs that are easy to repeat with the tools that you have. If you do not have a sheet metal brake, bend the sides by clamping each leg between scraps of 2 × 4 wood held in a vise or clamped to a table.

Tack your patch into the target panel. Take your time to make sure the panels stay in perfect alignment throughout the tack-welding phase.

Beginning with a 12 × 12-inch blank, I bent my legs once at 2½ inches from the edge and then again at 1 inch from the edge because those dimensions conveniently lined up with two painted lines on the bending bar of our sheet metal brake. Next, I taped off a rectangle along one side of my panel, cut out the inner portion with a 4½-inch cutoff wheel secured in an electric angle grinder, and filed the edges until they were clean and free of burrs. I bent a second panel to the same leg dimensions as the original blank and clamped it behind the panel with the cutout. Smart strategic thinkers could simply bend an 18 × 12-inch version of the panel and cut off 6 inches from one end to use as a patch for the center. As more of an arts, letters, and interpretive dance–type guy, I didn't think of that until after I had already bent the second piece. Remarkably, I have had at least a dozen students do this exercise and I have not thought of making it out of one piece until now. No doubt you'll be smarter.

Scribing around the perimeter of the hole with the "patch" clamped behind gave me a perfect line for trimming. I cleaned the panels with acetone prior to welding. Any foreign material or filler will compromise the strength of the weld. Consider wearing nitrile gloves, not oil-stained welding gloves, while welding. I clamped the "patch" in place and carefully tacked it around the perimeter. On a patch that crosses a bend

or body line, consider putting a tack on the bend or body line as early as possible. Welding always causes shrinkage. Despite your best efforts to stretch the welds with a hammer during the tacking phase, however, a panel may shift and the misfit will be noticeable. If you do not have much experience with patch panels, tacking on the bend or body line secures the panel's position at these critical points before the panel can wriggle out of alignment.

An oft-repeated phrase my students hear in our sheet metal lab is "Be the taskmaster." By that I mean that you must stay in complete control of every phase of the setup, welding, and finishing process. You must monitor every variable and respond to each situation as it unfolds. If you become complacent, you will lose control and things will go awry. Thus, time spent fitting any patch is time well spent. Learn this lesson now and reap the benefits forever.

The stepped panel is easy to clamp, so secure its alignment with Vise-Grips and begin the tacking process. Do not leave a gap for a TIG weld; for a MIG weld, leave a gap approximately equal to the thickness of the metal. Place your tacks about 1 inch apart for TIG or ¾ inch apart for MIG. To make certain that the patch and the larger surrounding panel stay in the same plane at all times, stop and assess panel alignment after each tack weld. Tack the entire seam before welding anything completely. Misalignment will be the result of shrinking at the tacks, so stretch out the metal by hitting it with a steel hammer against a steel dolly, but hammer only enough to get the metal flat. Too much hammering will stretch the metal and result in a tumor.

Much like choosing the wrong spouse, welding missteps will lead to long-term anguish. They might even cost you money. Follow these steps to make sure your weld is as small and as easy to finish as possible. As for welding technique, I recommend either the MIG or TIG methods described in *Professional Sheet Metal Fabrication*. Oxyacetylene welds are very ductile and easy to finish, but they are less suitable for patch panels because of the high heat they bring to the panel and the area around the repair. To MIG weld thin sheet metal, use a series of hot short welds laid adjacent to each other between the original tacks. With the voltage turned up, the MIG weld will be flat and centered within the thickness of the metal. The MIG will require a lot of careful grinding on both sides of the weld and it will not be as deliciously ductile as the TIG, but it will work.

A small TIG weld, without an excess of filler rod, will behave exactly like the parent metal in its pristine, unwelded state. For tiny welds on old-car sheet metal in the 18- to 20-gauge range, choose 0.040-inch tungsten. Smaller tungstens can stabilize the arc at a lower amperage. Start with about 35 amperes and adjust from there. The 2 percent thoriated tungstens (red striped) give the most stable arc and keep their tips the longest. Their ground dust is also slightly radioactive, however. Ceriated (usually gray striped) is probably the next best, though a distant second. At home I use thoriated exclusively on steel. While teaching I use ceriated for steel to protect the health of the young whippersnappers in my care.

In addition to the small tungsten, choose a small filler rod: 0.023-inch, 0.030-inch, or at the most 0.035-inch. These can often be purchased in straight rods, but I use ER70 S-6 MIG wire because it is easier to get locally. A $\frac{1}{16}$-inch-diameter filler rod will leave a large weld bead behind. If you feel the smaller wires are a hassle to straighten by hand, wrap a length around a screwdriver bit chucked up in a drill. The bit allows the drill chuck to grip the thin wire, which would otherwise be too small to hold. Secure the opposite loose end of the wire in a vise or in a pair of Vise-Grips held in a vise. Spin the drill at a slow speed and pull back against the wire to straighten it.

Watch the panels very closely as you apply heat with the TIG torch. If a hole starts to open, immediately add a dab of filler. If there is a slight gap to begin with, make an arc but do not try to create a puddle. While the arc is crackling, you'll be able to see what you are doing. Bring in the filler and melt a miniscule droplet about the size of a ball in the tip of a ballpoint pen on top of the seam. Keep the TIG torch over the ball with the arc crackling so that the argon protects the filler from oxidizing. Add more heat to the ball of filler and direct the melting ball across the seam with the TIG torch until it spans the gap and joins the two panels. This technique works splendidly when you need to join a new piece of metal to clean original metal on an old car. The arc will naturally go to the droplet of filler and will make joining old and new metal very easy. Otherwise, the TIG arc seems to prefer the old metal on one side of the seam and you will have trouble burning holes.

Begin welding by striking an arc on the first tack and create a puddle about $\frac{1}{8}$ inch in diameter. The diameter of the puddle is your heat indicator. A diameter of $\frac{3}{16}$ inch means the puddle is too hot. Keep the tungsten close—about $\frac{1}{8}$ inch or less—to the panel. The farther away the tungsten gets, the hotter and bigger the pool will be because the gap adds resistance, just like the air gap on a spark plug. Tilt the torch no more than about 15 degrees to the right of perpendicular if you are right-handed. More angle than that will spread out the pool and the shielding gas. Move the weld puddle down the seam like a robot from right to left. On thin steel in the 18- to 20-gauge range, there is no need to move the torch in any direction besides down the seam. Do not move it back and forth. Do not swirl it around in circles. The $\frac{1}{8}$-inch-diameter puddle will penetrate. Additional torch gyrations only add time spent heating the panel unnecessarily, which means more heat distortion to stretch out later. This simple robotic TIG-welding approach is contrary to what is customarily done on thicker steel, such as $\frac{1}{8}$-inch plate and thicker, where torch movement improves penetration, but this approach is the hot ticket for thin metal.

Keep the angle of the filler metal low—about 15 degrees in relation to the panel—as you introduce it to the puddle, and don't let the end of the filler rod ball up from heat. Touch the rod to the leading edge of the puddle about every count of "one Mississippi, two Mississippi, three Mississippi." Just touch the rod to the pool and it will melt. If you consciously try to melt the rod, you will melt off far more than you need or want. If you do not add too much filler, the TIG weld will be small, flat, and a breeze to finish out. Keep the tungsten pointy and regrind it if it gets contaminated. A nasty tungsten will require more heat to stabilize, and when it does, the panel will look like a great white shark has taken a bite out of one side of the weld seam.

Following the elaborate ritual above, take a crack at the stepped panel. Do not be disheartened if you do not succeed at first. Sheet metal has a way of finding the most tender, vulnerable parts of your psyche and chomping on them. Persevere. Analyze your mistakes. If you learn *anything* from each attempt, it will have been worthwhile. I often tell students that sheet metal projects can take as many as three or more attempts to complete successfully. You may emerge victorious on the first attempt, but the struggle will seem like a barroom brawl. Glad to be alive, you'll shake your head in amazement and wonder what happened. On the second attempt, you'll be more aware of what's going on and you'll emerge from the experience with a few coherent thoughts and most of your teeth. On the third attempt, you won't necessarily have the thing "wired," but you'll understand what has transpired. The surge of adrenaline that follows one of these contests spurs us on in pursuit of the next challenge.

SNEAKING UP ON THE PERFECT FIT

Whether a panel is an aftermarket piece or crafted by you, try to get it to fit on the problem area like two Solo cups nesting together, unless flanges dictate otherwise. Recently I have been pleasantly surprised by the quality of aftermarket panels that students have acquired to repair their personal cars. I hope this is a growing trend and not just an illusion fostered by inhaling too much acetylene. Nevertheless, let's explore some minor modifications that may need to be made to a panel that you have purchased from the aftermarket.

HOW TO HEAT SHRINK

Despite your best efforts, you may have stretched some metal along the weld seam during the tacking phase or while hammering your welds. I discussed heat shrinking extensively in *Professional Sheet Metal Fabrication.* A short description of the process is as follows: (1) heat a dime-size spot red-hot with an oxyacetylene flame; (2) while the metal still has color, hammer the red spot down against a flat steel dolly held behind the panel. Use the lightest flat-faced body hammer in your possession and hit the spot only about as hard as you would drive a tack. Continue hammering very lightly to smooth out the shrunken spot.

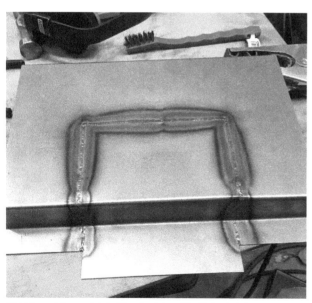

Weld the patch completely. Stopping intermittently to stretch out the inevitable shrinkage that occurs along the weld seam is probably an easier way to maintain complete control than welding without stopping.

Carefully grind and file any superfluous weld seam that stands proud of the base metal. Use extra care on the bends—overgrinding there will be very noticeable. Once the weld is ground, trim away any extra metal along the edge of the patch.

PATCH PANEL CHECKLIST

If your self-esteem is intact after the stepped panel exercise, or if you are already skilled enough to apply some of the techniques just described to cars you are working on, here is a checklist of things to consider before attacking your next patch panel:

You must be the taskmaster at every step along the way.
Plan what will happen and monitor your progress as you go. Sheet metal has a way of sneaking up on you and turning the tables before you realize what's going on.

Strive to hang on to the old stuff as long as possible.
Resist the temptation to cut away old rusty metal just because it's rusty. The status quo, though rusty, contains valuable information that will be forever lost once the panel is altered.

Plan for weld seams so that you'll be able to stretch them out. Welding inevitably involves shrinkage. If the shrinkage is not stretched out, the weld will end up lower than the surrounding metal. Gaining access to the back of the weld might require making a larger patch to move the weld seam to a more accessible spot or cutting out an access hole behind.

On multilayer repairs, try to address the layers one at a time to maximize fit and access. This will typically involve tacking the new exterior layer in place, removing the underlayer, welding and finishing the exterior layer, then addressing the underlayer.

On panels that are both rusty and dented, fix the dents before repairing the rust. If you do not, the shape of the repaired panel will most likely be off.

Frequently, aftermarket panels are made to fit comfortably over the original panel. Perhaps this is intentional. The producers may be assuming that the average person is simply going to pop rivet the new piece over the old, slather the seam with plastic filler, and call it good. Second, a slightly oversize panel is much easier to accurately place in relation to the original panel than an exact duplicate, which often cannot be superimposed over the panel it replaces. If your panel is oversize or not quite right, do not fear; this can be changed.

To change a flange or body line, draw or lightly scribe the new intended line for the bend, support the line you want to keep with the crisp edge of a dolly or hunk of steel, and hammer above the supported line. My favorite hammer for this process is ground on a gradual curve from the top of the face to the bottom on a 1½-inch radius. The face has no radius horizontally. This technique comes in handy all the time. In teaching, I try to use the same langauge repeatedly to help students generalize from the particular. In a future moment of need I hope my words will suddenly manifest themselves and help fix the problem at hand. Say this phrase out loud: "Support the line you want to keep. Hammer the unsupported metal" and commit it to memory. If the edge of the new panel does not quite match the panel to which it attaches, do not hesitate to re-form it against a stake held in a vise. The edges need to be spot-on or the patch will be very obvious.

When patch panels are made from original panels, the patch often ends up larger than the original, which leaves one or more flanges in the wrong place. An easy way to move a flange on a patch panel is to support the line you want to keep with a piece of steel and then hammer over the unsupported adjacent metal.

By hammering the unsupported metal next to my preferred bend line, I moved this flange over about ⅛ inch. A hammer with a face ground prominently in one direction can help ensure that the metal is finessed into position as opposed to mauled on top of the steel fulcrum.

If you are happy with the fit of an aftermarket patch panel superimposed over the original, you can sneak up on the perfect fit by cutting off only the edge of the old panel. Removing the edge allows the new panel to be fitted perfectly without overtrimming.

Imagine that your panel is magnificent: it *seems* to be an exact duplicate of the thing it replaces. Unfortunately, the presence of flanges on the pieces involved prevents you from securing the new piece *exactly* in its intended spot. Don't worry, you need not commit yourself to hacking off the original yet. Sneak up on the perfect fit by cutting off just one or more edges of the original panel to allow the new one to slide into place. Clamp the new panel with Vise-Grips. Step back and assess the fit. Remember, you are only cutting off an edge of the old panel. You have not yet committed to trimming the panel off for welding.

If you are happy with the fit of the new piece superimposed over the old, carefully scribe *once* around the perimeter of the patch and make a few registration marks across the edges to ensure that there is only one true home for the patch. Scribing once is the best way of marking. For average or substandard work, use a marker. For maximum anal-retentiveness, use spring-loaded temporary rivets called Clecos or self-tapping sheet metal screws for a three-point attachment across the future weld seam.

Once the patch is located, you may cut away the old metal. Don't be afraid to file the last bit by hand if needed. Leave no gap for a TIG weld or a gap equal to the thickness of the metal for MIG. The setup process is critical to achieving good results. Tack-weld the patch in place, hammering gently as you go to maintain a perfect fit. Do *all* of your tacks, but don't weld anything. It is okay to mix MIG and TIG as needed if your seam requires it (e.g., MIG welding a spot that has a hair more gap than you'd like). When MIG welding, I find it helpful to start tacks in the middle and work out to the edges. This allows you to lightly file the panel edges if they creep together in response to the shrinkage caused by welding. If the gap closes too tightly to file easily, enlarge the gap with a ¹⁄₃₂-inch-wide cutoff wheel, the edge of a thin abrasive disk mounted in an angle grinder, or a reciprocating saw.

If there is a second layer, you may now remove it by carefully cutting it out from behind. Keep heavily used small-diameter cutoff wheels for this purpose; they allow you to sneak behind 90-degree bends and cut through a single layer in a two-layer sheet metal sandwich. Cut

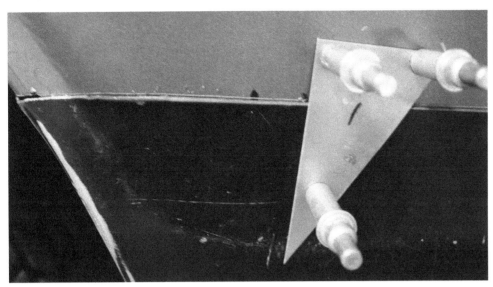

With the edges of the old panel removed and the new panel held in place with Clecos, finding the exact trim line is a breeze.

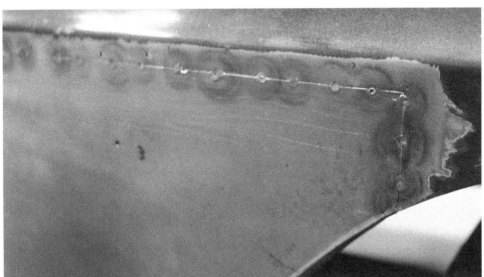

If all our patch panels fit like Greg's, the world would be a better place. Aside from the wee crater in one of the tacks, this is what a perfect TIG seam looks like. Greg welded this sitting on the ground with the TIG amperage pedal under the back of his knee.

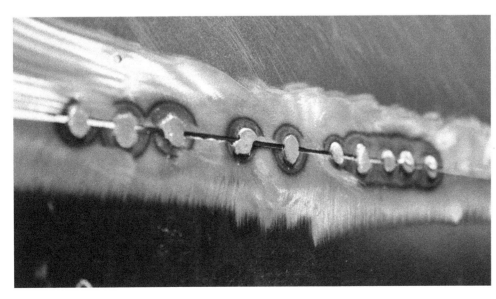

The panels at the center of this image are crawling slightly out of alignment. Andrew caught this potential goof and hammered the panels back into place before welding.

out a larger area on the back of the repair area to leave plenty of room for finishing the weld on the topside. Weld the topside completely, hammering as you go to maintain a perfect fit. File or grind it as needed. Once the topside is complete, replace the back.

The last phase of installing the patch panel is removing any evidence of your weld. A well-executed TIG weld seems to finish itself with a single dramatic wave of a file. If this doesn't quite do the job, or if you have a MIG weld to contend with, keep in mind that you are removing *only* the metal that stands proud of the parent metal. Ideally, the only metal removal will take place directly on the weld seam. If you do not see any pinholes or gaps in the seam that require welding, scribble on the seam with a black Magnum Sharpie permanent marker. As you file away the weld, the ink will serve as a guide coat defining the panel's topography.

There are many options for removing the extra weld. Electric and pneumatic grinders remove material rapidly—sometimes too rapidly. A 36-grit flap wheel in an electric grinder will remove a fat MIG weld in just a few passes, but keep in mind that the work surface in contact with the metal is very small, which makes flatness difficult to achieve. Coarse body files cut satisfactorily at a slower, controllable rate, and the work surface of a file is many times larger than that of most rotating tools. I recommend an aggressive tool to remove the first 75 percent of the proud material, then switching to a file to zero in on a perfect finish. Resist the temptation to continue filing until everything is shiny. You will remove too much material.

During filing, a guide-coated panel will take on an increasingly splotchy appearance as highs and lows are identified. Use hammer-off dolly techniques as much as possible to get all the metal into the same plane. Any spots that do not respond to hammer-off dolly work will likely be extra material that needs to be shrunk with heat. Grind the back of the weld so that the bead does not interfere with your panel-straightening efforts. Don't hesitate to guide-coat your panel with more Sharpie on the front and the back of the panel as many times as needed. Chasing high and low spots along a weld seam can be tedious work for some people, but this kind of analysis is good for improving your eye and feel for shape. It will also dramatically reduce the amount of plastic body filler needed to cover your welds.

A PRACTICE PATCH PANEL WITH A FLANGE

As promised earlier, I have designed a simple exercise that anyone can do to practice the aforementioned steps of patch panel installation. This project has the added benefit of polishing your flange-turning skills. The ability to create a clean 90-degree flange on a curved panel with hand tools is a great skill to have. On this piece you'll get to do it twice.

My second patch panel exercise allows you to practice your flange-turning skills in addition to your welding and finishing skills. Cut one corner of a 12 × 12-inch panel to a 2½-inch radius and scribe a ½-inch line around the sides with the curved corner.

Cut a sheet metal blank approximately 12 × 12 inches. Smaller pieces are slightly more challenging because they will distort more from the heat. Scribe a line ½ inch in along two edges of the panel for a flange and cut one corner to a 2½-inch radius as measured to the outside of the flange. This panel represents an original fender needing a repair. Repeat this operation on a second piece of metal measuring approximately 8 × 8 inches. The second panel is our patch.

The first step in turning a 90-degree flange cleanly by hand is to thin the metal along the bend line in a bead roller. If all you have to create a flange is a pair of Vise-Grips, the work can be accomplished, but you will need to bend only a short portion at a time and stop periodically to shrink the extra material around the corner. This shrinking is easily done in a Lancaster-style hand-operated shrinker, but you could also trap any wrinkles that appear during flange-turning against a steel dolly. In addition, you can use your shrinker jaws like a giant set of Vise-Grips to clamp the metal for bending and shrinking where needed.

If thinning the metal is an option, choose a thin metal bead-roller die with an edge radius of approximately ¹⁄₁₆ inch against a flat steel die. On steel, pinch about halfway into the metal and make one pass along the flange line (make one pass only or you will have multiple thin lines and the metal will not bend cleanly). Bend the flange toward 90 degrees between the wheels of a wheeling machine or between two

To facilitate bending the flange, thin the metal on the bend line in the bead roller.

Bend the flange to 90 degrees using a wheeling machine, bead roller, or Vise-Grips.

A Lancaster-style shrinker can be used simultaneously to bend and shrink a flange on an outside curve.

If you lack a shrinking machine, the flange can be hammered up against a steel cylinder or dolly. The extra material that needs to be shrunk will bunch up in wrinkles. Gradually cold shrink them until the flange is smooth.

Hammering straight down onto the flange from above thickens the flange slightly and drives the material down toward the bend, defining the bend in the process.

If stubborn wrinkles develop, correct them as soon as possible by supporting one side of the wrinkle with a dolly and hitting next to it with a hammer. These wrinkles must not be allowed to fold over themselves or you will never get a clean flange.

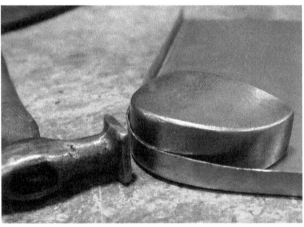

Final planishing of the flange against a steel dolly is permissible as long as you don't stretch the flange by overeager hammering.

The finished panel with a flange on one side should look like it was stamped by a soulless machine rather than a sheet metal enthusiast with a twinkle in her eye and a song in her heart.

flat-bead roller dies. Shrink the metal in the corner to prevent wrinkles from forming. If you do not have a shrinking tool, hammer the flange up evenly around the corner and cinch it in past 90 degrees. You will create a small ring of overshrunk metal that will help you compress all the metal in the flange against a steel dolly. Work out any small wrinkles by cold shrinking them against the dolly with a hammer. Scary wrinkles may be heat shrunk against a dolly using an oxyacetylene torch. Make the second panel identical to the first and test its fit on top of the original. The fit should be fantastic.

If your practice patch fits the original panel, mark the points where the new piece overlaps the first panel on the flanges. Carefully cut away the flange from panel one with any suitable tool you have. Doing so allows you to sneak up on perfect alignment between old and new before you have committed to cutting too much from the original panel. Dial in the perfect fit along the flanges and clamp the panels together. Consider also securing the panels with Clecos through metal tabs to prevent shifting. Scribe a trim line before disturbing anything. If you forego the Clecos, add a couple of vertical registration marks to assist with realignment. In practice, the Clecos trick seems more conducive to MIG welding than TIG welding because a thin gap wants to form once the old metal is removed and the new metal is in the proper plane.

Repeat the flange exercise on a smaller piece of metal and superimpose it over the first panel. I have colored my second panel black to represent an aftermarket patch panel. If you are satisfied with the fit, cut the edge off the bottom panel.

If you feel a three-point attachment might help you on future MIG repairs, use Clecos to secure your patch in position and scribe a line around its perimeter.

Separate the panels and cut away the repair area of panel one. If a cutoff tool is your weapon of choice for removing the repair area, lay a strip of tape along the cut line ¼ inch inside of the final dimension before cutting. Trim the last ¼ inch by hand with aviation snips. Note that snips are designed to curl the scrap to one side or the other. Orient the snips so that the scrap curls away from the cut, rather than having the jaws fight the main body of the panel.

You might wonder why you shouldn't first cut away the area to be repaired, place the patch behind, scribe a line on the patch, and then trim the patch. After all, trimming the outside edge of the patch would be easier than cutting the inside edge of the hole. I don't recommend this course of action on this practice panel for two reasons. First, on old cars, there is invariably some additional structure behind the original panel that gets in the way. Second, by cutting away the original panel first, you have committed yourself and there is no going back. If you discover that something has been overtrimmed or is otherwise unsatisfactory, righting the wrong will be much more difficult.

Tack-weld the patch in place, maintaining perfect alignment throughout the process.

After welding, utilize all your metal-finishing skills to recapture a perfectly flat surface. Stretching will be necessary along the weld seam. Heat shrinking will likely be necessary beyond the intersection of the weld.

Place your practice patch in position on the panel and secure it with Clecos or Vise-Grips. Take your time tack-welding the seam, stopping frequently to assess the situation. The alignment between the panels must remain perfect the entire time or you will not get a satisfactory result. Hammer the tack welds as needed to counteract the shrinking that naturally occurs with welding. Once your tack welds are complete and you are satisfied that you are still in control, weld the panel, stopping frequently to check for misalignment. On a small panel like this, heat distortion will be a formidable foe. The good news is that if you can tackle this practice patch, many real patch panel situations will seem easy by comparison. Welding heat will be dissipated out into the panel if the repair is on a door, quarter panel, or other large surface. Do not be intimidated by larger panels. In fact, larger repairs are often easier from a heat-control standpoint. Use this opportunity to fine-tune your heat-shrinking and weld-finishing skills. If your first attempt does not go as well as you hoped, critique your work and try again.

TIPS, TRICKS, AND OTHER SORCERY

Having covered the essentials of patch panel installation, I would like to offer some other tips that might be useful in your future repair efforts. One recurring problem is the need to remove rusty fasteners and accurately locate fastener holes in an area to be patched. If there are no impediments to heating the fastener, such as glass, wiring, gasoline, a hippie's hidden stash in a rocker panel, brake fluid, or interior trim pieces, heat the fastener red-hot and let it cool completely before applying any force to it. If you discover the hippie's stash only after inhaling several plumes of smoke, take a break for a few hours before continuing. Heating fasteners red-hot will force the oxides to separate from the base metal. If you attempt to turn a nut or bolt at this time, however, the fastener will be at its softest and it will likely twist off. Let the metal cool and the fastener will back out easily.

If you need to remove a threaded stud that is snapped off flush or almost flush, sand or wire brush the exposed end of the stud to remove any oxidation. A wire brush spinning at high rpm in an electric or pneumatic tool is infinitely better than scrubbing it with a handheld wire brush. Be sure to wear safety glasses. Strive for a silver bare-metal finish. You will weld a nut onto the end of the broken stud or screw, but if you hurry and do not do a thorough job de-rusting the broken shaft, you are likely to get a deficient weld that peels off even more of the end of your shaft when you try to back it out.

Welding down into a nut is not easy, so do not settle for just any nut to weld onto the stud. A jam nut is a low-profile nut that will outperform any standard nut for this task. The low profile allows you to get a better weld between the end of the stud or broken screw and the nut. If you do not have any jam nuts, hold a standard nut against a grinder with a pair of Vise-Grips. You want a nut that easily fits over the diameter of the broken shaft without undue slop but is as low profile as possible while still having enough surface for your wrench to grip. To exacerbate the situation for educational purposes, I've chosen a stripped Phillips-head trim screw that required an extra dollop of trickery. The small, round, low-profile head was adjacent to a prominent ridge in a strip of stainless trim that prevented us from welding a nut on it. As a result, we first welded a flat washer to the screw head, then we welded a nut to the washer. Once the piece was cool, the screw backed out without any drama.

When attempting to free a stuck fastener, a low-profile jam nut like the one at right is the hot ticket. Weld the nut to the fastener. Allow it to cool, and back out the fastener.

On frozen fasteners with missing or very small heads, weld a washer to whatever is left of the fastener, then weld a nut to the washer. Once the assembly is cool, it will back out easily.

Removing a forlorn fastener is sometimes just the first step. If the holes the fasteners pass through are corroded beyond use, an easy way to locate them for reinstallation is to draw or scribe two lines through the center at 90 degrees to each other. Extend the lines well past the edges of the repair for accuracy. Patch the panel. Redraw your lines, drill new holes or mount studs as needed, and celebrate your glorious success.

Occasionally, you will encounter a repair where some of the original panel is missing entirely. Hopefully, you will at least have one side intact from which you can make templates. My student Richard's Studebaker quarter panel provides a great learning opportunity because it gives us a chance to solve a new problem: how do you copy the shape of something that is missing?

For as long as he has owned the car, Richard has been perplexed by the abnormally swollen lower rear quarter panels on his bullet-nose Studebaker. He knew plastic body filler was present, but he didn't know what it concealed until he sanded one panel down to bare metal. Beneath the filler, Richard found a patch panel crudely bashed from a sheet of ⅛-inch-thick steel.

After a significant amount of careful cutting, Richard peeled away the armored excrescence with as little damage to the remaining original metal as possible, leaving a large hole in the process. To re-create the missing panel as a guide for shaping a new one, Richard glued some Styrofoam to the back of the piece with Weldbond white glue and sanded it to the correct shape. Because both quarter panels were a mess, he had no original shape from which to make templates,

so his foam sculpture would have to suffice. Richard is an artistic sort, so filing the foam to shape was not difficult for him. Artist or not, anyone with a flexible sanding block could do the same on a part like this. Be sure to use a flexible block on a panel with any crown. Guide-coat the foam by scribbling on it with a Magnum Sharpie if you need more feedback during sanding.

With the Styrofoam standing in for the missing part of the panel, Richard stretched the highest crown of the new piece on the English wheel. To speed the process, he shrunk the rear edge with thumbnail dies mounted in our Dake machine. Richard intermittently superimposed his patch over the Styrofoam-filled quarter and rocked it back and forth to identify places that needed additional stretching. He continued stretching until his patch sat firmly over the Styrofoam-enhanced original. The last step was to create the detail along the bottom edge of the piece by creasing it in the English wheel.

I used this Styrofoam technique to help another student visualize wheel arches for his car and it worked beautifully, so it would be useful in customization as well. The Weldbond glue securely adheres the foam to metal or plywood, thus any solid surface is a good candidate for building whatever you want as long as you can work with flat blocks. If your substrate is curvy, consider the two-part pourable taxidermist polyurethane foam I discuss later in this book. It too clings to any clean surface, and filling a void around your curvy substrate might be a better way to add material than gluing blocks to it.

If an area in need of a patch panel has holes that you need to relocate, draw lines through the centerlines and extend them out past the repair area. Once the new metal is replaced, reconnect the lines and drill the holes.

Richard's Studebaker quarter panels both have lengths of ⅛-inch-thick steel pipe welded onto them.

After Richard lopped off the excrescences of steel pipe from his quarter panels, large holes remained. He filled the void with Styrofoam, which he sanded to the appropriate contour for use as a guide during shaping.

This patch required stretching at the deepest part of the crown and shrinking along the rear edge. Richard installed the crease along the bottom of the patch by bending the panel in the English wheel.

A welding rod makes a great flexible straightedge to mark a curved body line across a patch panel.

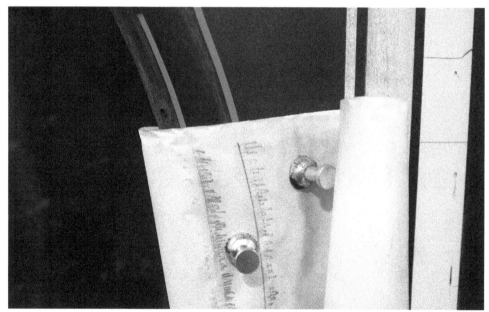

To copy multiple details on a panel, place strips of fine tape along all prominent features. Stick a piece of paper over the panel with magnets and transfer the details to the paper with a pencil or grubby finger. The details from your paper pattern can be transferred to metal with a prick punch.

On Richard's quarter panel, re-creating the crease running along the bottom was not too difficult with the Styrofoam assist. Without a foam model, you can accurately eyeball a crease across your patch panel with a length of welding rod or strip of sheet metal. Either will readily follow a consistent arc; just lay it across your piece and trace the curve.

Knowing that these kinds of problems frequently come up in real life, I gave my student Josh a VW hood and asked him to make a patch panel along one side of it that included the prominent crease near the hood edge. Josh made a crowned panel that he superimposed over the original hood and clamped in place with Vise-Grips. To mark the location for the crease that defines the body line, we held a ⅛-inch-diameter welding rod against the panel and manipulated it until we felt confident that we had an accurate template to trace. Josh drew a line along the template, creased the edge of the panel along the line between two flat wheels in the English wheel, and then continued wheeling the short flange to stretch the metal enough so it would lie flat like the original.

What do you do when there are multiple body lines in a patch panel? Brian Ellis's pickup provides the perfect opportunity to find out. Brian had rust holes above the rear wheel arches on his Ford. The damaged area stretched from the lip of the wheel arch up a few inches into the bedside. Although aftermarket panels for this popular truck are probably available, Brian wanted to make his own. First, he ran two strips of flexible vinyl auto body tape along the critical body lines he needed to replicate in his patch panel along the top of the wheel opening. He secured a piece of paper over the tape lines with magnets and scribbled across the tape lines with a pencil. The paper pattern he ended up with was a perfect blueprint for laying out his patch panel on some steel.

Brian transferred the lines from his paper pattern onto a flat sheet of steel with a spring-loaded prick punch. Using a very flat lower anvil wheel on the English wheel, Brian pushed down on the side of the panel to create a bend along the deepest body line, the one farthest from the wheel opening. Because the metal on the wheel opening side of the bend had to occupy a shorter radius curve than the flat metal on the other side of the bend, the metal had to be shrunk to create the first part of the detail. Brian repeated this procedure for the second body line, the only difference being that the metal had to be stretched to account for the increase in length as the metal is folded down almost perpendicular to the original surface. The finished patch panel is so handsome it will be a shame to paint.

Another important consideration for this repair was maximizing access to the back of the panel to facilitate finishing out the weld bead. Brian cut away enough of the support structure behind the repair area to ensure that he could get a body dolly behind the weld seam to hammer against once the welding was complete.

Pushing the panel down alongside the anvil wheel creates a clean crease that convincingly replicates details stamped at the factory.

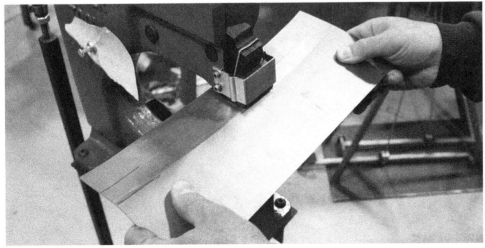

After creating the first crease line, the metal on the wheel-opening side of the repair must be shrunk because we are now asking it to assume a curve in a tighter radius, rather than to remain flat.

Brian created a second crease and began folding over the second portion of the flange. This time the metal must be stretched because the radius of this curve is greater than that of the curve adjacent to it.

After welding, the finished repair will be unnoticeable.

Oftentimes a patch panel is needed across a raised bead or a wire-wrapped edge of a fender. Ever since I read John Glover's book, *The Practical Sheet Metal Worker*, I have longed to try a technique Glover describes for addressing this situation. A wire edge was often combined with a small bead pressed into the fender on American cars of the 1920s and '30s, and in some British cars as recently as the 1950s. These details helped fenders withstand vibration and reinforced the overall stylistic theme of the car, like a calligraphic line drawn around the vehicle's edge.

Over time, as fenders suffered abuse, well-meaning owners and others tried with varying degrees of success to reverse the ravages of time. My student Derek's '32 Chevy fender is a classic example. A crack along the fender edge has been welded numerous times with no attempt to recapture the contour of the sheet metal.

Following Glover's sage advice, I instructed Derek to unwrap the old fender edge and hammer the bead flat. Some heat shrinking was needed to get the old bead flat again. Derek fabricated and welded in a patch panel while the panel was flat, then he rolled the bead across the patch. The brilliance of the Glover method is the smooth transition from the old bead to the new metal. This method is easier than welding in a patch with the bead already in it, although the latter method will work in situations where the finished piece will not fit in a bead roller.

Repairing beads and details pressed into factory sheet metal can be intimidating, but if you can support the edges of a detail where it meets flat sheet metal, you can usually raise the needed shape out of the flat panel with a homemade tool. I refer to these tools as "bonking tools," because they exist outside the normal realm of tool categorization. While they sometimes derive from broken punches, chisels, and legitimate tools, the better ones emerge from the fertile mind of the creator in direct response to a need at hand. Much like a rocket booster, golf putter, or ballet shoe, the bonking tool

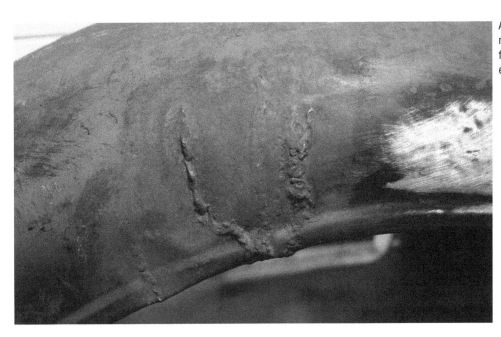

Although likely to give you nightmares, Derek's '32 Chevy fender is typical of what you can expect to find on a 1930s car.

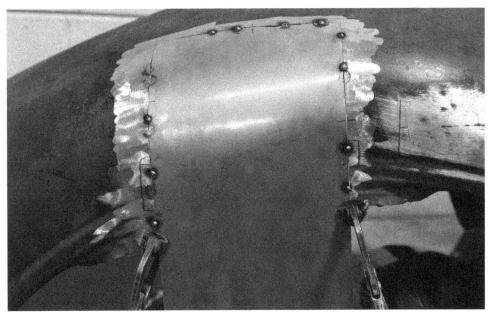

Derek fabricated a patch by shrinking along the top edge of his blank and rounding it over a stake with a mallet. With the original bead hammered out on both sides of the patch, we have our sights set on a smooth transition across the repair when we reinstall the bead.

Derek seamlessly blended his patch into the surrounding metal by wheeling across the repair with the flattest anvil wheel that would fit without leaving marks.

Following John Glover's advice, rolling a bead across both the old metal and the new makes for a nice transition.

The finished repair is indistinguishable from the surrounding metal.

Peter quickly and easily repaired the bullet-shaped ends of his rusty Austin-Healey Sprite seat pans with some custom tools: a wood silhouette beneath the bead detail served as a crude die to define the shape. A thin piece of sheet metal on top of the wood kept the wood from crushing. A second piece of wood clamped the metal against the form so that the stretching was localized in the detail.

Peter started with soft brass bonking tools and finished with a dull steel tool for maximum crispness.

is a specialized piece of equipment perfectly suited to its job. Luckily, crafting effective bonking tools is well within the capabilities of the average do-it-yourselfer and is downright simple for people who care enough to read books about crafting bonking tools. My favorite materials for crafting bonking tools are, in order: hardwood, brass, aluminum, and steel. Hard thermoplastics, such as DuPont Delrin, work exceptionally well too, but most people don't keep rods of Delrin around. Soft woods such as pine typically do not perform well and only serve to disparage the good reputation of bonking tools generally. Hardwood excels at most bonking tasks, but you can move to a harder material as the job demands.

Peter Holbrook's rusty Austin-Healey Sprite seat pan was a prime candidate for a bonking tool. While the half-round beads in the seat pan were straightforward to re-create, the nifty bullet-shaped ends posed a minor threat. Peter cut the appropriate silhouette out of two pieces of plywood, one slightly larger than the other. The smaller cutout perfectly matched the damaged original piece, while the larger cutout functioned as a clamp to keep the sheet metal flat as Peter stretched the appropriate raised detail out of the steel. Starting in the deepest portion of the bullet, Peter worked his way out toward the perimeter with a selection of fine handmade brass and steel bonking tools until he had sufficiently raised the metal to match the rest of the bead.

We could have spent a couple of hours crafting a set of dies for our Pullmax that matched the Austin-Healey seat pan beads perfectly, but Peter decided that route would have been overkill. If you are striving to be competitive at the Pebble Beach Concours d'Elegance, then of course perfection is the only option. However, for the average guy or gal restoring a car they want to drive and enjoy, there is usually a satisfactory sane solution. Patch panels meet that need perfectly.

Chapter 10
Shiny Trim Repair

Repairing aluminum and stainless trim might seem intimidating because the end result must be finished to such a high degree. Yet, shiny trim is just like any other old-car sheet metal that needs to be pushed back into place. In fact, as an eternal optimist, I like to think of trim repair as a situation in which you have an unusually clear idea of where exactly the displaced metal must end up. The road map for your journey is right before you. In this chapter, I will demonstrate how to straighten a piece of stainless-steel trim. I will also illustrate a more complicated aluminum repair involving a welded-in patch, and create two trim pieces from scratch.

One mistake that is easy for the well-meaning novice to make is investing in all the cute hammers and tiny anvils that are sold for trim repair. Ironically, small steel tool surfaces are likely to make repairing trim more difficult because you will inevitably leave tool marks in the metal that are hard to remove. For snuggling on the couch on a wintry afternoon, the precious baby anvil and pointy hammer are perfect. They will fit next to the cat on your chest, but for fixing trim there is a better option. Always start with the least aggressive tools you can find. The best ones will be chunks of hardwood that you've lovingly crafted with a belt sander. If you need a more aggressive tool, try a brass or aluminum rod. A steel tool against a steel surface should be your last resort.

As with any dent repair, try to make as much headway as possible with pure *form* (i.e., no thickness change) before you shrink or stretch anything. This will mean lots of hammer-off hammer-and-dolly work rather than smashing the trim against a steel surface with a steel hammer. Eventually, some light planishing will probably be needed, but try to leave that for the last 3 percent of the repair.

SAVING A SAD SIDE SPEAR

When my student Patrick asked if we could fix his bent 1956 Oldsmobile side spear, I knew it would make a terrific demonstration piece. The front third of the spear veered off course at a 45-degree angle while the rear third boasted a significant bow.

To overcome the natural tendency of metal, especially stainless steel, to spring back, you often need to push the material a little past where it needs to end up. Thus, to remove the bow in the rear third of the side spear, we placed a small spacer made of ¼-inch-thick dense rubber under the spear several inches past the highest point of the bow on either side, and we pushed down on the bow at its peak. Thanks to the rubber spacers between the trim and the table, we were able to push the piece slightly past flat. Because of the pliability of the spacers, we did not mar or kink the spear, and when we released the pressure, the side spear was flat along its rear half.

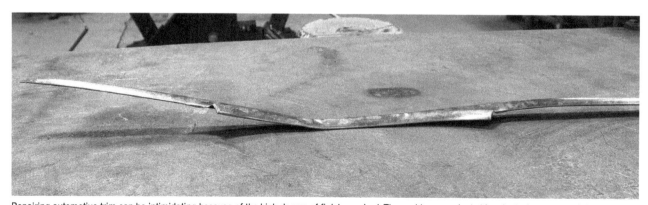

Repairing automotive trim can be intimidating because of the high degree of finish required. The problems are just shiny dents, however, and they respond to the same straightening techniques as non-shiny dents.

ABOVE: Trim repair is an area in which your creative energies should be exercised. Semihard surfaces allow metal to form into place without stretching.

LEFT: Make a tool like this to peel back the short 90-degree bend typically found on trim pieces. Peeling back the bend allows you to fit the work between the jaws of a Lancaster-style shrinking tool and affords better access for hammering.

The sickening bend at the front of the side spear was more challenging. Because the trim was flattened out at the worst part of the bend, we needed to peel back the edges of the trim where the sides were turned under at the factory to retain clips installed in the fenders. Create your own low-profile tool for this common operation by making a small cut in a piece of scrap square or round stock. With the edges peeled back, you can put bent trim between the jaws of a Lancaster-style shrinker or stretcher. We expected to use the shrinker sparingly.

With the turned-over edges temporarily removed, we placed the piece facedown and pushed out some of the worst bend against a wooden tabletop. Using the same rubber spacers we employed at the rear of the side spear, we continued working the dent along the forward end with a wooden tool that we shaped to the contour of the metal on a belt sander. As with the rear, we spaced the piece off the table with the rubber blocks so that we could work the dent a little past flat. As our dent improved, we employed

To reverse the ghastly bend at the front of this side spear, we spaced the piece facedown on top of dense rubber spacers on a tabletop and gently hammered behind the damage with a wooden tool.

For maximum accuracy and control, we placed a cross-peen body hammer behind the last surface irregularities and struck it with a rawhide hammer. We hammered against a piece of aluminum.

The finished piece is at bottom. The piece from the opposite side of the car is above. For final buffing, tape long, skinny trim pieces to a piece of wood to keep them from getting snagged by the buffing wheel (and curled up like a pretzel).

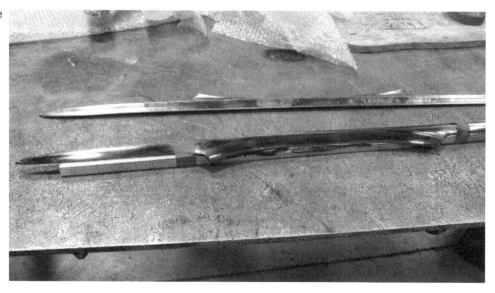

firmer surfaces to hammer against: a hard rubber hammerhead and a block of aluminum. We also used a Sharpie for a guide coat and gently sanded with a worn-out piece of 320-grit sandpaper to identify high and low spots. A cross-peen body hammer, tapped with a rawhide mallet, made an effective forming tool for pushing up the low spots from the back against a hard rubber hammerhead and an aluminum block. To refine the crisp line running down the center of the spear, we secured a dull cold chisel in a vise and gently hammered next to the crease. The critical point here is to support the line you want to keep and hammer on either side of it. This is a forming operation, not a stretching one.

RESTORING THE BLING TO A HEADLIGHT RING

The damage to Patrick's trim was rightfully earned in a traffic mishap. Some damage, unfortunately, comes by way of well-meaning but inept hands. My student Andrew's '66 Chevy II headlight trim ring is a classic example. In an effort to straighten some dents along the top edge, a previous owner hammered the back of the damaged areas with a sharp pick hammer against a metal surface, which left the topside grotesquely bumpy, like a plucked chicken. This person then filed most of the bumps whisper-thin in an attempt to level the surface. Pick hammers will be useful for dispatching ill-tempered zombies after the apocalypse, but they usually do more damage than good on sheet metal.

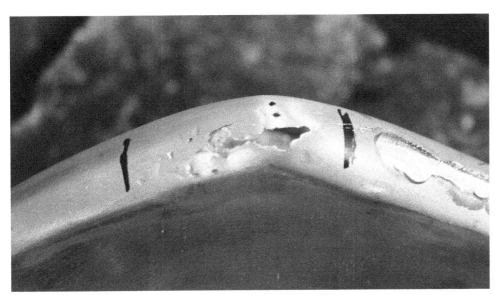

The top edge of this headlight trim has been violated with a pick hammer and filed through.

The back of the Chevy headlight trim is worth looking at if only for comic relief. If you ever have a piece of trim to repair, remember this catastrophe and be thankful it is not yours.

Once we recovered from our initial nausea, we cut a small piece of 1100 alloy aluminum 0.040 inch thick. A little shrinking along one edge of our intended patch gave us the correct shape almost immediately. We carefully scribed around the patch and cut away the damaged portion of the trim. When welding thin aluminum, I recommend clamping a piece of copper behind the repair to support the thin metal and help dissipate the welding heat as you approach the edge. In addition, leaving the patch extra long will make welding all the way to the edge easier. Otherwise, the edge of the panel will liquefy with alarming speed and you'll be left wondering where it went. After filing down the weld bead and trimming the extra metal from the edge of the patch, a little hammer and dolly work was all that was needed to get this repair perfectly flat.

We successfully welded one thin area adjacent to the main repair. Andrew shrunk the top edge of a small aluminum rectangle to curve the patch.

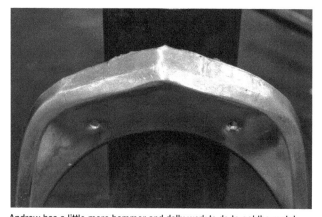

Andrew has a little more hammer and dolly work to do to get the metal perfectly flat and to clean up the body lines, but at least the panel is now solid and usable.

PULL-THROUGH DIES

If repairing your trim is possible, sing a song of praise, because sometimes there is no choice but to re-create a mauled or missing piece from scratch. One method of making trim pieces that readers might find useful is the pull-through die technique. This method incorporates a homemade die through which the user pulls a partially shaped strip of metal with a winch. The die, typically made of two pieces bolted together, represents the finished profile of the desired piece.

Although the technique is not limited to making trim pieces, these objects lend themselves well to this process because so many pieces are based on a common long shape. I first learned of this technique from Tim Barton's *The Lost Sheet Metal Machines* series. Cass Nawrocki describes his liberal use of this technique in *Any Impossibility in Shaping Metal*. I demonstrate this technique in class using a length of stainless-steel trim off, I assume, an American car of the 1950s.

The research and development phase of die-making and blank-sizing can be time-consuming, but if the piece you need to make is not readily available, the payoff is worth the effort. My chosen piece has the profile of an elongated C, which I knew could be achieved in a single pass through the dies. A more complex shape might require two passes through two different dies. The shortest path to a relaxed C shape is a modified channel with one wide side and two short legs. A channel-shaped blank is easily achieved with a sheet metal brake. Due to the shortness of the sides, however, I discovered through trial and error that I could not bend the sides to their final length from the beginning; they were too short for the brake to bend. Instead, I left the legs long and trimmed them with aviation snips after bending. If I planned to use this trim piece in a restoration, I would use stainless steel, of course, but for the purposes of testing and demonstrating the technique, mild steel suffices.

As for my die, I whittled out a steel center piece to create a slight bulge in the main body of the C. With the die halves bolted together, the center piece met a corresponding strip of concave steel that I shaped with a file. At times like this, my propensity for hoarding any and all pieces of scrap metal is a blessing. To curl the short sides of my channel shape into a C, I scrounged two more metal scraps to act as ramps to create the needed transition. I welded this assemblage together and began running test strips to optimize results.

For long trim strips common to classic cars, pull-through dies are a low-cost, low-tech option. The original trim piece is at top. The demonstration piece I made with a pull-through die is at the bottom.

The top half of the die, at rear, has a thick midsection to squeeze a radius into the piece and keep the metal blank aligned during pulling. Short ramps on both sides of the center fold over the short sides of the blank.

As long as the inner surfaces of the die are filed smooth, the blank passes through cleanly and takes on the new shape.

I likely could not have pulled my steel blank through the dies without an adequate clamping apparatus. The bolt-on clamp I used is of a type commonly sold by auto body tool suppliers. During pulling, the sheet metal will tear before this type of clamp gives way. I made a mount for the die out of scraps of square tubing and secured it in a vise on a large steel table. I hooked a hand-operated come-along winch to the table opposite the vise and pulled the metal through the die. I was careful not to pull from an angle because that would unintentionally curve the piece. Viewing the process in a photographic sequence belies the thorough testing that went into reproducing this trim piece, and yet, the new piece is a faithful reproduction that could be achieved by anyone with a minimum of tools.

If your pulling apparatus is in the same plane as your work, the piece will remain straight. Otherwise, you will inadvertently introduce a curve.

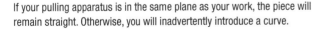

The demonstration piece is taped in place on an MGB hood. The original is beneath it.

MAKING TRIM WITH A RECIPROCATING MACHINE

Another useful but more grandiose tool for fabricating trim pieces is the Pullmax machine. Dave's MGB lacked the aluminum strip that typically runs horizontally across the front of the hood. Although Dave had a couple of damaged original trim strips, he asked if I could make a new piece using the side profile and end cap appearance of his samples for reference.

Although the Pullmax is beyond the reach of most do-it-yourselfers, some readers will have access to one of these machines and might find this demonstration interesting. Furthermore, I expect this same piece could be made using a hand-operated come-along winch with a set of pull-through dies that look exactly like the dies I made for the Pullmax machine, only wide enough that they could be squeezed together with bolts threaded vertically through the dies on both sides of where the metal slides through. The technique would be exactly as I demonstrated on the previous trim piece. Also, I think you could install both details found in the trim piece in a single pass with a pull-through die, rather than in two passes in the Pullmax (with a die change in between).

The trial and error on a project like this can be considerable, because you must run a test piece for every die modification, but persistence eventually pays off. I whittled my dies out of ¾-inch hot-rolled square

These incredibly sophisticated dies were hacked out of ¾-inch hot-rolled square stock with a grinder and some files. The left set forms the first profile along the front visible edge of the trim. The right set forms the hidden offset underneath.

steel bar with a grinder and some files. Although there are more complicated and certainly more accurate ways of shaping dies, it is hard to argue with the speed of this simplistic approach. Once I had run several test pieces

The first pass through the dies defines the look of the trim piece as seen from the front of the car. The extra material along the top edge helps register the uppermost detail and provides a surface for stretching the piece with a Lancaster-style shrinker to curve it. The new piece is above the original.

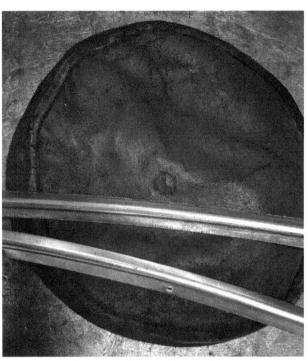

The second pass through the other set of dies installs the small recess for the trim-attachment screws. Shrinking along the open edge curves the piece. The new piece is above the original.

and tuned in the die faces to the appropriate shape and finish, I inserted a length of 0.040-inch aluminum bent at 90 degrees. My first pass established the profile of the piece as a bystander sees it while facing the front of the car. I left each leg of the angled piece longer than necessary to ensure that all the bends came out sharp. I noticed during testing that if the blank was cut to size before installing the detail, the bend farthest from the 90-degree bend turned out a little softer than if I left extra metal to help register the bend. In addition, the extra metal outside of the finished size gave me a flange on which to use a shrinker or stretcher when curving the piece to fit a hood. I swapped out the dies for a second set, flipped the blank over, and installed the small bead that goes on the engine side of the trim piece.

With both front and bottom profiles installed, I shrunk the bottom flange with a Lancaster-style machine to curve the piece to match the hood horizontally. I stretched the extra metal along the top edge to curve the piece vertically as well. The ends of the original part were easy to replicate by trimming them to the appropriate shape and bending them over with a pair of Vise-Grips.

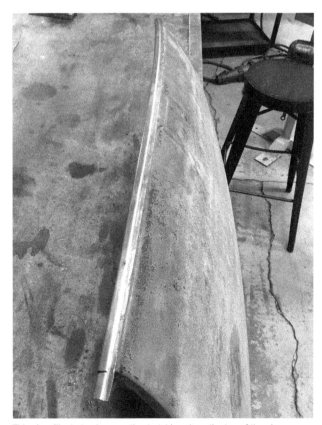

This view illustrates how gentle stretching along the top of the piece introduced a subtle curve that perfectly matches the hood.

Chapter 11
The Nayslayer Model T Speedster

One of the greatest joys in teaching is meeting young people who are passionate about automotive restoration and helping them channel their enthusiasm in a productive way—ideally toward a project that exceeds their and the instructor's wildest expectations.

Recently I was blessed with four super-students who couldn't seem to get enough of the metals lab. They put away tools and swept the lab long after their three-and-a-half-hour evening class was over. As the semester drew to a close, I worried that their zeal for sheet metal might be displaced once they became bogged down in more mundane academic classes such as calculus, history, or political science. In hopes of further stoking their enthusiasm, I suggested that they try to build a Ford Model T speedster body outside of class the following semester, thinking that such a project would be just right for students with one semester of sheet metal training under their belts. Much to my delight, these students eagerly accepted the challenge. Once work began and word got out about the project, however, the doubtful grumbling of

naysayers was heard in the shadows. Undaunted, the students persevered and finished the car in plenty of time for the annual student-organized car show at the end of the school year. Christened "the Nayslayer" in response to the doubters, my students' snappy sobriquet fit the car perfectly and reaffirmed that these kids have something special.

In hindsight, this was a great project. Building things from scratch inevitably creates all kinds of new problems to solve and forces a person to be creative. If you have ever dreamed of building your own speedster body of any type, the Nayslayer is a good introduction. The metal shaping involved was not overly complicated, the body could be built with just a few tools, and the problems we had to solve were typical for a basic scratch-built body.

We chose to build a brass-era 1915 Model T body because early cars need more exposure, especially among young audiences. Because our goal was to build the body in four months, from the outset we were interested in minimizing welding, weld-finishing,

A Ford Model T speedster is a terrific beginner project because it can be altered to suit your tastes, abilities, and budget.

This stack of Model T frames illustrates the differences between early frames and those built between 1923 and 1926. Later frames have a significantly wider rear crossmember compared to pre-1923 frames. The narrower frame looks sleeker on a speedster.

On the finished car the early rear crossmember barely protrudes past the body.

and complex metal shaping. In addition, we knew we would not have time to paint the car, so we felt that the body should be capable of being easily disassembled, painted, and reassembled by a future owner. Securing the body sheet metal with brass machine screws gave us a visually appealing temporary method of holding the car together. Once the car is sold, a future owner can disassemble the car, paint the body panels individually, and reassemble the car with brass rivets set cold so as not to damage the paint. Last, we wanted to build a body that could be adapted to any T frame without making irreversible changes to the chassis.

MODEL T SPECIAL CONSIDERATIONS

Model T speedsters make wonderful do-it-yourself projects because parts are plentiful and widely interchangeable, and the complexity of the project can be tailored to fit one's skills, budget, and available tools. Moreover, the Ford Model T was the first production car extensively modified and hot rodded on a vast scale from the very beginning, so period photographs and written materials are easy to find. The abundance of original source material is great for ideas on body shapes, construction details, and solutions to problems one is likely to encounter.

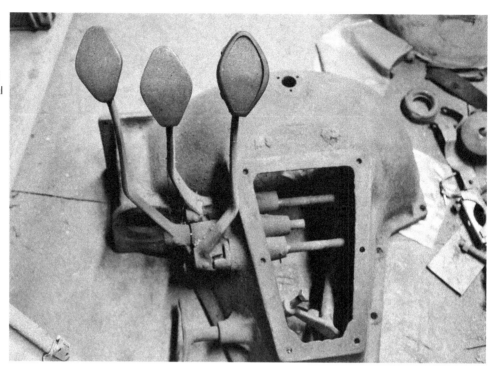

Pre-1923 Model Ts had smaller pedal pads. Although later pedal pads fit giant twenty-first-century feet, they become a liability when you lower the steering column. You could cut them down, but the moral thing to do is find an early pedal assembly like this.

If you are contemplating building your own T speedster body, you might be wise to choose a pre-1923 frame. While the longitudinal frame rails on all Ts are the same distance apart, the rear crossmember is much wider on frames built between 1923 and 1926; it projects out past the frame rails an extra few inches on each side. This may not make any difference on the body style you have in mind, but I mention it because the wider frame might limit your options. Thus, the Nayslayer body could be bolted on a later frame and be completely functional, but there would be more frame stick-out above the rear axle.

Other details to consider before embarking on your own T build are the pedal assembly and the handbrake lever. As with the frames, there is an early and a late pedal assembly. Though interchangeable, the pedal pads on the earlier assembly are smaller, which provide a little more room for the driver's feet if the steering column is lowered. The later pads can be cut down, of course, but it is easier and more tenderhearted to choose the earlier assembly. In addition, if a speedster body is narrower than stock, and the steering column and dash are lowered, the handbrake lever will need to be straightened at the least and possibly shortened. We heated a lever red-hot at the point we wanted to change its shape and easily bent it in a vise. This bend could be reversed if we ever have a change of heart.

SOLVING THE HOOD-TO-COWL CONUNDRUM

Once we mounted a brass-era radiator and firewall on an early frame, we hit our first snag. Because of the disparity in width between the firewall and the radiator, a smooth transition between the two seemed impossible. On early Ts, the hood meets the firewall at 90 degrees, and the firewall rises above the hood line for at least an inch or two all the way around the hood. As we laid pieces of poster board between the radiator and the top of the firewall to simulate a hood, we quickly realized that any attempt to use a stock firewall was going to end in miserable failure—the change in width from the back of the radiator was just too drastic.

After a prolonged period of panicky brainstorming, an easy solution emerged. We realized that the steel firewall from mid-1923 to 1926 Ts is about 4 inches narrower than the steel firewall of 1917 to mid-1923 Ts. Because the two firewalls share an identical mounting arrangement on the frame, they are interchangeable— assuming you are prepared to build an entire new body to fit the smaller firewall. With the later, smaller firewall installed, the transition between radiator and firewall was dramatically improved, but we now needed to redesign the cowl to fit the narrow firewall. Fortunately, another easy solution presented itself: we used the shape of the original brass-era firewall to define the shape of the cowl where it passes over the dashboard. The two firewalls in sequence gave us a beautiful shape from the radiator back to the dash that anyone hoping to build a T speedster could easily copy. Visit the Model T Forum (www.mtfca.com) for drawings of Model T firewalls with dimensions.

We traced the brass-era firewall onto a piece of plywood, cut it out, and clamped the plywood in place on the frame. Like a station on a wood buck, the plywood defined the exterior body surface so that work could progress.

DEFINING THE TAIL

Pleased with the proportions of the front half of the car, we turned our attention to the rear. We knew we wanted a pointed tail of an approximate length past the rear axle, but we had no predetermined shape for the body at the rear of the cockpit. Starting with an outline of the brass-era firewall on a piece of cardboard, we sketched out various options. After considerable trial and error, we cut one half of the intended shape out of cardboard, folded it over for symmetry, and cut out the other half. Once we had checked the template in place on the body, we cut a matching station out of plywood and clamped it to the frame to define the body shape at the rear of the cockpit.

To clarify the body contours at the sides of the cockpit, we used another template-making technique that could easily be applied to any number of situations. We bent a long piece of ³⁄₁₆-inch-diameter steel rod and laid it along the length of the body from the radiator

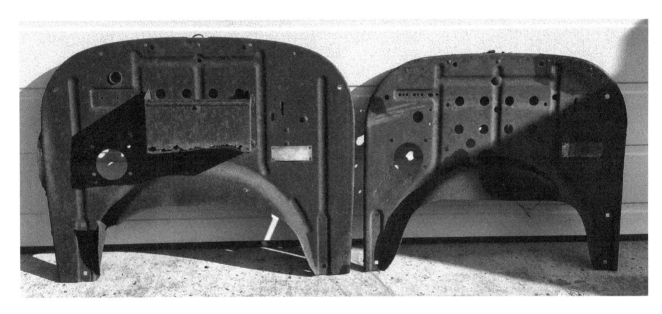

ABOVE: The 1917 to mid-1923 Model T steel firewall is about 28 inches wide, while the later one is about 24¾ inches wide. We used the two like stations on a station buck to define the cockpit shape of our body. We put the narrow one behind the engine bay and the wide one at the cowl.

LEFT: We determined the contour of our body at the cockpit by bending a length of ³⁄₁₆-inch-diameter steel rod and tracing it onto plywood.

all the way back to the rear of the cockpit. Generally speaking, in order to bend a gentle arc in a rod without creating kinks, do it with your hands spread far apart. We experimented with different curves until we found one we liked and then traced it onto a piece of plywood to use as a template for the cockpit sides. We used this template to cut four identical plywood stations to run alongside the cockpit. With our body defined from the radiator to the back of the cockpit, we addressed the tail.

Using a technique I described in detail on the small gas tank project in *Professional Sheet Metal Fabrication*, we created a 6-inch-diameter steel disk and mounted it on plywood approximately 10 inches shy of the tip of our planned tail. We flanged the disk by squeezing it between two lengths of 6-inch-diameter pipe in a hydraulic press and cold shrinking the flange down against the sides of the bottom pipe. Because we were determined to have the end of the tail finish in a point,

we reasoned that the flanged disk would give us a mounting point for a conical tip, as well as a place to secure longitudinal stringers to which we could screw the exterior body sheet metal. In hindsight, this worked quite well.

With no budget for this car build, we had to be resourceful at every turn. With plenty of thin steel sheet metal available, but not a lot of other materials, we made longitudinal stringers for the tail section out of 20-gauge steel and bent them into a U shape to stiffen them; 18-gauge steel would have been stronger, but we used what was plentiful. Regardless, the finished body shell is incredibly stiff, yet lightweight; three people can lift it on and off the frame relatively easily. We placed the stringers in areas where we anticipated fastening the exterior sheet metal as the build progressed. In addition, because the stringers defined the exterior surface of the body, there was no need for any buck building for the tail.

The shape of the body's rear half emanated from a 6-inch-diameter disc placed at an arbitrary distance behind the cockpit according to our taste. To minimize metal shaping, we planned to form the rear sheet metal and screw it to longitudinal stringers connecting the disc and cockpit.

The plywood silhouette at the rear of the cowl is traced from a 1917 to mid-1923 Model T steel firewall. The steel support structure for the cowl is made of 14-gauge steel and 1-inch square tubing.

On the underside of the tail, behind the rear axle, we made a single semicircular station out of plywood and secured it to a plywood spine running through the center of the tail. For the leading edge of this station, we bent a strip of 18-gauge steel to 90 degrees and shrank one flange to curve the strip until it hugged the station. With the leading edge of the strip snug against the plywood, the adjacent flange needed to be shrunk somewhat as well so that the exterior sheet metal would lie flat against it. Because sheet metal gets more difficult to shrink as the gauge of metal gets thicker, we used thumbnail shrinking dies. Gathering jaws in a hand-operated shrinker would have worked, but the thumbnail dies were faster.

BUILDING A SIMPLE STRUCTURE FOR THE BODY

Now that the general parameters of the body were established, we began building a steel support structure for the cowl and body sheet metal. With the help of the plywood body template that we used earlier on the cockpit sides, we cut curved pieces of 14-gauge steel to run along the bottom of the body. A vertical strip of 14-gauge was welded along the length of these to provide a rigid L-shaped member to which body-to-frame mounts could be welded. We also used 14-gauge steel to create a structure behind the dash, supplemented with a crosspiece of 1-inch square tubing to aid in securing the steering column.

Because the body gets wider as it approaches the cockpit from the firewall, a little shaping needed to be done to our cowl structure: (1) we stretched the upper corners of a 20-gauge strip with a hand-operated Lancaster-style stretcher and secured it with temporary rivets to the firewall, and (2) we shrunk the upper corners of the cowl support by hammering them while hot. By stretching our support at the front of the cowl and shrinking it at the rear, we created a taper in the structure to allow the exterior sheet metal to lie flat at all points along it.

Mounting our rapidly developing project to the T frame could not have been easier. We made two rear metal body mounts out of ⅛-inch-thick angle iron and

Because the cowl tapers from front to rear, the supports beneath the sheet metal must also taper. Behind the firewall, the support needed stretching to flare out to meet the sheet metal. The 3/16-inch rod represents the plane occupied by the finished exterior sheet metal.

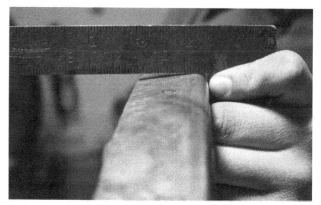

At the rear of the cowl, the support beneath the sheet metal needed to be shrunk to follow the taper of the cowl. We heated the forward edge of this support at the corners and hammered it evenly to shrink it while the metal was red-hot.

In this view of the cowl support, the outward flare of the recently stretched front member is evident. The horizontal supports at the sides of the cowl and along the body are strips of 20-gauge steel with beads rolled into them for stiffness.

four forward mounts out of 14-gauge steel. Because our firewall was narrower than stock, however, we needed to narrow the front factory body mounts on the frame by about ½ inch on either side. Rather than remove any material from the mounts, we simply heated the outer ½ inch of each mount and bent them down to 90 degrees with a crescent wrench while they were red-hot.

In the event we someday decide to return the frame to its original configuration, these bends can be reversed by reheating the metal and bending the mounts back.

To support the sheet metal along the sides of the cockpit, we took two wide strips of 20-gauge steel and installed two opposing offsets in them for stiffness. The resulting cross-section resembled a flattened top hat.

We used a set of joggle dies in the Pullmax machine to make the offsets, but a bead roller would have worked as well. By pulling down on each strip as we pulled it through the dies, we were able to put the correct curve into the piece, which we confirmed by comparing each strip to the plywood cockpit side template that we made earlier. (Pulling down on the piece during beading would accomplish the same thing.) Another option for creating a curve would be to install the beads with the piece flat and then shrink along the top and bottom edges with a Lancaster-style shrinker.

Thus far, our body support structure was coming along beautifully, but it was a little flimsy due to the thin gauge of the metal we had been forced to use for much of

it. Fortunately, we came up with a handsome, easy way to make stiffening members. We bent lengths of 20-gauge steel to a U shape that fit snugly over a small section of square steel pipe. Placing the round head of a body hammer over the metal with a void at the center of the pipe behind, we tapped on the hammer with a rawhide mallet to create a series of clean dimples that dramatically stiffened the steel. The dimples work to harden the metal and serve the same purpose as beads in the floor pan of a modern unibody car. Using a nifty 2¼-inch punch from Mittler Brothers, we fabricated small brackets to bolster our body-support structure even further.

We made stiffening members for the body by hammering dimples into 20-gauge steel over a pipe. To facilitate centering, we made the edges of the members fit the pipe and then slid the pipe along at measured intervals. We used the round end of a body hammer like a punch and hit it with a rawhide mallet.

Jon Bubnis's fabricated body mounts slid over the factory mounts and lowered the body in relation to the frame. Jon welded these mounts to the lengths of fabricated angle running along the bottom of the body.

Thanks to our swank dimpled supports inside the tail, the finished structure was remarkably stiff and light.

EXTERIOR SHEET METAL

With our body framework complete, we made patterns for the exterior sheet metal out of poster board, which behaves like sheet metal—it buckles and refuses to cooperate wherever shaping is needed, which gave us an accurate picture of where shrinking or stretching needed to happen, and where seams ought to be placed. With the exception of the reverse scoop on the top of the cowl, the Nayslayer's body from the radiator to the dash is all form, meaning that the metal was bent into the proper contours without changing its thickness. No special tools were needed for this operation; we simply bent the metal over an empty welding gas cylinder.

Once we had formed the metal for the cowl, we secured it with Clecos. Jonathan Bubnis spent quite a long time planning out the spacing and the placement of the Clecos, because we wanted our many fasteners to harmonize with each other. Clecos come in various sizes that correspond with common rivet diameters and are color-coded for easy identification. We used gold ³⁄₁₆-inch Clecos because they best complemented the brass machine screws we had already purchased. (If you use brass screws on your project, be sure to shop around. When I first began searching for brass fasteners, I was horrified by how expensive they seemed to be—sometimes $1 or more per screw! Fortunately, I discovered brass screws online at Fastenal at 70 percent off. I checked my local store's inventory online and then

promptly went there and bought every screw they had.) Before drilling any holes, Jon clamped each panel with Vise-Grips to prevent shifting. Then he installed each Cleco one at a time and trimmed the panel edges last, because each panel moved slightly as the Clecos drew it down tight against the support structure.

We installed the cowl sheet metal temporarily without a problem. The hood presented an unusual puzzle, however. While the firewall was curved along its top edge, the radiator had five distinct facets. How could a hood be curved at one end and faceted at the other? Jake San Martin made the aluminum hood by bending it against an empty welding gas cylinder. By trimming the hood sides to a scallop, he solved the hood paradox by eliminating the need to replicate the radiator's many facets.

The reverse scoop on the top of the cowl, while more complicated to make than the panels formed thus far, was not so difficult to shape that any beginning metal student should feel intimidated by it. In fact, one would be hard-pressed to find a better panel on which to become familiar with reverse curves. Because we were shooting for a large reverse curve of a general size, and not trying to re-create an existing panel, we enjoyed a degree of artistic freedom that one seldom has in pure restoration. Normally, an original panel is the objective standard against which your work is measured, which is a much more demanding standard than, "I'm happy

Jon laid out the sheet metal for the cowl and carefully determined how the screws holding the assembly together should be spaced. The cowl scoop is a piece of metal cut from a large reverse curve panel.

with the way that looks." Our reverse scoop panel was inspired by images of British race cars we found on austinharris.co.uk, a repository of hundreds of vintage automotive photographs. Visit this site with caution, however, because you may find yourself powerless to resist its spell. Like an illicit drug, it will keep you coming back for more until you neglect all your responsibilities and find yourself penniless and alone. On the bright side, at least you'll come away feeling inspired to shape metal. In case you do not have a wheeling machine or power hammer, you can find images of cars on the site that used a half-cone in place of the reverse curve scoop we used. You can make a cone purely by bending, with delightfully sinister results.

We decided roughly how large of a scoop we would need to add interest to our cowl, cut out a square blank of sheet metal, and drew an X with a permanent marker across the diagonals on both sides of the blank. The Xs ensured that we worked each region evenly. Although our blank seemed abnormally large, we planned on cutting away much of it. Ironically, the size of the panel made it easier to shape, especially in the English wheel. It was easy to hold and roll through the machine, and we did not have to worry about wheeling right up to a finished edge, which can result in no work directly on the edge and too much work slightly shy of the edge. We could have been more persnickety in our planning by making a poster board model of the intended scoop, but knew we could

fine-tune the finished size considerably by trimming, so we worked directly on the metal without a model.

The shape we were striving for resembles a giant potato chip or McClellan saddle: two ends of the rectangle sweep dramatically up, while the other sides swoop down. Regardless of the tools one has, this shape is achieved by stretching the two long sides in relation to the very center of the panel. The form part of the equation—the bending that must take place—involves manipulating the two stretched edges one way and the two unstretched edges the opposing way, like the edges of a potato chip. The easiest way to make the shape is with a linear stretching die in a power hammer, but an English wheel will do a nice job at a slow, controllable rate. If the wheel is too slow on its own, you can speed the process by bashing with a big hammer the areas you know will need extreme stretching. You can supplement your hammering with a hand- or foot-operated stretcher applied to the outer edges of the panel. Do your pummeling over a shot bag or sandbag so that the metal has somewhere to go. While the lumps that inevitably result from bashing of this sort can be planished out by hand with a spoon over a large steel stake held in a vise, such work is tedious and time-consuming, especially if you plan to work with steel, and the finish will not be as nice as work done on a machine. A planishing hammer would be a helpful upgrade over pure handwork if a wheeling machine or power hammer is not yet in your arsenal.

Jake San Martin's aluminum hood cleverly sidesteps the problem of how to join the irregular surface of the radiator to the cowl.

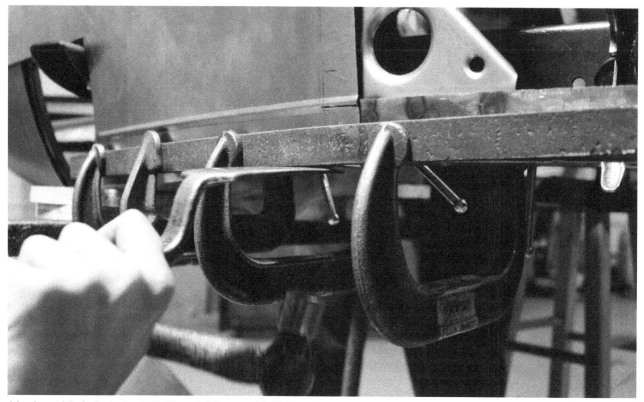

Jake clamped the body sheet metal tightly against the support behind it and hammered over to 90 degrees along the length of the body. Spreading the blows out by hammering a spoon left a perfect finish. The small triangular gusset was made with a Mittler Brothers punch and die set.

As we stretched the edges of our steel blank, the reverse curve of the panel became more extreme. Once we felt we had achieved sufficient swoopiness, we began trimming the edges until we could set the panel in place on the cowl and check its fit. For our final trimming, we left approximately ½ inch of metal for flanges along the sides to attach the scoop to the cowl and ⅜ inch along the cockpit side of the scoop to wrap around a length of ⅛-inch-diameter wire. We made the scoop's side flanges by squeezing each flange area against a flat anvil wheel in the English wheel and bending the panel up against the side of the upper wheel. The wired edge along the scoop's rear was accomplished using the technique I demonstrated in *Professional Sheet Metal Fabrication*: we thinned the metal on the bend line in the bead roller, bent it into a U shape, trapped the wire at both ends, and gradually squeezed the metal tight around the wire with a homemade wiring tool. The wire can be trapped with Vise-Grips as well if you have not made a wiring tool. We attached our scoop with temporary rivets and moved on to the rest of the body.

The sheet metal on the sides of the cockpit was mostly form, which made the sides easy to mock up, but they were boring to look at because they were such large expanses of plain metal. We rolled a small bead 2 inches from the bottom of each side panel to add some visual interest. Moreover, adding a 90-degree flange along the bottom edge of the body sides added stiffness and gave the panels a very clean appearance. We created the flange by using the body support structure as a hammer form. We sandwiched the body sheet metal between a thick strip of scrap steel and the bottom edge of the body support structure. By hammering a spoon held against the flange, we were able to bend the metal over without leaving any marks. Furthermore, because the sheet metal was trapped in the hammer form, any shrinking or stretching that took place over the relaxed S curve of the body's profile was confined to the flange; the cockpit sides remained pristine. This technique worked beautifully and was infinitely easier than putting a 90-degree flange in the panel first, and then trying to shrink and stretch the flange with a hand-operated machine to match the curve of the entire panel to the body structure. We did use the hand-operated shrinker along the rear vertical edge of the cockpit sides, however. Because the rear of the cockpit is the point at

114

which the body begins to narrow as it approaches the tail, we wanted the cockpit sides to taper in at the rear and anticipate this transition. Thus, as seen in cross-section, the body circumference gets smaller as you move from the cockpit to the tail. Because the body was closer to a cylinder resting on its side than a cone, shrinking was needed at the rear.

FINISHING THE TAIL

Like the cockpit sides, the sheet metal for the tail was predominantly form, though we could see that shrinking would be needed where the tail met the cockpit. Without shrinking, our tail would have resembled a cone against a cylinder, with an abrupt transition. This might have looked satisfactory, or even good, but I wanted the students to have a chance to use thumbnail shrinking dies on this project. The minor shrinking we had done at the ends of the cockpit sides with gathering jaws set the stage for the transition, but we needed an additional 3 to 4 inches of smoothly flowing metal to clean up the body where the tail met the cockpit. Because gathering jaws are not very effective past about 1 inch from the edge, we knew thumbnail shrinking dies were the best

choice for shrinking several inches into the panel. In hindsight, smaller panels would have been easier to handle in the machine, but we thought we were making life easier by having fewer panels to join.

Three panels made up the tail section that meets the cockpit: two sides and a top panel. We marked the leading edge of each of these panels with carefully measured shrink marks at 2 inches and 3½ inches deep. By treating each panel very evenly, we obtained a uniform result that obviated the need for laboriously comparing one side to the other with templates. The metal at the upper rear corners of the cockpit needed a few more shrinks than the rest of the panels, but this did not pose a problem because we shrunk both corners the same amount. We intentionally shrunk the ends of all three panels more than we needed, and then gently stretched them back out to "just right," with a perfect surface finish. We were guilty of stretching a little past "just right" on one side and had to heat shrink the resulting tumor. With thumbnail shrinking dies you typically want to shrink a little more than necessary so you can smooth out the evidence of your shrinking with a wheel, planishing hammer, or power hammer.

We shrank the rear edge of the cockpit sheet metal to create a better transition between the cockpit and the tail.

We made two more panels for the underside of the tail by bending flat sheet metal over an empty welding gas cylinder.

With the tail almost complete, we were eager to finish off the rear with a polished cone. Not wanting to fight any more metal than necessary, however, we carefully planned out the cone with poster board. Bending the cone was very challenging because the small end was only about 1 inch in diameter, which made the slip-roll machine out of the question. As one of my students wrestled the cone, I was reminded why modern cars are plastic and why plastic body filler is popular among some folks repairing old cars. Adam Mashiach obtained the best results by bending the metal blank around a steel rod held in a vise. If you attempt to make a cone yourself, be sure to file off all burrs and sharp edges and wear gloves, unless you're a masochist. Once Adam was happy with the cone shape,

We shrank the leading edge of the tail sheet metal with thumbnail shrinking dies to increase the taper of the body where the tail meets the cockpit. If you can live with a more abrupt transition, a Lancaster-style shrinker would work too.

Jake San Martin and Adam Mashiach smoothed out the areas shrunk with thumbnail dies in the power hammer, but a wheeling machine would work too.

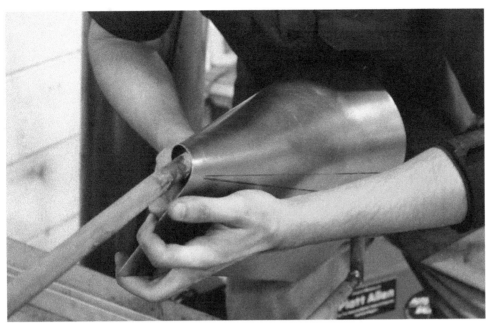

Over a rod held in a vise, Adam bent a cone for the extreme end of the tail. He polished the metal before bending because it was easier to sand and polish it in its flat state.

The finished tail cone looks charming and handmade, perfect for the spirit of this car.

he plug-welded it together and ground down the welds. To finish off the cone's tip, he inserted a large bolt with a round brass-plated head—probably an old bumper bolt with its chrome sanded off—and tack-welded a nut inside the cone to retain the bolt.

RESOLVING THE TOP EDGE OF THE COCKPIT

The Nayslayer was coming together nicely, but the cockpit needed a surround to pull everything together. We considered running a bead through all the panels around the cockpit opening and then wrapping a wire in the edge, but we thought a separate strip of metal, held by screws or rivets, would look even better. We made paper patterns for strips of sheet metal 3 inches wide for the cockpit surround, cut metal as needed, and installed a ¾-inch flange along the cockpit side of each strip. First we thinned the metal on the bend line in the bead roller, bent the flange to 90 degrees in the English wheel, and then used a hammer and dolly to clean up the bend.

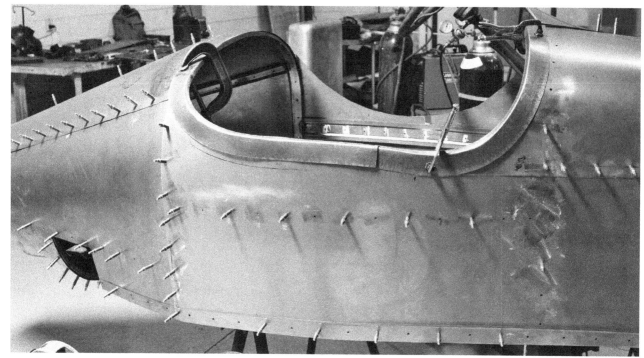

We finished the cockpit edge with a 3-inch-wide band of sheet metal shaped to hug the curves of the opening. After installing a short 90-degree bend and shaping the band to fit, we ran the strip through a set of dies in the Pullmax for a decorative flare.

When installing a flange on a curve, expect to shrink the metal on outside curves and stretch the metal on inside curves to keep the overall shape with which you started. Furthermore, whenever you install a flange in the edge of a panel, be mindful of how soft or sharp the bend needs to be. In this instance, the crispness of the bend did not matter as long as it was even. We planned to run our metal strips through a set of dies in the Pullmax that re-form an existing 90-degree angle. As such, the dies dictate the resulting appearance of the bend and the original bend merely helps guide the metal through the dies and gets changed in the process. If we had wanted a very sharp bend, we would have created it with a hammer and dolly or used different dies in the Pullmax.

The dies we chose were recycled from an earlier project and re-create the profile of a 1965 Chevy truck front-wheel opening. After installing the bead with the Pullmax dies, we stretched the short flanges with the hand-operated stretcher as needed until each strip fit its intended spot around the cockpit opening. We intentionally made the cockpit opening asymmetrical for looks. (Asymmetry is also much easier to achieve than symmetry.)

As a final step, we thinned the metal about ⅛ inch in from the edge of the short flange in the bead roller and folded it back against itself for a clean, safe edge facing the car's interior. In the absence of a Pullmax, a similar result could have been obtained with a bead roller by rolling a half-round bead near the cockpit side of the strip and bending the extra metal down at 90 degrees, shrinking as needed to account for the smaller radius on the inside of the curve.

With our cockpit almost complete, we addressed the problem that every T speedster body builder must solve: the steering column must be lowered. In its stock location, a Ford Model T steering column is too tall and upright for speedster use. Fortunately, early hot rodders had this conundrum solved by the time Prohibition came around. The usual practice was to insert a wedge between the steering box and the frame at the front end of the steering column, and then fabricate a mount somewhere under the cowl to stabilize the steering column. The change in column angle necessarily involves modifying the firewall, but this is a simple modification; nowadays, various companies sell kits that include the steering box wedge and a bolt-in mount for the firewall. Naturally, we chose to fabricate a sheet metal mount out of 16-gauge steel to affix the column to the firewall. In addition, we bolted a steel strap under the column behind the dashboard, where a piece of 1-inch square steel tubing runs across the body.

For the dashboard, Zane Luekenga machine-turned a stainless-steel panel. Though the end product looks as if it were made by magic, the engine-turning process is not complicated, though it does require patience. First, Zane made a poster board pattern of the dash panel that he traced before cutting the panel from stainless steel with a plasma cutter. Next, he glued the panel back-side-down on a piece of plywood with construction adhesive. With the stainless firmly secured to the plywood, Zane sanded the dash panel all the way out to its edges with successively finer grits of sandpaper—180, 320, 600—using a dual-action palm sander. Sanding gave the panel a blemish-free surface that would appear uniform and shiny after turning. Zane mounted the board in a Bridgeport milling machine and slowly lowered a spinning ¼-inch-diameter wood dowel against the stainless panel. Spinning at 400 rpm with a dollop of valve-lapping compound on its tip, the dowel rod

A common method of changing the angle of a Model T speedster steering column involves inserting a wedge between the frame and the steering box. Were we to put this car on the road, we would cut and insert a wedge to match the gap of this spacer block.

Lowering the steering column on a Model T requires cutting out the bottom of the firewall and installing a new mount where the column passes through the firewall. Jon Bubnis made ours.

Zane Luekenga called upon his heroic patience to machine-turn our stainless-steel dashboard with a wood dowel and some valve-grinding compound.

Despite the gold leaf graffiti in the lower right corner, the finished dash looks stunning. I think it is worth every hour of work Zane put into it.

created a semi-satin swirl on the stainless with each pressing. Zane pressed the dowel down twice, moved it over 0.125 inch, and repeated the process. When he got to the end of a row, he moved over 0.180 inch and went back across the panel. Without a milling machine, I suspect a person could perform this operation on a drill press, though you would have to resituate and clamp the panel for each decorative flourish.

MAKING HOOD STRAPS

If you have read this far and feel inspired to build your own T body or other type of speedster, you will need hood straps. While various types of hood straps are sold

on the aftermarket, this book is for people who want to make their own stuff.

We were intrigued by a set of straps we saw on an early-1930s Duesenberg-powered Indy car and felt that their simple design would be easy to replicate. At the local department store we bought four leather belts with buckles that looked believable for what we were trying to do. Then we gathered together four ¼-inch bolts measuring 8 inches long, four washers, four small stiff springs, and eight nuts. We cut the heads off the bolts and welded a short length of ¼-inch-diameter steel rod horizontally in their places, thus creating a rod that could retain a leather strap at one end and bolt through the frame

Jake made the hood straps from four belts looped around lengths of brass rod secured to the aluminum hood with roll pins. The other end of each belt is secured to a long bolt with a short length of steel welded across it to form a T. The bolts pass through holes in the frame. Not visible in the image, a spring on the end of each bolt, secured with a washer and nut, provides tension.

at the other. Jake San Martin reinforced the hood sides with an extra layer of 0.063-inch-thick aluminum. At the extreme ends of these reinforcements he mounted short lengths of ¼-inch brass rod to act as strap-attachment points. He drilled through one end of each aluminum mount and each brass rod and drove a small roll pin into each hole to secure the rods in their locations. With the hood centered on the body, Jake carefully cut the belts to uniform lengths, looped each strap around its mounting point, and fastened the doubled-over leather with the same brass screws and nuts that we used on the body sheet metal. The threaded ends of the rods were inserted through holes in the frame, then a spring, washer, and two nuts finished off each assembly.

Once the body was fully assembled with temporary rivets, we replaced all the Clecos with machine screws. Although nyloc nuts did not exist in 1915, they were a compromise in authenticity we were willing to embrace to facilitate assembly and to keep the body secure. We then slathered wheel-bearing grease all over the bare steel panels to prevent rust. For the final touches, Jake lettered the car with pinstriping enamel and we proudly rolled it out onto the show field. If ever the skeptics get you down, think of the Nayslayer and go build what's on your mind.

The combination of brass, aluminum, and steel is pleasing to the eye. A set of yellow wooden wheels borrowed from another student completes the package.

Chapter 12
Re-creating an Indy Race Car

More than eighty years ago, *Automobile Racing* author Ray F. Kuhns advised aspiring race car builders to shape body panels "in the usual fashion" with a power hammer. Kuhns would not likely have imagined that college students would be following his advice so many years later, but that is exactly what we do every day in my classroom. Although modern technology certainly has its place in automotive restoration, learning traditional techniques, such as the use of the power hammer, is an indispensable part of our students' training. Thus, when James Long of Grass Valley, California, asked if we could re-create the body of an old Indy car from scratch, our students eagerly seized upon the opportunity.

Our Indy car project is a good model for anyone wanting to build his or her own '20s- or '30s-era speedster or a scratch-built body. The shaping involved was more complicated than what was required for the Nayslayer Model T (see Chapter 11), yet none of the shaping was so complex that anyone should feel intimidated. Hopefully, the chapter that follows shows how this entire build simply applies the lessons from previous chapters to a new set of circumstances.

BUILDING A BODY BUCK

By the time he called us, Long had made significant progress in his effort to re-create Kelly Petillo's 1935 Indianapolis-winning car. Long had assembled a rolling chassis using the correct Rudge wire wheels and a period-correct set of frame rails. Long selected Petillo's car because 1935 was the first of many Indy-winning cars powered by the Offenhauser 255-cubic-inch engine, a powerplant developed by Harry Miller a few years earlier. Long reasoned that if he couldn't obtain the appropriate 255-cubic-inch engine, he already had a 110-cubic-inch "Offy" that could be substituted and remain within the Miller/Offenhauser lineage. Long's goal for the completed car was to travel to different events and allow young passengers to experience the exhilaration of riding in an Offy-powered open-wheel race car. Understandably, assisting this man on his most noble of quests became a moral imperative for my students and me.

Using an assortment of screenshots from newsreels of the 1935 race, as well as Miller body drawings reproduced in Mark Dees's *The Miller Dynasty*, we created drawings for our car that we felt would

My students' re-creation of the 1935 Indianapolis-winning car was a terrific learning experience that required research and plenty of creative problem solving.

A speedster-type design is a perfect candidate for your first full-body build. We transferred 1/8-scale drawings to gridded gift wrap paper glued to plywood. We followed the drawings to cut out stations for a buck.

keep it faithful in appearance to Petillo's car while accommodating the chassis, radiator, and gas tank that Long provided. If the thought of designing a body out of thin air makes your heart skip a beat, relax! If you have ever given birth, potty-trained an emotionally scarred mastiff, or successfully zipped a new cover on your futon, this is much easier. Simply accumulate data for as many of your hard points as you can—frame dimensions, drivetrain dimensions, cockpit dimensions, and so forth—and start plotting them on graph paper. You will need a top view, a side view, and a view from each end. For dimensions you are not sure about, such as the finished contours of the body panels, try to find dimensions of something similar, or make some sketches using curves of known radii to get you in the ballpark. For our car, there were enough drawings in *The Miller Dynasty* to get an idea of what dimensions and radii would be believable from one area of the car to the next. I also found a detailed drawing of a two-seat Studebaker Indy car from about the same period, which was very helpful. By comparing the Miller drawings to the Studebaker, we got an idea of which dimensions and details were commonly used and those that were unique to a specific car. If you have design experience and the appropriate software, make the most of those resources. If not, I will outline a method that anyone can follow successfully.

Make your body drawings on graph paper at a scale that will be easy to translate to inches or centimeters with whatever level of exactitude you require. On the graph paper we used, one square equaled 1 inch, which made the drawings ⅛ scale. By adjusting a compass to a given number of squares and drawing a series of arcs onto poster board, which we then cut out, we compiled a selection of radius gauges at ⅛ scale. If you are fortunate enough to live in a city, you can probably buy large rolls of gridded paper. I do not, so I glued smaller sheets of graph paper together until I had the size we needed. If you aren't opposed to spending a little money, you can probably buy a set of radius gauges. Using the fixed data points that you know, start sketching in body shapes using your radius gauges until you are satisfied with your design. As automotive designers have always known, drawings at ⅛ scale look vastly different when translated to three dimensions at full scale, hence the history of clay models in automotive design.

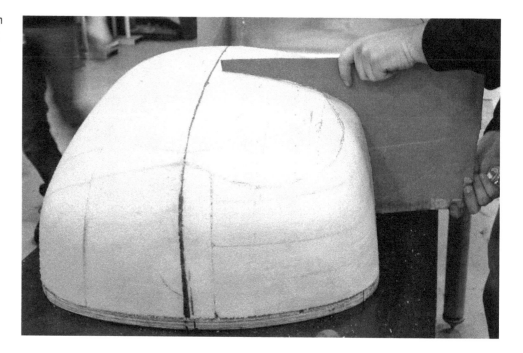

Zach ensured symmetry on both sides of his grille shell by using cardboard templates to check its contours at several points in relation to a flat surface.

Real life often contradicts what two-dimensional drawings dictate. With his foam buck in place, Zach shaved the surface to his liking.

Nevertheless, up through the wood station buck phase, you will have invested very little money, so changing course is always an option. Consider any time invested as part of your education.

Enlarging and transferring our drawings to plywood for a body buck was simple. We scaled up the ⅛-scale drawings on the back of 1-inch gridded gift wrap paper. We attached the paper decorative-side down to plywood sheets with spray adhesive, cut out the stations

with a band saw, and assembled a buck to use as a guide in shaping the body panels. Generally, a buck is not used as a form to bend metal against, but rather as a three-dimensional placeholder indicating where the finished sheet metal surfaces should lie in space. Once the metal is shaped, the buck is removed. A buck can function as a hammer form, however, as long as it is adequately reinforced, so take that into consideration if there is some part of your build where this would be useful, such as a drip rail around a hood opening or a 90-degree flange around a wheel opening. Using the gift wrap paper method, we created a station buck for the engine bay, belly pan, and tail section.

With a lot of shape change in a small area, the grille shell would have been difficult to represent accurately with a handful of plywood stations on a conventional buck, so Zach Oller carved a grille shell facsimile out of Styrofoam. The three-dimensional foam model allowed us to visualize our design on the car more completely, which seemed prudent for several reasons. First, the finished shell needed to clear the front axle during suspension travel. It also needed to house a radiator designed for a flathead Ford, and it had to resemble Petillo's very distinctive original shell with its heart-shaped grille. Psychologically, I like the additional visual information a solid buck can provide when a lot of shape change is anticipated. Although reading the fit of a panel is a little trickier over a solid foam block than it is over a wood station buck (you can't see anything from behind), I think you will prefer the added information it provides, especially if you are new to metal shaping.

For foam bucks, I like 2-inch-thick builder's insulation that comes in 4 × 8-foot sheets. I have tried dozens of adhesives with varying degrees of success; some glues attack the foam, while others don't harden adequately. I strongly prefer Weldbond white glue, which can be obtained in 3-liter jugs. Cut a few slabs of Styrofoam to encompass your intended design, slather some glue between them with a paintbrush, place a weight on the entire sandwich, and allow it to dry overnight. Carve the Styrofoam with surforms, disc sanders, files, and/or a hack saw blade with a handle made of duct tape. Weldbond glue is water-soluble until fully dried, so clean your brush right away. Weldbond also bonds Styrofoam beautifully to wood and metal, which can be helpful if you need to combine it with an existing wood buck or even add it to a missing area on a damaged automotive panel.

With a foam buck for the grille shell and a wood station buck for the engine bay, belly pan, and tail section, only the cockpit and cowl were undefined. Knowing that the steel support structure under the cowl was going to be substantial, we decided that there was no need to build a buck for the cowl; we would shape the metal to fit the understructure directly. The steel support structure beneath the cowl on Indy cars of this era appears to have been almost standardized in design and is well documented in period photographs. Interestingly, many of the body drawings specify ⅝-inch square steel tubing for the cowl structure, but we—and apparently many of the builders of the time—used 1-inch tubing for enhanced rigidity. We built a simple jig to facilitate the bending of the tubing by arranging pieces of steel on a tabletop in our intended curve and welding them in place. Because we had no way to shrink the tubing along our intended arc, Coye Savell cleverly suggested that we heat one section at a time and hammer the inside wall to push it inward in relation to the adjoining sidewalls. This technique worked surprisingly well. By collapsing the innermost wall, the tubing followed our jig perfectly. We made the cowl support behind the firewall out of two strips of 12-gauge steel welded to each other so that they formed an L-shaped cross-section: one leg of the L behind the firewall and the second leg beneath the cowl sheet metal.

We welded random hunks of steel following a chalk line on a tabletop to create a jig for bending the square tube under the rear of the cowl.

Sharp students enable perceptive instructors to feign competence. Coye's brilliant suggestion to cave in the inside wall of our square tubing allowed the tubing to follow the jig effortlessly.

STARTING ON THE BODY SHEET METAL

Draping large sheets of paper over the wood buck allowed students to anticipate what would need to happen to each piece of aluminum for it to conform to the correct shape. Large wrinkles indicated that the metal needed to be gathered, or shrunk, while tears indicated that the metal must be spread out or stretched. If the paper lay undisturbed over the buck, such as along the length of the hood center panel, the metal only needed to be formed.

Coye Savell cut the two hood side panels to size and installed the necessary bends with a sheet metal brake: a 90-degree bend along each panel's bottom edge, a 90-degree bend facing the engine along the top edge on the right panel for mounting a hinge, and a Z-shaped bend along the top edge of the left panel for capturing the movable hood top panel. Coye formed the hood top panel by bending it against an empty welding gas cylinder.

We obtained aluminum hinges for the hood from the Yard Store (www.yardstore.com), an aircraft surplus and metal supply in Wichita, Kansas. Indy car builders of this era often used hinges in a novel way that is worth emulating. By mounting one half of a hinge on a hood side and the other half on the firewall or radiator support, the hood is made removable by pulling out the pin that runs through the center of the hinge. The hinge combination is very secure when the pin is installed, but takes only moments to remove.

We used 14-gauge aluminum for all exterior body panels, as specified in an original Miller drawing we found in Dees's *The Miller Dynasty*, with the exception of the belly pan, where we used 12-gauge aluminum. Typical of this type of car, the cowl became wider as it joined the cockpit, where the sheet metal swept up in an asymmetrical curve above the dash. Where the body widens, the sheet metal is thus required to assume a greater radius and needs to be stretched. Because the shape change on our car was quite drastic, we made the top cowl section out of two separate pieces of metal. James Virzi stretched the rear of the large main piece of metal with a linear stretching die in the power hammer perpendicular to the edge of the metal, and with a semi-flat anvil wheel in the English wheel. The long, skinny footprint of these tools thins and thus adds length to the material in the same way that a rolling pin squeezes out dough. In our case, this meant the added length expanded the rear edge of the panel to conform to the structure beneath. Similarly, James stretched the small second panel that sweeps up above the dash, accentuating the rise on the driver's side by working that area more.

With the exception of the forward end where it met the firewall, the belly pan was all form. Bobby Robertson bent the sides against a length of pipe of the appropriate diameter clamped to a table. The forward end of the pan was made from a separate piece that required shrinking at the corners. To use my running

Our hood sides were held in place just like crafty Indy car builders did it back in the day: we used hinges mounted vertically with removable center pins.

James Virzi wheeled the rear edge of the cowl sheet metal to make it flare out toward the cockpit.

The cowl sheet metal was composed of one large sheet across the body and two smaller pieces welded to the cockpit side of the cowl.

track analogy, we were asking the metal at the corners to move from the outer lane, where the metal is flat, to the inner lane, where the edges are drawn in. We used thumbnail shrinking dies in the Dake machine for this operation. In the absence of those tools, we could have moved the weld seam to split the shape between two adjacent panels and thereby divided the total amount of shrinking between two panels instead of doing all our shrinking on one. Gathering-style jaws might have accomplished this, though the metal was quite thick (0.071 inch). A third option would have been to cut out most of the corner, bend and shrink around the void, and fill in the missing portion with a bowl-shaped piece of metal stretched to shape.

Nervous that a modern driver could easily weigh as much as the jockey-sized Petillo and his slender riding mechanic Jimmy Dunham together, I encouraged Bobby to add ribs to the belly pan. He used a die in the Pullmax machine to create ribs with a softened hat shape cross-section for stiffness (think of Boy George's hat). To the extent that dies are able to trap the metal, they can be used to stretch and shrink. By bending the rib at the appropriate point while it was in the machine, Bobby brought the rib to 90 degrees without losing the hat shape. Minor stretching between the dies prevented the rib from becoming kinked. In the absence of dies to trap the metal, one could place a weld seam at the apex of the corner and shape the end of each rib piece as needed for a seamless appearance. Once installed on the car, the belly pan did not flex in the slightest under the author's ponderous 230-some pounds.

Bobby formed most of the belly pan from two pieces of aluminum bent along a length of pipe clamped to a table.

Bobby made the forward end of the belly pan from a single large piece of aluminum. He shrank the corners to 90 degrees with thumbnail shrinking dies.

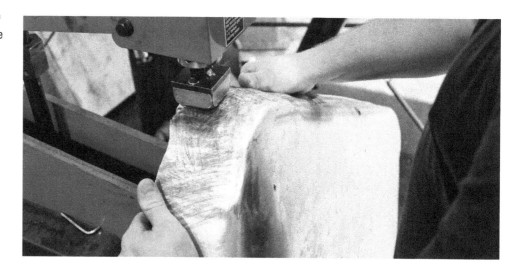

Bobby made a set of dies for the Pullmax having the same radius as the bend along the bottom edges of the belly pan. Then he ran his belly pan endcap through the dies.

Proper fitment is about 90 percent of successful welding. When completed, Bobby's belly pan looked like one homogenous pressed piece of metal.

Bobby made numerous belly pan ribs in the Pullmax. He gradually bent the ribs to 90 degrees as he ran the pieces back and forth between the dies.

Bobby's belly pan turned out beautifully. With the added ribs, the car owner will be able to transport sumo wrestlers with ease, should the need arise.

CRAFTING THE TAIL

Oscar Voorhees fabricated the tail section and the rear belly pan in several pieces using the wheeling machine for stretching and thumbnail dies for shrinking. The boat tail is such a universal vintage race car shape that it is worth describing in a little more detail. On our car, and I suspect many vintage race cars of this type, the sides of the tail were form except along the top edge. Thus, a ruler would sit flat if placed vertically anywhere along the sides of the tail. If turned lengthwise, the ruler would go hollow under either end due to the curve. Where the sides joined the top panel, shrinking was needed because we were asking the metal to move into a tighter-radius curve as it moved toward the longitudinal center of the car. The depth of Oscar's shrinks was determined by the beginning of the highlight line, the transition area where the flat side begins to curve over in a tight radius to meet the gradual radius of the top panel. The area of the highlight line is the area of the tightest radius. Oscar used thumbnail dies here because they are fast and work the metal evenly

through its thickness, but he could have used gathering jaws or even tuck shrinking. To keep the weld seam in a flat area to facilitate stretching and weld finishing, Oscar intended for most of the shrunken metal to get trimmed off the side panels, so he made them large to leave plenty of room for trimming. A large, pie-shaped, deeply crowned panel made up the top of the tail. Oscar wheeled and raised the center of the panel in relation to the edges, where again he shrank in from the edge up to the beginning of the highlight line with thumbnail dies.

The underside of the tail section was fabricated much like the top, except that the radius where the side of the body met the underside of the tail was tighter than on top of the tail. We reinforced our edges at the joint between the tail and the belly pan with 1/8-inch aluminum angle that could be bolted to each other and to the frame to support the rear of the body. As was common practice on these cars in the 1930s, we made most of the finished tail section a single, removable unit with the cockpit and cowl sheet metal by riveting the

Oscar shrank the top 2 inches of the tail side panels. The rest of the sides was form.

Because the panel across the top of the tail was quite deep, Oscar shrunk in several inches from the edges. He stretched the metal above his deepest shrinks.

Oscar smoothed out all the evidence of his shrinking in the wheeling machine.

By now the car looked convincing as an old Indy racer, but James was too busy documenting his time and work to notice.

The sheet metal for the underside of the tail was a repeat of the topside, though the transition along the sides was more abrupt. Oscar placed the buck for the underside of the tail upside down to facilitate working.

two together. Where the rear two-thirds of the body met the cowl sheet metal, we joined the two body sections by riveting them to a backing plate of 12-gauge aluminum, one piece per side. A removable body makes maintenance much easier. To finish the cockpit edge, we rolled the outermost ¾ inch of sheet metal around a ¼-inch-diameter aluminum rod. The wire-wrapped edge stiffened the top of the panels and left a safe, cut-proof surface for white-knuckled riders to grasp.

Car owner James Long supplied an aluminum gas tank that we modified and installed inside the tail section. The tank, presumably from an old dirt-track car, had a very deep sump that we sectioned 6 inches. Jared Thurston built a tank mount from square tubing, fabricated a long filler neck out of exhaust tubing, and cut a filler hole in the top sheet metal panel of the tail with a plasma cutter. To obtain a clean hole with a professional-looking rolled edge, Jared made a two-piece hammer form out of wood. The bottom piece of the hammer form, placed beneath the sheet metal, had a hole cut to size with a routed ¼-inch-diameter lip around its perimeter. The top piece of wood was

merely a squeezing apparatus to hold the metal and the hammer form in the right orientation. Jared gradually worked the lip around the perimeter of the hole down against the hammer form with an air hammer.

THE GRILLE SHELL

While Jared was finishing up the rear of the car, Zach Oller was hard at work on the grille shell at the opposite end. Zach made each side of the shell from one piece of metal that he indexed to the buck with a metal tab screwed into the buck's plywood base. The tab ensured that each panel was always in the same place on the buck every time Zach checked its fit. Keep in mind that shaping to a moving target is impossible. If your panel is not positively indexed with your buck, you are chasing a moving target. The side panels were mostly form with some shrinking at the corners. The top and bottom panels both curved, so shrinking was needed to force the metal to assume a shorter radius where it wrapped around the front of the shell. With the grille undetermined, Zach wheeled out a crowned panel and filled in the hole in the front of the shell. The smooth

Jared Thurston's front fuel tank mount was notched to clear the rear differential during suspension travel. The seat mounts were welded to a crossmember bolted between the frame rails. A small piece of ¼-inch-thick steel welded beneath the seat fronts improved comfort considerably.

Jared hammer-formed a hole for the fuel filler neck in a piece of wood. The plywood clamped on top prevented any distortion from occurring around the hole.

The finished fuel tank filler hole looks like it was made with a costly, sophisticated tool, but you know better.

front gave him maximum flexibility when it came time to fit a grille.

Zach determined the correct grille heart shape through trial and error. He cut several large hearts out of paper and taped them one at a time into position with the shell installed on the car. Once satisfied, he traced the heart's outline on the car with Sharpie permanent marker and kept the paper heart as a pattern. Zach made the outer border for the grille from solid aluminum bar stock supplied by the car owner. The bar stock, having a half-oval cross-section, required annealing and cutting to wrestle into shape. To anneal the metal, we scribbled on it with a Sharpie and heated it until the ink burned off at 600 degrees Fahrenheit. Because shrinking was impossible, we made some cuts through the inner half of the stock at the sharpest curves with a cutoff wheel. We sandwiched the aluminum between two pieces of wood in a vise and fashioned a bending tool out of 1 × 2-inch hardwood. We modified the wood for our application by cutting a notch in one end so the tool resembled a wooden pipe wrench. The notch ensured that the half-oval profile maintained its correct orientation as

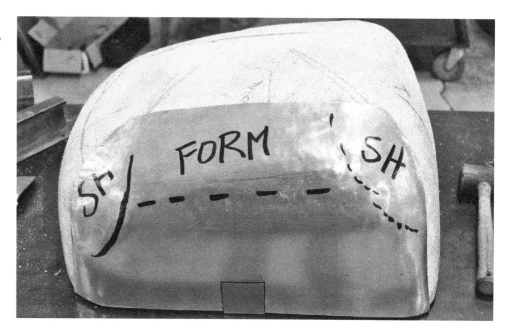

The sides of the grille shell required shrinking at the corners, which Zach achieved with thumbnail dies.

The front of the grille shell required shrinking across its width.

After shrinking the front of the grille shell, Zach wheeled a nice finish into the panel.

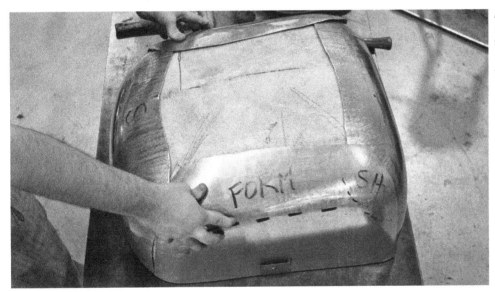

At my request, Zach mocked up the pieces for the grille shell. Because the heart-shaped opening was yet undefined, he filled in the front of the shell with a crowned panel.

we bent the metal into two half-heart shapes. Thanks to the cuts we had made earlier along the inside of the aluminum bar stock, the metal followed the heart shape without the need for shrinking. The metal along the outer half of the stock stretched on its own as we bent it to shape with our wooden tool. As soon as our two heart halves matched the paper template, Zach welded them together, along with the various cuts we had made, and filed the surfaces smooth. We secured the grille surround to the shell by drilling and tapping several holes, running threaded aluminum studs into the holes, cutting the studs flush, and welding up the holes. This worked beautifully. The connections were strong and invisible from the exterior.

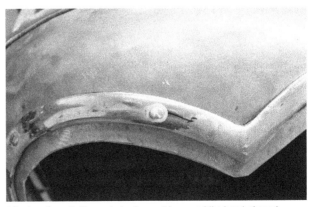

After bending a half-round aluminum strip around the heart-shaped opening, Zach threaded small aluminum studs all the way through the strip and welded the exposed end. This technique worked beautifully.

Tony DiValentin and Zach McClure riveted their seatbacks to ¼-inch aluminum plate. The hammering force on the ³⁄₁₆-inch-diameter round-head rivets was supplied by a 4× rivet gun.

A bucking bar held against the back of the rivet transferred the rivet gun's energy and thickened the rivet shaft.

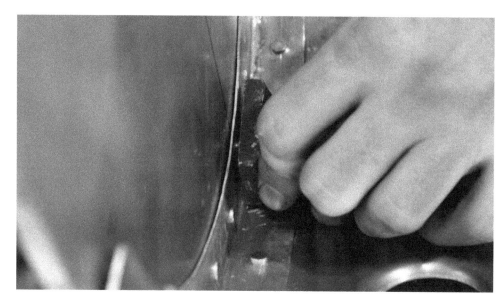

CUSTOM SEATS

The problem of seating was daunting in this two-person car. Fortunately, we had only a general idea of how Petillo's seats looked, so we had a lot of creative freedom. To make the most of our confined cockpit, we situated the mechanic's seat slightly behind and below the driver's. We made the driver's seat about an inch wider than its neighbor and added enough material to the seatback to keep the driver from spilling over into the mechanic's lap during left turns. The seat design Zach McClure and Tony DiValentin came up with could easily be adapted to any hot rod or custom car. They cut flat bases out of ¼-inch aluminum plate and formed backs from 14-gauge aluminum stiffened with a series of beads and tapered holes using a Mittler Brothers hole punch. They finished the seatback edges by wrapping the outer ¾ inch around a ¼-inch-diameter aluminum rod. To avoid the need for shrinking at abrupt corners, they cut away the seatback and left the rod exposed at the corners. Unfortunately, after the seats were built, but not covered, we decided to remove several inches of height out of the car body in the rear, which left the seatbacks protruding above the cockpit sheet metal. Zach and Tony good-naturedly lopped a few inches off the tops of the seatbacks and riveted a strip of ¼-inch aluminum across them for stiffness. The seatbacks were riveted to the bases between two L-shaped strips of aluminum per seat, with one strip on the inside of the seat and one on the outside.

SEAT, GAS TANK, AND BODY SUPPORTS

The methods we used to attach our seat-supporting crossmember and gas tank mount to the frame are worth describing because they may be useful for anyone building a custom speedster or hot rod. The universally accepted way of stiffening an old ladder-style C-channel frame is to box in the open side. Our frame was mostly boxed with ³⁄₁₆-inch plate when we began work. Once we had mocked up a seat-supporting crossmember out of 2-inch square tubing, we drilled and tapped the ³⁄₁₆-inch plate at the appropriate points to mount the crossmember. Similarly, we drilled and tapped two blocks of ½-inch steel for the forward gas tank mount and welded them on the inside of the frame on both sides. For the rear gas tank mount, we used two large U-bolts to secure the mount to the crossmember at the extreme rear of the frame.

In direct imitation of Petillo's car, we secured the body to the frame with lengths of ⅛-inch-thick aluminum angle riveted to the body and tightened down over threaded studs screwed into the frame rails. This angled aluminum was much too thick to shrink or stretch in a handheld shrinker/stretcher machine. As a result, when shrinking was needed at the rear of the cockpit where the frame curved up over the rear axle, we cut out the leg of the angle that would have otherwise needed shrinking. We bent the remaining leg of the angle to fit the curve and then filled in the gap with a piece of ⅛-inch aluminum plate. After welding, the angle looked like one piece. To cover up the gap between the frame rail and the tail at the rear of the car in an era-consistent manner, we welded a triangle of

⅛-inch plate to the angled aluminum and secured it to studs threaded into the frame rails. Besides enhancing the appearance of the rear of the car, these wide plates served as rugged body mounts for the rear of the body. When stretching was needed from this point to the rear of the car, we used a linear stretching die in the power hammer with the die perpendicular to the edge. This process directly mimics the S-curve exercise described in *Professional Sheet Metal Fabrication*.

Monica Ewy and Dalton Whitfield effortlessly stretched the legs of ⅛-inch-thick aluminum angle with linear dies in the power hammer. Stretching was needed to curve the angle to match the car's frame.

Where shrinking was necessary forward of the rear differential, we cut out part of the angle and later welded in a filler piece. Otherwise, stretching allowed the angle to follow the curves of the body and frame.

A single large panel was affixed across the frame behind the rear differential. The rest of the body sits on top of this panel and can be lifted on and off the frame for servicing.

The complete body looks like it just rolled out of 1935. The owner wanted the grille opening left alone so that he could install the vertical bars with his own students.

Where welding was needed, panels were fused either by the TIG process or with the oxyacetylene torch. When confronted with the innumerable rivets found on this car, we were blessed to have a veteran military helicopter mechanic in our midst to help us refine our riveting technique. Clecos were used to maintain panel alignment until all the riveting was complete.

After he installed the engine, Long brought the car back and asked us to make an exhaust cutout in the right hood side panel. Ken Hamel and Chris Brous cut a template for the plasma cutter from ¼-inch luan board, leaving 3/16 inch between the edge of the template and the desired cut. With the template clamped tightly to the panel, they made a perfect cut.

WRAPPING UP

Over approximately eight months, thirteen students contributed time and energy to the Indy race car. Working steadily at various times of day and night, they made consistent progress without getting in each other's way. We finished the body in time to display the car in Gasoline Alley during the Sportscar Vintage Racing Association's Indianapolis meeting in June 2015. I was delighted with the car, of course, but by far the best part of the build was being immersed in the energy and enthusiasm that comes with helping young people reach a shared goal. Despite the widely held perception that students today are enamored with, and sometimes enslaved by, the latest technology, in my experience they prefer a power hammer to a smartphone any day. The responsibility falls on all of us who love restoring old cars to put the right tools in their hands and show them what can be done.

Once the owner installed the engine, he brought the car back to have one hood side cut out for exhaust clearance. Ken and Chris made a thin wood guide for the plasma cutter.

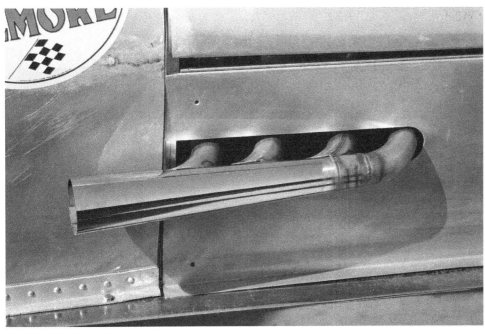

My students did not execute the fancy paint job on the car, but it goes well with their craftsmanship on the body.

Chapter 13
Building an Aluminum Motorcycle Fairing

When one of my colleagues saw Drew Ross's hand built motorcycle fairing taking shape, he remarked, "It looks like you're putting a $40 saddle on a $10 horse!" True as that statement might have been, in my opinion it only underscored the vision, creativity, and desire of the craftsman doing the work. This direct link to passion is one of the main reasons why teachers teach. Life can easily pass you by if you wait to build your dreams until you have the ideal this or that.

Drew started his project by constructing a wire-frame buck around the borrowed motorcycle to use as a guide during metal shaping. Although wire bucks are not as accurate as some other forms of bucks, it worked well for this project because it came together quickly and was easy to change. Like any great sculptor, Drew has a good enough eye to look at both sides of his fairing and make accurate shaping decisions based on his observations.

A book like this should both educate readers on developing their skills and encourage them to pursue their goals. By starting with the humblest raw material, Drew Ross's motorcycle fairing is an inspiring piece of craftsmanship that anyone should find motivational.

Drew's choice of a wire buck was a great one for this project. Practically transparent, the wire buck enabled Drew to assess both the aesthetic and the practical qualities of his proposed design.

If you are at all uneasy about your ability to do the same, an alternative is a Styrofoam buck, which captures more surface detail and is rugged enough to make cardboard templates against. As I described in *Professional Sheet Metal Fabrication*, you can make an accurate template of an existing shape by dragging a compass held perpendicular to the surface against a flat piece of cardboard. With templates, you can objectively confirm that you have achieved symmetry rather than relying on your eye alone. At first glance, the highly irregular surfaces of a motorcycle may seem unlikely substrates to which to attach Styrofoam, but all you need is some flat surface somewhere on which to spread some glue. Weldbond white glue bonds wonderfully to wood, metal, and Styrofoam. If there are bolts somewhere on the engine or frame that can be temporarily removed, fabricate some metal or thin plywood sheets that you can fasten in place with the bolts you removed. If you use sheet metal, degrease it of any oil and sand it to give it some tooth for the glue

to adhere to. Glue pieces of 1- or 2-inch Styrofoam builder's insulation onto the sheets, leave a weight on them overnight, and drill through the Styrofoam from the back of the support. Reattach the bolts to the bike with a socket on an extension, then carve the Styrofoam with surforms, files, disc sanders, or a saw blade.

STRETCHING, SHRINKING, AND FORMING

Using 0.063-inch 3003 aluminum, Drew began by shaping the portion of the fairing over the handlebars. He made this section out of two pieces of aluminum that he stretched into deeply dished shapes using a hammer and a shot bag. As classic high-crowned panels, some shrinking around the edges of these two pieces was needed, which Drew accomplished with thumbnail shrinking dies in our Dake machine. In the absence of thumbnail dies, he could have used tuck shrinking around the edges of these panels, though it would have taken longer. He smoothed out the rough shapes in the English wheel.

Drew made the upper portion of the fairing from two identical high crown panels. He shrunk the outer edges of each panel with thumbnail shrinking dies and stretched the middle, checking each panel periodically against the buck.

Once each half of the upper fairing fit the buck, Drew welded them together and ran the piece through an English wheel to stretch out the weld. Finishing the upper portion as a unit gave Drew better access than if he had waited until he was further along in the process.

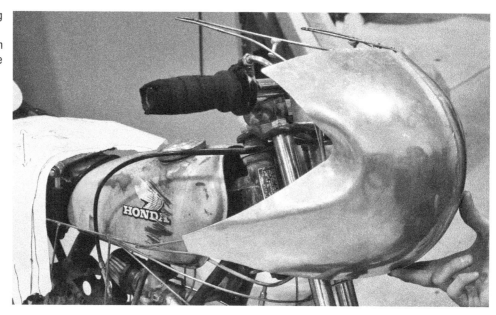

Again using the English wheel, Drew introduced a crown into the large fairing sides. The bottom and front of the fairing sides were mostly form. Where the metal had to assume a tighter radius—at the bottom front corner of the fairing—a lot of shrinking was needed to wrap the sheet metal around the motorcycle completely. Conversely, where the metal had to assume a greater radius—at the top of the fairing where it swells to meet the handlebars—stretching was needed. Drew executed a few quick stretches in a Lancaster-style hand-operated stretcher and wheeled the panel with the wheels perpendicular to the edge. To refine both panels,

Drew alternated bouts of wheeling with checking his panels in place on the bike. Because Drew had access to thumbnail shrinking dies, he was able to shrink the bottom front corner of the fairing to almost 90 degrees. Without shrinking dies, the alternative would have been to make the bottom front of the fairing from a separate bowl-shaped piece made through stretching instead of shrinking and then weld it on.

Depending on one's level of experience, the process of making a panel appear "flat" can be laborious and test one's patience, or it can go quickly. I use the term *flat* to refer to the state of being in the correct plane, meaning

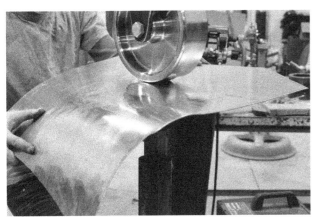

Drew raised a low crown in the fairing sides with a wheeling machine. Because a low crown is just a controlled lump, Drew did not obsess about the direction of his passes, only that he kept his tracks close together to achieve an even result.

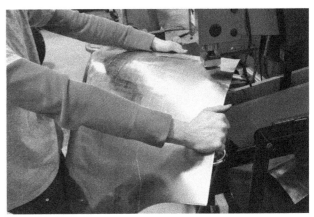

Because the lower front corner of each fairing half was a softened 90-degree turn, significant shrinking was needed here.

This illustration maps out which parts of each fairing half were stretched, shrunk, or simply bent.

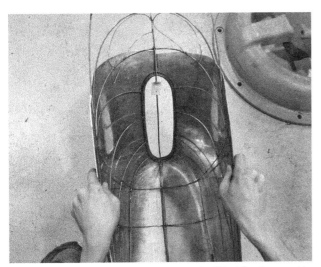

Looking down into the fairing with the wire buck off the bike, Drew could easily check how well the pieces fit the buck and how well they would meet each other for welding.

Drew made sure the fairing halves met perfectly. Although sometimes forgotten when power tools are available, a sharp file is an efficient and controllable tool. Drew removed all proud areas of the weld seam by filing to avoid inadvertently removing too much material.

that there are no high or low spots in the panel. Thus, a flat panel may not literally be as flat as a tabletop, but its surface will read as a continuous, blemish-free plane. Tumors and low spots will show up as waves in the surface. If you are just starting out in metal shaping, lightly sand the surface with very fine sandpaper (320 to 600 grit) on a sanding block. For even more clarity, scribble on the surface with a Sharpie or spritz it with a guide coat before sanding. You are sanding for information, of course, rather than removing material; the scratches tell you the topography of the panel. You must decide whether the scratches indicate that an area of the panel is high or just right. Any method for raising the low spots in a panel is okay, but larger tool surfaces, such as a wheel, are easier to control and will give you a better finish than a handheld hammer with a dolly behind the panel.

High spots will need shrinking. If you find that you have a high spot somewhere on an aluminum panel, do not despair. The 3003 aluminum sheet is incredibly easy to work with and simple to shrink. Scribble on the high spot with a permanent Sharpie. Burn off the ink with an oxyacetylene welding torch or a handheld MAPP gas torch from the hardware store. The Sharpie ink will burn off at 600 degrees Fahrenheit, which is hot enough to anneal the high spot. Trap the high spot against a dolly or piece of wood that is flatter than the panel and hit it with a flat-faced wood or rawhide mallet. The metal need not be hot. The relative softness of the high spot in comparison to the surrounding metal will cause it to yield and upset into itself, or "shrink."

Normally you must overshrink such spots and then stretch them back out to achieve the right shape with a nice surface. Drew finished his panels to a high degree before welding them together because his access would be limited after welding.

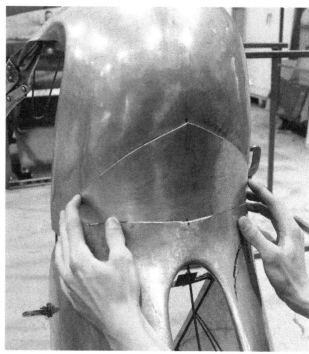

Drew joined the upper and lower portions of his fairing with a small diamond-shaped reverse curve panel. He wheeled the upper third and lower third of this panel to stretch those edges in relation to the horizontal strip running across the middle.

Through trial and error on his wire buck, Drew determined that kidney-shaped cutouts were needed for front fork clearance. Drew slid his fairing over the buck, transferred the shapes, cut away the metal as needed, and rolled about ¼ inch of metal back around the perimeter of each hole.

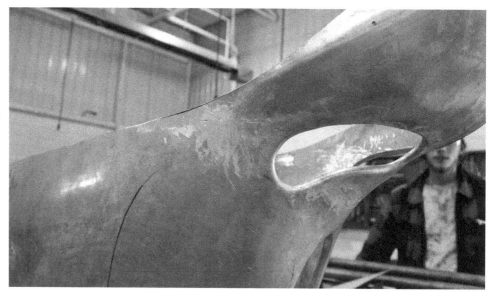

Drew made a separate small panel with a reverse curve on the English wheel to finish the transition area where the lower fairing met the upper fairing. To gain front fork and front tire clearance, Drew cut out openings in the aluminum with aviation snips and then hammered the edges of the openings over a homemade steel T-dolly with a ¼-inch radius. The dolly gave all the openings a clean, rounded, professional appearance.

Drew fabricated some mounts and temporarily attached the fairing to the bike so he could begin working on the seat pan. He was anxious to replace the misshapen lump of foam and duct tape that comprised the original seat. Once he had identified the ideal rearward location for his posterior, Drew built a simple wire outline of the shape of his intended seat pan as if it were seen in profile. He cut a piece of aluminum for

Starting with an extra-long seat base mounted on the bike and a piece of wire bent in the silhouette of the seat in profile, Drew identified his optimum seating position and bent the rear of the pan up to match his template.

Drew made the rearmost part of the seat by pummeling an annealed sheet of aluminum into a shot bag and shrinking its edges with thumbnail shrinking dies. He then wheeled the surface until it was even. Without a buck or template to go by, Drew simply clamped the oversize piece in position on the bike and trimmed metal off the bottom until he was satisfied.

Seen from the rear, the seat pan harmonizes nicely with the rest of the bike. A long rectangle of 12-gauge steel beneath the base of the pan adds rigidity. Drew's design could easily be adapted to fit any number of custom projects.

the base of the pan and bent it around a piece of pipe to create the upward curvature it needed.

For the deep rearmost portion of the seat pan, Drew stretched a large piece of aluminum by hammering it into a shot bag. Shrinking the edges of this highly crowned panel with thumbnail dies pulled the edges of the panel up tight in relation to the center. Drew made the piece oversize so that it would be easy to trim in relation to the bottom of the pan.

After trimming the rear of the pan and welding it to the pan bottom, Drew folded over all the raw edges of the pan and the fairing for a finished, professional look. To fold the edge of a panel over, gradually work your way around the panel's perimeter, bending a small flange to 90 degrees with a pair of Vise-Grips. Finish the job with a hammer and dolly. You can also very lightly thin the metal at the bend point with a bead roller and then bend the flange back with a hammer and dolly, or in a wheeling

machine or with a planishing hammer. When working with steel, thin the metal for a flange about halfway through its thickness on the bend line. On aluminum, leave only a light indentation during thinning or the metal will have a tendency to crack. Regardless of the technique you use to get the flange started, work the entire perimeter or length of the flange in small increments and finish by hammering the flange over on itself against a dolly. Stop hammering as soon as your doubled-over flange looks clean and even. If you over-hammer a doubled edge, it will become thin and uneven and look terrible.

For the finishing touches, Drew sanded his fairing and seat pan with a dual-action sander using 320- and then 600-grit sandpaper. He buffed both pieces with a spiral-sewn cotton buffing wheel loaded with Tripoli abrasive. To remove any remaining fine scratches, Drew polished his work with a loose-section cotton wheel loaded with white rouge.

To encourage approximately ³⁄₁₆ inch of metal to fold over evenly around all the remaining raw edges, Drew gingerly ran the edges through a bead roller with light pressure, lifting as he rolled. Too much pressure can cause a crack to form.

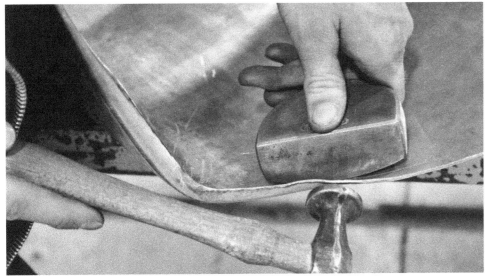

With a bend started around the perimeter of the fairing, Drew supported the bend line with a dolly and hammered the loose edge over 180 degrees.

A doubled edge can be wheeled, planished in a planishing hammer, or simply hammered against a steel dolly. Overzealous crimping with any of these tools will crimp the edge too much, however, and the damage will be impossible to reverse.

Chapter 14
Building a Pair of Early Cadillac Fenders

To illustrate a diverse range of sheet metal problems the vintage-car enthusiast will likely encounter, this step-by-step demonstration shows how to build two fenders from an early car, in this case a 1913 Cadillac. As the fenders on this car are flat, meaning that they are pure form, I did not expect to perform much shrinking or stretching. This was true for the most part, but as is the nature of old cars, expect the unexpected.

BUILDING A SIMPLE BUCK

The flatness of the fenders made the construction of a wood buck straightforward. Though very little shaping was involved, the number of small pieces and the method of construction on these fenders underscore the usefulness of accurate paper patterns for assembly and locating surface details. Moreover, because of the symmetry of the rear fenders, one set of paper patterns was used for both fenders, and using one pattern is a handy way to ensure that two panels come out alike. Finally, as is often the case with fenders on early cars, the panel's construction relies heavily on wrapping and crimping wire-edged panels. Because most tooling used to carry out these operations was probably obsolete by the beginning of Woodrow Wilson's second term, this

These 1913 Cadillac fenders were a great exercise in careful pattern making, measuring, beading, and wire edging—techniques that are needed to make any prewar fender.

While checking the fit of the original fenders on the car, I noticed a significant gap near the forward end of both. Unfortunately, the absence of fasteners near the problem areas meant that I could not simply snug the metal tight with a bolt. Instead, shaping would be needed to increase the curvatures.

piece gives me an opportunity to demonstrate realistic solutions for the average hobbyist dealing with these kinds of panels.

As with any fender reconstruction or patch panel, the first step is to check the fit of the piece on the vehicle. I couldn't have asked for a better example of real life. Although the wheel center caps boldly proclaim, "Cadillac Standard of the World," the fenders did not fit particularly well. After elongating several bolt holes with a carbide cutter mounted in a die grinder, the fit improved somewhat, but there was still a ¼- to ⅜-inch gap along the inside edge where the forward end of the fenders met the body. I observed interference between the fender and the bottom of the body tub and made a mental note to account for this misfit later during construction. Had this been my car, I would have modified the original fender to get the fit spot-on before replicating the panel. I would also consider adding one more fastener near the front of both fenders. In stock

condition, the first 2 feet of the fender are not bolted to the body tub. Although the fenders attach to splash aprons on the front inner edge and to the running boards on their leading edges, there is a long expanse of unsupported metal with a tendency to sag away from the body.

To facilitate construction, I built a simple wood buck. Buck building can easily get out of hand, especially for enthusiasts with an inclination toward anal-retentiveness, but I restrained myself. Because the fender's outside edge is at 90 degrees to its bottom, I knew I could trace its profile with the piece sitting upright on a table or the floor. Also, because there is no crown (shape) in the fender, I knew I could use one profile for both sides of my buck. I cut two identical profiles from ¾-inch plywood and affixed them parallel to each other with enough spacing so they would support the stock fender. I left sufficient material around the perimeter to keep the buck stiff, but not so much that my view

To facilitate construction, I built a simple plywood buck that could be used for either rear fender. The essential dimensions were the width inside the wire-edged border and the curve of the fender from front to back.

from the underside would be obscured. The horizontal supports running between the two profiles did not need to be shaped to lie flush against the underside of the fender because the profile pieces already defined the fender's contour.

TESTING, TESTING . . . 1, 2, 3

With the buck complete, I moved on to the research and development phase, which involved making small test panels to determine how much material I would need for each piece of the fender, which tooling to use, and what order of operations would achieve the best result. Avoid the natural tendency to cut metal first. Your mind tells you to cut metal because you perceive that cutting material is progress. In reality, prematurely cutting metal is a shortcut to greater frustration, material waste, and lower self-esteem. Further along you will come to realize your mistake and feel like an idiot. Metalcraft is challenging enough without self-loathing.

The small half-round bead that outlines all the fenders and the hood of this car probably could have been reproduced with a bead roller. I didn't bother measuring the bead with a radius gauge, but I suspect a ⅜-inch-radius die would have gotten me close.

If a commonly available die does not match your application, there are people, such as Dave Williams of Williams Lowbuck Tools, who will machine a pair of dies to your specifications for around $100. I looked forward to the opportunity to make a die for the Pullmax machine instead.

I made an accurate mold of the fender bead by taping some cardboard in place on the fender in the shape of a box. I squirted some oil on the box and the fender to prevent my mold material from sticking to either of them and filled the box with plastic body filler. I then used the resulting female mold of the bead to guide me as I carved a male die out of a piece of ¾-inch hot-rolled square stock. One could use a mill, if available, but I've found that I can usually make an accurate die in an hour or less using a grinder and a selection of files.

The sharp corners in the beads at the rear of the fenders presented interesting challenges. Again, a bead roller would have been a good choice because it navigates around corners very well. Because I was determined to use the Pullmax machine, however, I needed a suitable way to guide the panel through the dies around the corners. I could have made a guide from sheet metal or thin plywood and attached it to the panel. Or I could have guided off the outside edge of the panel, either by pushing the panel edge against a guide or pulling back against the die. I achieved the best results on test pieces by installing a short 90-degree flange along the outside of the panel and pulling the panel back against the lower, stationary die in the machine. I welded a short length of curved steel on the lower die to ensure that the bead stayed a consistent 1 inch from the outside flange as I dragged the panel against the die. On the Pullmax and the plasma cutter, I have noticed that pulling along a guide usually produces a steadier result than pushing. I anticipated using a long fence for the straight sections of bead.

With my beading figured out, I measured the two wires wrapped into the original fender and made several test pieces to experiment with how much metal I would need for the various wrapping operations. Most wrapped wires call for three times the diameter of the wire (circumference = 3.14 × diameter). The bottom edge of the fender's side panel carries a wrapped $3/16$-inch wire, which would require $9/16$ inch of material for wrapping. The top edge of the fender's side panel carries a wrapped $1/8$-inch-diameter wire, which is then wrapped into the perimeter flange of the fender's main panel. I needed $7/16$ inch for the upper wrap.

Once I had discovered exactly how much metal I needed to match the original fender's dimensions plus the additional material for the wrapped wires, I made accurate paper patterns of each panel. I usually use either white freezer paper or banner paper for patterns. Freezer paper is slightly transparent, which is helpful for capturing surface details, but when wider pieces are needed I use banner paper. I held the freezer paper in place with strong magnets and transferred the fender's details to the pattern by carefully rubbing a grubby finger over all the bolt holes and beads. I trimmed the edges of all my patterns even with the edges of each panel without any wire edges, and then wrote the necessary dimension for each wire edge or flange in the appropriate place on the paper pattern.

Matching the bead on the new rear fenders to the bead on the original front fenders required that I make a die for the Pullmax. I built a cardboard box around a crisp section of the original fender bead, slathered some oil on the area, and filled it with plastic body filler.

I whittled a die out of ¾-inch hot-rolled square steel stock. To navigate the sharp corners at either end of the fender, I made the die's contact area very small. I also added a curved guide to the bottom die against which to pull the panel.

I made an accurate paper pattern of one original fender by embossing the surface details into the paper with a grubby finger. I trimmed the outer edge of the paper to the exact dimensions of the piece and made notations where additional material would be needed for wire edging and flanges.

STARTING THE BUILD

Because these fenders are almost identical, I will describe the construction of one fender (the right rear) and the taillight mount I had to add to the left rear. Using the same magnets that I had used to hold my pattern to the fender, I affixed my paper patterns to a large sheet of steel and outlined all the relevant details with a spring-loaded prick punch. I cut out the main top panel for the right rear fender and installed a 90-degree ⁷⁄₁₆-inch flange around the perimeter. There are many ways to bend a flange to 90 degrees, but the basic steps usually involve thinning the metal along a line where the bend is intended, bending the flange gradually with a tool, and shrinking or stretching to account for the thickness change that will always occur around corners. I used a bead roller to thin the metal on the bend line, then I bent the short flange over about 45 degrees in the wheeling machine. I used a hammer and dolly to bend the metal to 90 degrees down the long straight sides. Around the sharpest

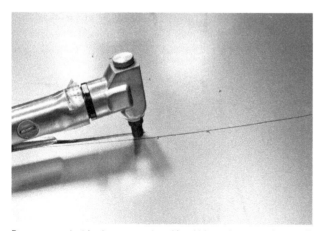

Because our electric shear was not working, I trimmed generously around my pattern with a pneumatic nibbler. Although these tools cut quickly and easily navigate curves, the shower of tiny crescent-shaped shards they spew forth diminishes their usefulness in my opinion.

I scribed a ⁷⁄₁₆-inch border around the edge of the first blank with a set of dividers and thinned the metal along this line with a bead roller. Thinning the metal ensures that the bend will happen in the right location.

Bending a 90-degree flange around a corner requires shrinking when the flange must come inboard, as here. You can bend and shrink the flange simultaneously in a Lancaster-style shrinking tool or cold shrink the wrinkles against a dolly. A wood mallet shrinks particularly well and does not leave marks.

corners, I placed the short flange between the jaws of the Lancaster-style shrinker and both bent and shrunk the metal until I had achieved a clean 90-degree flange. I took care to see that the flange was clean and even all the way around the perimeter of the panel because I intended to guide the piece against this flange when beading in the Pullmax machine.

I liberally sauced my sheet metal blank with oil and ran the long straight side through the Pullmax. Because the panel was unwieldy at 6 feet long, I hoped that adding the long bead would stiffen the panel before I attempted to bead around the corners. The bead in the Cadillac fender is not particularly deep and could probably have been pressed in one pass, but I made two or three passes down the long side, gradually tightening the dies each time to make sure the bead came out cleanly. Thanks to the rigidity added by the long bead, the panel tracked smoothly through the Pullmax on the corners; the only trick was to keep the panel exactly perpendicular to the die throughout each curve.

I installed the long straight bead in the Pullmax by pushing the edge of the panel against a straight fence mounted on the machine. I beaded the curvy end by pulling the panel back against the guide attached to the lower die.

With the beading complete, I shrunk the perimeter flange of the main panel to make it hug the buck. At the rear of the fender I stretched the perimeter flange to introduce a kick-up. Whenever you shrink or stretch along an extended gradual curve, numerous small nibbles will give you cleaner, more controllable results than a few dramatic clamps of the jaws.

In imitation of the original fender, I made the side panels out of two pieces with a joint in the factory location. If you have access to a machine with very powerful gathering jaws, such as an Eckold piccolo or Kraftformer, straight wire-edged panels can be quickly turned into curved panels by shrinking or stretching the edge opposite the wire. Lacking these tools, I wire-edged curved pieces cut out to match the contours dictated by my paper patterns. Because working with narrow 2-inch-wide strips of metal would have been very challenging, I left my metal blanks as large as possible. Installing a wire along one side of my oversize blank stiffened up each piece sufficiently that I could then trim them down to size and wire the other edge along the bottom of each panel.

I shrank the short perimeter flanges to curve the fender to match the buck—a good 10 feet of shrinking—in a kick-shrinker. At the rear of the fender the panel changes direction, so stretching was necessary to introduce the racy reverse curve. Best of all, extended bouts of kick-shrinking and stretching on a project like this are sure to give you buns of steel.

As previously noted, I can be relied upon for one good idea annually. This time it was making the fender side panels out of extra-large pieces of metal. The extra material made wire-edging a breeze. I started with a paper pattern that captured the entire curve of the fender, even though in the end only about the outer 3 inches of metal would be used.

I installed the first flange on the fender side panels with a kick-shrinker. I used the shrinker jaws as a bending device and shrank only as much as needed to account for the minor thickness change taking place in the flange.

I cleaned up the flange along the top of the side panels with a hammer and dolly. I made this flange as even as possible because it had to fit the curve of the adjacent flat panel perfectly.

Before I wrapped a wire into the flange I created along the top edge of the side panels, I degreased the metal, rubbed it with a Scotch-Brite pad, and liberally coated everything with a weld-through primer to prevent oxidation. I use self-etching primer for wire edges if I will not be welding.

For hand-wiring operations, I typically use one or two pairs of modified nippers. With the sheet metal bent into a U shape, I normally make one pass down the wire to trap the wire. Changing the angle of the tool, I make a second pass to tighten up the roll. Sharp jaws focus leverage at the risk of damaging the surface. Protect exterior surfaces with a sliver of scrap metal as needed.

In imitation of the factory side panels, I made a series of cuts in the top flange along the curves at the rear of the fender. These cuts were originally made, no doubt, to eliminate the need for shrinking flange material along this inside curve and to make the wired side panel easier to install. I used the same wiring technique for both the top and the bottom wires: I thinned the sheet metal along the bend line in the bead roller, gripped the flange for wrapping the wire in a pair of Lancaster shrinker/stretcher jaws, and bent the flange to 90 degrees, shrinking or stretching as needed to account for the thickness change of the metal around curves. Once I had bent each flange to 90 degrees, I hammered them over into a U shape against a homemade dolly. I painted each wire and the channel in which it would ride with zinc weld-through primer before closing the flange around the wire with another homemade tool. The weld-through primer prevents corrosion from starting in this inaccessible area.

With the wire installed along the top of each side panel, I checked the fit against the fender top panel. Satisfied, I cut away the extra metal, leaving enough material for the height of the side panel ($1\frac{5}{16}$ inches) plus metal for a larger wire edge along the bottom ($3 \times \frac{3}{16}$ inch = $\frac{9}{16}$ inch).

The next wire edge I needed to install was opposite the first, which required stretching. The Erco kick stretcher easily massaged the flange over to 90 degrees.

Where the original fenders curve abruptly, the metal wrapping around the wire was slit at the factory, presumably to facilitate bending around corners.

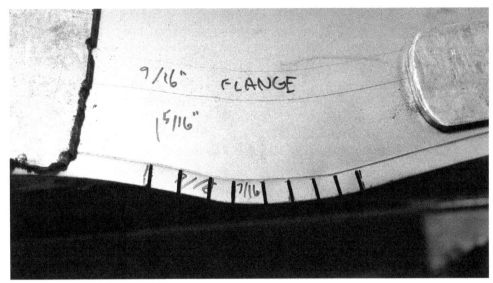

I cut my steel blanks with a thin cutting wheel in imitation of the original fenders at the sharp corners.

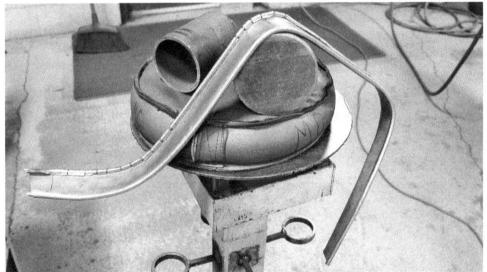

With the sheet metal already wrapped around the wire, I bent the fender side panels over a steel cylinder to match the original fenders.

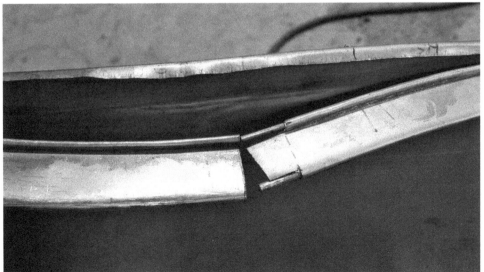

Both fenders had a single joint in each pair of side panels. The wire edging from one panel slides into a corresponding void in the adjacent panel.

As far as I could determine, the factory side panels were retained on the fender by wire wrapping alone; I did not see any welds. Dubious of my ability to replicate the factory's manufacturing process, I decided to plug-weld my side panels in place through the fender top panel. I drilled a series of ³⁄₁₆-inch holes along the length of the panel at intervals of about 8 inches. I was careful to locate the holes on the top surface of the fender, rather than on the curved highlight line along the edge,

because I would need to grind the welds later without leaving any evidence. I sprayed the side panels and the underside of the fender top panel with weld-through primer, clamped the side panels in place on the fender, and welded the side panels in position. The many cuts in the upper flange of the side panel at the rear of the fender made this panel much easier to bend into the correct shape and adjust as needed. By bending the side panel into the sharpest corners after the wire was

Doubtful of my ability to secure the fender side panels by crimping alone, I drilled a series of ³⁄₁₆-inch holes through the top panel for plug welds.

After crimping the side panels in place and checking their fit on the buck, I executed the plug welds, identifiable in the image by the small blue dots along the fender's outer exterior.

These Cadillac fenders have an additional 18-gauge support at the front for attaching the running boards. I made a paper pattern, fabricated the necessary pieces, and plug-welded them in place.

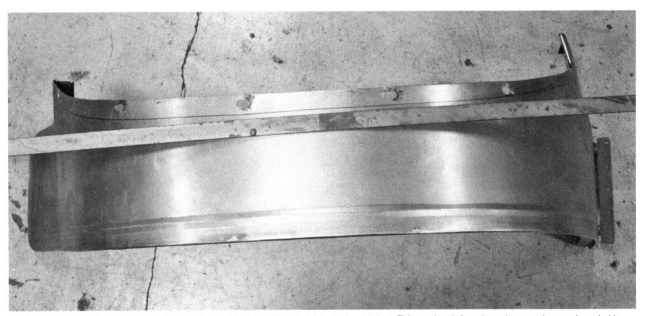

The inner edge of each original fender has a 1-inch-wide strip of ⅛-inch-thick steel welded on. This overhead view shows how much curve I needed to give the strip to match the fender.

already installed, I did not need to hassle with shrinking or stretching any flanges. Where the side panel along the forward end of the fender met the side panel at the rear, I copied the factory seam.

With my panel finally starting to look like a fender, I was anxious to test its fit on the car, but the piece was still a little floppy. For additional strengthening, the original fender has a steel support behind its front edge where it meets the running board, as well as a 1-inch-wide strip of ⅛-inch-thick steel running along the inner fender edge. The fender is bolted to the car through this steel strip. I made a paper pattern of the steel support at the front of the fender, copied it in 18-gauge steel, and plug-welded it in place on my fender. I then bolted the stock running-board mount in place.

I stretched one side of each steel strip with linear dies in the power hammer to curve the pieces as needed. The outer side of the strip was made thinner and longer as compared to the inner side, hence the curve.

I periodically checked the curvature of the steel strip by clamping it in place on the fender with Vise-Grips.

I first attempted to shape a ⅛ × 1-inch-wide strip of steel by heat shrinking the inner edge, but this was agonizingly slow, so I moved to the power hammer and stretched the outer edge with a linear stretching die held perpendicular to the edge. At the rear of the factory fender, this strip is abruptly twisted 90 degrees about 7 inches from its end. After a couple of failed attempts heating and twisting my steel strip, I cut off the end and fashioned the curviest section out of a second piece of metal.

Before welding the 1-inch strip in place on the fender, I wanted to test fit the entire assembly on the car again. I also needed to mark and install a joggle detail in the fender running along its top edge adjacent to the bolt holes. I traced the line where the body overlapped the top edge of the fender, installed a short offset joggle in the bead roller, and secured the 1-inch steel strip to the fender with countersunk machine screws. Not surprisingly, when I test fit the fender on the car, it fit exactly like stock, which is to say there was an annoying gap along the front about a foot above the running-board mount.

The 1/8-inch-thick steel strip along the inside of each fender abruptly twists where the fender projects out from the body tub. After twice failing to incorporate the twist accurately in the strip I just shaped, I made the twist separately and welded it in position.

I used a bead roller to install a joggle along the top inner fender edge. The joggle is on the topside of the metal directly opposite the ⅛-inch-thick steel strip, which I secured with countersunk screws until fitment had been checked on the car.

Disappointing and hilarious at the same time, my first test fit revealed a gap at the front of the fender exactly as I had noted on the original fender.

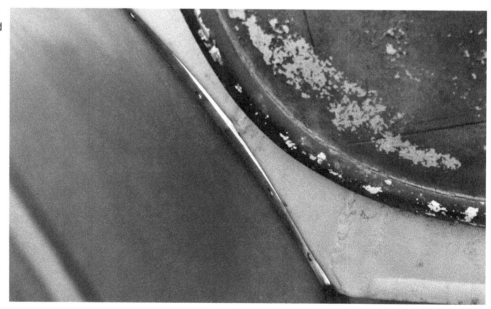

I concluded that if I could increase the radius of the fender in the problem area by about ³⁄₁₆ inch, I could close the gap between the fender and the body. I made a cardboard template to use as a reference. I traced the existing curve of the fender on the cardboard and then drew a second arc ³⁄₁₆ inch above the first.

Lancaster-style stretching jaws or a wheeling machine would have worked acceptably for stretching the panel edge, but I used the power hammer with linear stretching dies held perpendicular to the edge. After stretching the edge to match the template, I reinstalled the edge bead and shrunk a handful of times with the

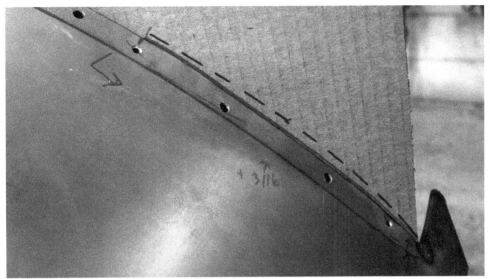

I made a cardboard template to identify the location and amount of stretching needed on the forward inner edge of the right rear fender.

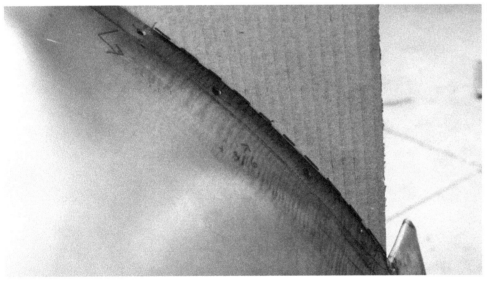

Stretching the edge of the fender in the power hammer caused it to swell and occupy a larger radius curve than it had a few moments earlier. I later performed this same operation on the left rear fender.

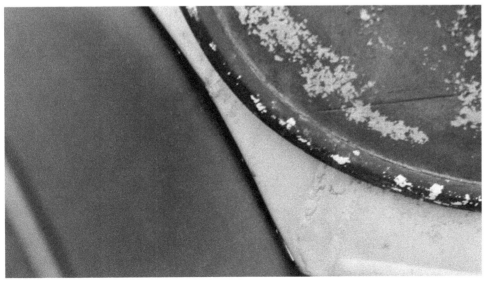

After stretching the problem area on the right rear fender, the gap between the fender and the body disappeared.

Lancaster shrinker. The metal on the low side of the joggle along the fender edge was forced into a slightly shorter radius than the metal comprising the fender proper, thus a little shrinking was required to change length into thickness. I also stretched the 1-inch-wide steel strip in the power hammer to match the exterior sheet metal. I screwed the assembly back together, test fit it on the car again, and was pleased with the result. Having put my mind at ease regarding fitment, I plug-welded the thick strip along the fender's inner edge and welded up all the holes left by my small machine screws.

I constructed a simple jig to locate the taillight mount on the left rear fender. I situated the jig so that the pointed bolt at right in the image passed through the steel mount on the inside of the original fender. When I mounted the jig on the new left fender, all I had to do was tighten the pointed bolt to find the equivalent spot on the new fender.

The jig in the previous image was necessary to locate the fixed external mount on the fender's inner flange in this image. A wire loom attaches to the mount.

I soldered a bronze washer on both the interior and the exterior sides of the sheet metal where the wiring for the taillight passes through the left rear fender. The washer sandwich looks and should function like stock.

ADDING A TAILLIGHT MOUNT

The left rear fender was more or less a repeat of the right fender except for one detail: the taillight mount. I measured up from the rear edge of the fender and heat shrank twice to create a flat spot in the bead as on the original. I used the same paper pattern I had used to fabricate both fenders to locate the cluster of bolt holes that surround the light-mounting point. To mark the position of the small rivet-on steel bracket on the inner side panel, I made a foolproof jig out of 18-gauge sheet metal. In my stash of old hardware I found a pointed bolt that fit perfectly through the hole in the bracket meant for a tube wire loom on the original fender. Once the jig was in place on the new fender, I simply tightened the bolt to leave an impression in the new side panel with which to locate the bracket.

To ensure electrical continuity on the original fender, but without leaving bare steel open to the elements, the factory installed a large brass tube rivet through the center hole of the taillight mount. Unable to obtain a facsimile of the original brass tube rivet, I soldered one small bronze washer on each side of the hole on my fender instead. I tinned the steel with Eastwood Tinning Butter and applied a paste flux to the washers to make sure my solder would stick. (I used 95 percent tin and 5 percent antimony solder because it has a low melting point compared to silver solder.) Once the washers were secure, I ground them flat so that they would not interfere with the fit of the taillight bracket. Then I ground down all my plug welds, filed rough panel edges, and deemed the fenders complete.

Chapter 15
Building a '34 Plymouth Fender

Unlike the 1913 Cadillac fenders described in the last chapter, which were almost all form, the Plymouth fender has a lot of shape that requires plenty of shrinking and stretching. Its additional complexity makes it a nice complement to the Cadillac project. For anyone who wants to try to build a '34 Plymouth fender after reading this chapter, Speedway Motors sells a fiberglass version for a reasonable price. For the purpose of learning, a fiberglass fender would make a better model than a damaged original.

I chose the Plymouth fender for this exercise because it is one of my favorite projects for students who are serious about restoring vintage-car sheet metal. This fender lends itself to several shaping techniques and provides several valuable learning opportunities: buck building, shaping a high crown panel, shaping a reverse curve panel, fabricating a beading die, installing a bead, wrapping a wire edge, and welding multiple panels into a seamless whole. It does not contain an independent low crown panel, but otherwise is a terrific introduction to more advanced metal shaping.

This project also presents the opportunity to tackle sections based on available tools. As you become more skilled at metal shaping, you will wonder what

The '34 Plymouth fender in this chapter presents a great tutorial on several metal-shaping techniques that can be applied to other projects, but fiberglass reproduction fenders are available for anyone wanting a model on which to replicate the exercise.

difference it will make to have one tool versus another. As we work through this project, we will discover the strengths and weaknesses of different approaches.

Although this fender could be faithfully replicated by building on top of the original, I will describe the process using a wood buck as a model. The buck allows us to view our work from the front and back, which makes describing (and photographing) what is happening and what needs to happen much easier. Building a buck is time-consuming, tedious, and certainly not always necessary. Moreover, a buck is only useful if the fit of the original panel on the buck is excellent and the buck is not so complex that it obscures your view of the work. Nevertheless, an accurate buck is helpful for assessing your progress during shaping and for ensuring that everything stays in alignment as you weld together a multipiece panel. In a classroom setting, an accurate buck is helpful for teaching and it gives students a chance to at least shape something to a buck in case they never get around to making one of their own.

When using an original piece as a model for shaping, details such as beads and creases sometimes prevent you from assessing the fit of the piece you are making on top of the original. Ideally, the piece you make should slide down onto the original like two Solo cups nesting together. If beads and so forth create problems, the easiest solution is simply to add another weld seam in a nearby area you think would be a good place to finish a weld. Without a buck, I would shape the Plymouth fender the same way I would with a buck: I would make it out of several pieces that could be individually checked against the model and then clamped, trimmed, and welded together until I had a complete fender. Because there is a 1-inch-high band of flat metal above the bead along most of the Plymouth fender's length, I do not believe the bead would interfere with checking the shape along the way. The bead is probably far enough removed from the shape not to be a hindrance. If it did interfere, I would consider making a strip with the bead included that I would weld on after I had made the rest of the fender.

The buck we use regularly in class for the Plymouth fender is an amalgamation of two separate bucks, which is highly unorthodox, but it evolved naturally from student progress, and its fit is superb. This buck also features a sheet metal border that follows the wheel opening to facilitate transferring the finished fender edge to the panels that will eventually make up the new fender. At some point a student scrawled "The Buck of Happiness" on the back of this buck with a permanent marker. Such an endorsement, in my opinion, bodes well for the rest of us who hope to learn from it.

MAKING A HIGH CROWN PANEL WITHOUT A BUCK

The '34 Plymouth fender is composed of two main shapes: the front two-thirds of the fender are a deeply crowned panel; the rear one-third is a reverse curve. Applying a radius gauge to the high crown panel indicates that the tightest radius varies from about 3 inches near the front to 4 inches at the back along the exterior side of the fender. Depending on one's aptitude for swinging a big hammer, he or she could beat the deeply crowned portion out of a flat sheet and smooth out the resulting lumps in the wheel or raise it exclusively on the wheel. In a previous life I think I was either a Viking marauder or an ogre, as I often gravitate toward bashing processes even though I have easier methods at my disposal. Hitting things with a hammer is wholesome fun that cultivates a condition of inner jubilation that is still legal in all fifty states. You should try it on something.

I built an example of the center portion of the fender in two pieces to illustrate how you can build this fender if you do not have a power hammer or access to a machine with thumbnail shrinking dies. I also wanted to see to what extent the bead would be in the way if one decided to use the original fender rather than a buck as a model. I used one strip of metal to represent the top of the fender and a second strip for the beaded area over the wheel opening. I situated the long top strip of metal over a hollow in a stump and made one pass of vigorous hammer blows approximately even with the top of the 3-inch-radius highlight line. These strokes stretched the metal suspended over the hollow and raised wrinkles along the lower half of the highlight line. I then hammered the wrinkles flat, trapping them in the stump with a wood mallet. Trapping wrinkles shrinks them, but this method is highly inefficient with steel, so I followed this first assault with several rounds of bashing along the top panel with a Viking marauder hammer into a shot bag. I used the wheel to smooth out the lumps and to add shape slowly and controllably as needed. I used a hand-shrinker along the long edges quite a bit and did a little more of the same on the ends. I formed the highlight area to match the buck by wheeling across the panel and bending down as I reached that area. Physically, this was a lot of work that took about two hours. I mention the work and time

Without thumbnail shrinking dies, you could make the high crown part of this fender by breaking it into two separate pieces. I torch-welded these together in imitation of English coachbuilders. The seam at left is as welded, and then wire-brushed and planished where it is shiny. I did not file or grind the weld.

involved to put at ease readers who try this at home. Yes, it really is difficult to affect a significant thickness change in steel with these tools. You are not somehow deficient because it takes a while. You could also wheel out the deeply stretched top panel. It would be less work and easier on your body.

MAKING THE BEADED FENDER EDGE WITHOUT A BUCK

The beaded portion of the second panel of the sample required shrinking from the transition point of the flat area above the bead into the sharply radiused area known as the highlight. I used a deep-throated kick-shrinker to nibble the material along the transition from the flat panel to the 6-inch radius. Then I used a hand-shrinker on the outer inch of the panel. I formed the shrunken area over to the appropriate radius by cross-wheeling and pulling down on the panel as I crossed the highlight.

At this point, the fit of the panel against the fender was okay but not ideal due to the bead. When I felt I

had the lower panel close, I ran a bead down the side using the Pullmax. With a bead installed in the panel, fitting the new metal over the old was a breeze. Because the little bit of shape in this panel is so far from the beaded edge, you can put the bead in first and then do the shrinking and bending along the top edge. Moreover, the panel will be stiffer and easier to work with if the bead comes first. As soon as I was satisfied with the fit, I clamped the panels together, scribed a trim line on one of the panels, and cut it to match the other. I torch-welded the panels together as a traditional coachbuilder would have done.

The drawback to the approach I just described is the creation of a weld seam right on the highlight line—the area of the tightest radius—which, according to my mentor, Fay Butler, is more apt to reveal surface discrepancies than a weld placed in a flat area where it can be hammered out. Nevertheless, countless European coachbuilt cars were made this way. I suspect that because classic coachbuilt cars were torch-welded, the significant stretching that torch welds always require adequately planished any welds on a highlight line. In imitation of English coachbuilders, I did not use any filler on the weld, which leaves the seam a whisper low in some areas and calls for more planishing. Some modern restorers of coachbuilt cars insist on torch-welding for reasons of authenticity and for the ductility of the torch-weld bead. In any case, the highlight line on the finished fender needs to be as even as possible using whatever method you have available.

PREPARING A PAPER PATTERN AND GETTING BUSY

Whether shaping to a buck or an original panel, I am a firm believer in accurate paper patterns. A pattern will (1) reduce waste, (2) forecast what needs to happen where in terms of shrinking and stretching, (3) help you plan your weld seams, and (4) perhaps most importantly, force you to pause and think through the entire project. On a high crown panel like the shape

Plotting out the highlight line with a radius gauge helps you plan your shrinking. The highlight line indicates the area with the tightest radius. The sharpest radius on the Plymouth was 3 inches.

that makes up most of the '34 Plymouth fender, I have students identify the highlight line with an official Fay Butler radius gauge. In the absence of this tool, you can use a compass to make a selection of individual radius gauges out of poster board. Once the highlight line is identified, run a fine tape line along either side of it. These two regions are important to the definition of the part.

Because most of this fender is a high crown panel, let's examine the making of that shape first. The high crown panel represented here is usually my first choice for students who have successfully completed the required material in our introductory sheet metal class. Following Fay's advice, I secure sheet metal pockets to the buck to hold the bottom of our paper pattern and later our sheet metal blanks. The pockets prevent shifting of either the pattern or the blank during patterning and shaping. After all, if the pattern moves around, how accurate can we expect it to be? I have noticed that the more obtuse the angle of the pockets, the less well they secure the work. With the work area clearly defined, the paper pattern will be reliable and will only fit in one place. Strong magnets work best for securing the paper pattern to the fender, but you can also cut a few holes in the pattern where there isn't a shape change and tape the pattern to the fender. During the patterning process, strive to identify the location and amount of shrinking that will be needed to make this high crown panel. Extra paper can be carefully folded over in evenly spaced folds or cut with a razor blade until the pattern lies flat against the fender. Strive for evenness in patterning and shaping. Rubbing the tape lines with a grubby finger or writing instrument will accurately transfer the exact location of the highlight line to the paper pattern. I placed several evenly spaced cuts in the pattern perpendicular to the curve of the fender to allow the extra paper to fold over itself and hug the fender. Expect the cuts or folds to extend back to the lower border of the highlight line. Any time spent obsessing over your pattern is usually well spent.

The ends of my cuts met the beginning of the highlight line. Below the highlight on the Plymouth fender is a 1-inch-wide band of metal with a 6-inch radius. It creates a transition between the highlight line and a 1-inch band of flat metal above the bead. My standard procedure is to trace the various bands onto my paper pattern. On some fenders, the flat area with the bead will go immediately into the highlight without the extra band of 6-inch-radius material

found on this fender. In *A Century of Automotive Style: 100 Years of American Car Design*, authors Dave Holls and Michael Lamm cite the '32 Graham Blue Streak as the inspiration for the valanced fenders that adorned many cars in the years immediately afterward. I suspect the '34 Plymouth was a response to the Graham. To capture the band of metal just below the highlight line, I shrank from the outer edge of the panel to ½ inch from the beginning of the 6-inch-radius band. I know from experience that our thumbnail shrinking dies affect an area ½ inch past the end of each shrink. I did not discover this on my own and would have struggled for years making panels that fit ½ inch high of where they were supposed to had Fay Butler not pointed this out to me. Fay cautions that each set of thumbnail dies affects the metal a little differently, so it is important to know what to expect. To deal with the highlight and the short band of 6-inch-radius metal below it, I shrank about ½ inch short of each significant radius change on the panel. To obtain adequate shrinking plus a nice surface finish with thumbnail shrinking dies, don't be surprised if you need to shrink a hair more than "just right" and then stretch the panel to get it spot-on.

Because the effect of our shrinks would reach slightly past the end of the little tuck that the bump on the thumbnail die raises, I had to make a decision regarding whether to mark the actual highlight line on the panel or to mark ½ inch back of the essential radius changes. Like Fay, I transferred the highlight line exactly to the sheet metal blank with a prick punch and then drew stopping points on the metal with a permanent marker for shrinking ½ inch out from the highlight line. Fay gives additional thorough and detailed guidelines for patterning in his *Shaping Book #1* (www.faybutler. com). In my experience, all his recommendations, even regarding points a novice might find trivial, have proven true. Marking the actual highlight line makes sense so that when you go to check a piece on the model you can tell whether you correctly identified the highlight. I drew out a shrinking pattern that placed progressively more shrinks toward the edge of the panel. The number of shrinks placed next to each other from the front to the rear of the fender along the highlight influences the radius of the curve as seen from the side, as if we were watching the car drive by. The number and depth of shrinks placed from the highlight out to the edge influences the radius of the fender viewed as if we were standing directly behind the car. Other than

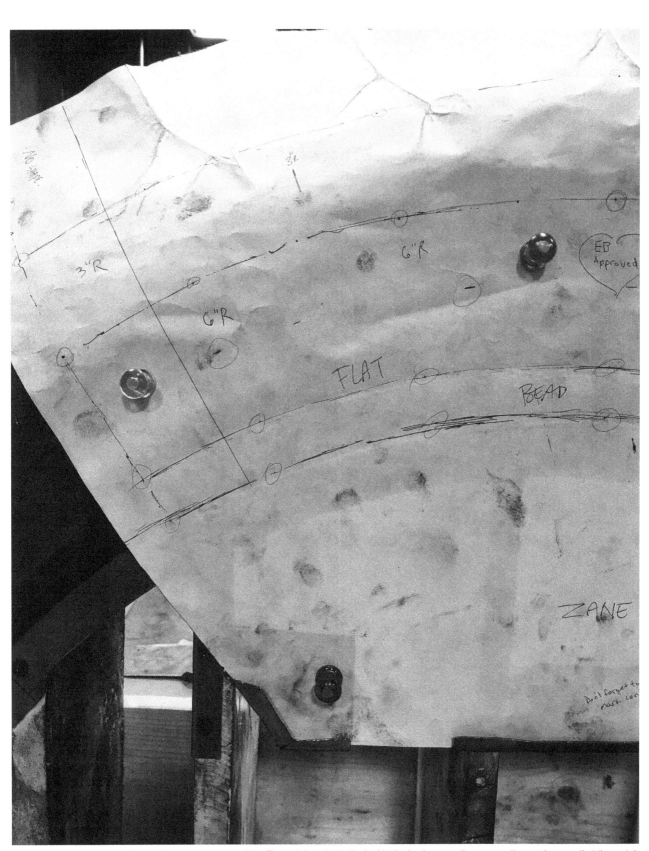

Transfer all relevant surface information to your paper pattern. The metal pockets attached to the buck secure the paper pattern and ensure that the metal blank is always checked in the same spot during shaping.

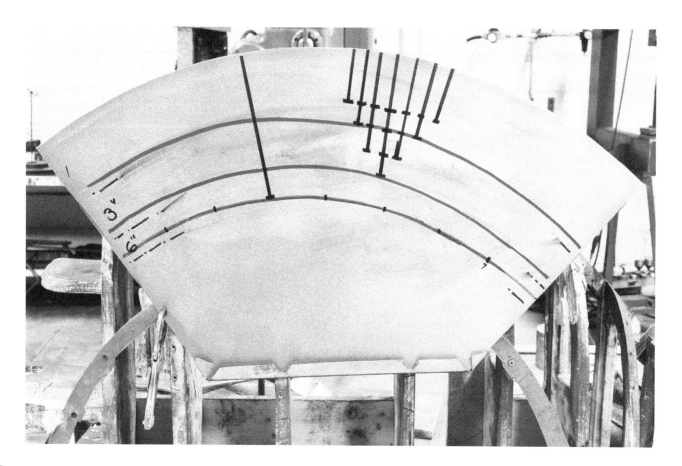

ABOVE: I transferred my paper pattern to a steel blank with a spring-loaded prick punch. The deepest shrinks define the radius change from the flat part of the panel to the 6-inch-radius band beneath the highlight. I did seven individual shrinks to ½ inch shy of this point. The remainder of the shrinking begins at the bottom of the 3-inch-radius highlight line. I did seven "trees" to ½ inch shy of that point.

RIGHT: To illustrate what Fay Butler means when he says that shrink dies affect an area deeper than the end of the shrink, I've brought back the sheet metal instructor and student from Chapter 4. I shrank to the black line, and yet the panel rose from the flat plane at the green line ½ inch back. Shrinking has brought the metal in the greater radius inward.

through experience, I do not know of an easy way to anticipate how much shrinking is needed until you are well underway. Fortunately, during shrinking a panel is not difficult to read, despite the ruffles resulting from the shrinking process.

One of the most transformational techniques I have learned from Fay is to change the form of a piece during shaping as needed to maximize die size. By changing the form, you can use larger, flatter dies with greater contact areas than you would otherwise think were possible. Large contact surfaces translate into more even stretching and better surface finishes. For example, if the radius on a panel is 6 inches in its normal relaxed state, you can use a 12-inch-radius die for smoothing and stretching. By shrinking with thumbnail dies, the first process I will describe on the Plymouth, the panel will shrink much more effectively folded up in a curve. When folding the panel up, the tuck raised by the shrinking die has nowhere to go and will shrink as you withdraw the panel. The metal will seek out the

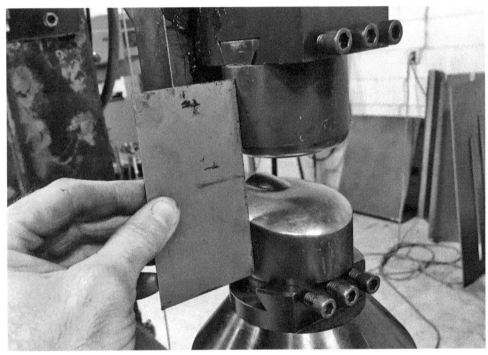

Before bringing thumbnail shrinking dies together under power, make sure they are aligned side-to-side and front-to-back. Misaligned dies will not shrink properly and will be damaged during use.

Curling a piece of sheet metal up in preparation for shrinking encourages the metal to seek out the tighter radius you are after. Grip the panel tightly against your chest so that the tuck raised by the lower die has no choice but to shrink.

Although it looks like something that just fell out of a garbage truck, the panel has been significantly shrunk and is moving in the right direction. Light stretching will follow.

tighter-radius curve that the folded-up position makes available. If you withdraw the panel at a controllable speed and do not hit it too hard, the shrinking will be palpable through your hands. I wear a homemade apron with a snap-on leather insert on the chest and hold the panel firmly there to keep it from bouncing or moving. I am convinced that securing the panel in this manner is essential to successful shrinking. In my opinion, when thumbnail shrinking in the power hammer, you can feel the metal collapse between your hands, although there is no observable cue (except the disappearing tuck) that the metal is getting thicker.

I have a difficult time impressing upon new students how several things must come together for shrinking to work on the power hammer. If the stars do not align, you might inadvertently stretch the panel.

Over the past few years I have concluded that using the power hammer is more difficult than it seems, especially for shrinking. The power hammer opens a broad spectrum of metal-squeezing possibilities that novices will not likely discern right away. As with ear training in music, practice over time increases one's powers of discernment. Thumbnail shrinking dies in a Pullmax-style machine with a fixed speed and stroke, however, are much easier to master. A folded-up panel will shrink better than a flat panel, and the panel must be moved in and out of the dies at a controllable speed. But if the dies are correctly adjusted, shrinking is assured. A high crown panel such as this Plymouth panel can be made by shrinking on a machine other than a power hammer, of course, as long as another tool is available for smoothing and stretching.

Having made this panel before, I had a vague idea of how much overall shrinking would be needed. First, I performed seven individual shrinks evenly spread out along the center panel. I inserted the panel in the shrinking dies until the end of the tuck created by the bottom die came to ½ inch from the origin of the 6-inch-radius band on the fender blank. The individual shrinks established where the flat part of the panel along the wheel opening changes to a 6-inch radius on the finished panel. I then performed six sets of staggered shrinks I call "trees" (because they remind me of evergreens) evenly spaced across the blank. I left the outer area at each end untouched. The deepest of these shrinks came to ½ inch from the origin of the 3-inch-radius highlight. Subsequent shrinks followed immediately in rows perpendicular to the panel edge consistent with the drawn pattern represented in the illustration.

The staggered shrinks work remarkably well. I tell students that it is better to remain in control and have a panel take a little longer than to overshrink. On high crown panels made predominantly through shrinking, try to get the highlight dead-on and march your way out to the edge. At any point during shrinking a high crown panel, you can smooth out the shrinks in the power hammer or wheeling machine and check the piece on the buck, but I knew from experience that more shrinking was needed. I did another row of shorter trees that came to ½ inch of the outer edge of the 3-inch-radius highlight. These shrinks were only two shrinks at their deepest point with one single shallower shrink on either side.

With the piece still curled up, I sprayed some light oil on the panel and smoothed out the ruffles left from shrinking in the power hammer with a 6-inch-radius die. Light stretching removed residual tension in the metal and evened out the panel's surface. In the absence of a power hammer, a wheeling machine does a very fine job of evening out a shrunken panel. I was careful not to overstretch the panel during smoothing, lest I undo the shrinking I had just performed. To prepare the work for checking on the buck, I pressed the piece down against

Stretching after a round of shrinking smooths the panel surface and relieves tension. Holding the panel in a curled-up state provides maximum die contact. With the panel curled up, a 6-inch-radius die can be used to smooth a 3-inch radius on the panel.

Although curling up the panel during shaping is standard practice with the power hammer, it is not widely done with the wheeling machine. Remember, form is easy to change. Curling up the form to achieve larger tool contact surfaces works beautifully with the wheel as well.

After smoothing a high crown panel with either the power hammer or the wheel, push the form back into the panel against the corner of a table and check its fit.

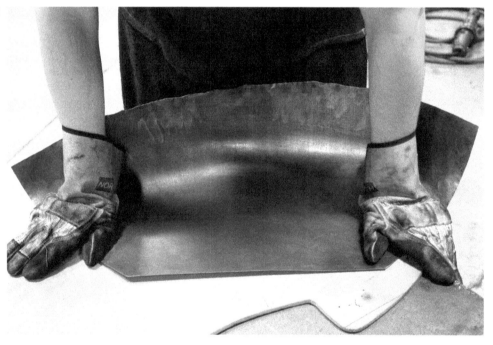

a table to return it to its proper form. Because I shrank the panel evenly in graduated stages that corresponded to the radius changes on the completed fender, the panel easily folded over in the right place.

Checking on the buck confirmed that the panel fit tightly from the flat area up through the highlight, but a gap along the outer edge indicated that more shrinking was needed there. When assessing your work against the

buck, change the form as necessary to achieve the best possible fit. Bend the piece over your thigh, a piece of pipe, or any object of the appropriate radius to establish a clear picture of whether remaining fit problems relate to shape or form.

Hopefully, on its first test fitting your panel will fit spectacularly well on the highlight and finishing it will require only additional shrinking somewhere between the highlight and the outer edge. On the Plymouth I did two more bouts of shrinking and smoothing along the outer edge of the panel before it fit the buck. For general smoothing and spot stretching on this panel, I normally use a 6-inch-radius bottom die. If I need to stretch the highlight specifically, I use a 4-inch-radius die. For smoothing and stretching along the outer panel edge, the 12-inch-radius die has seemingly magical qualities; with light pressure, it will shrink unwanted lumps by trapping them against the large die surface. With moderate pressure it smooths like a steamroller. Hitting harder with a 12-inch-radius die stretches.

Not surprisingly, even when I put the form back and was satisfied with the overall shape, the panel

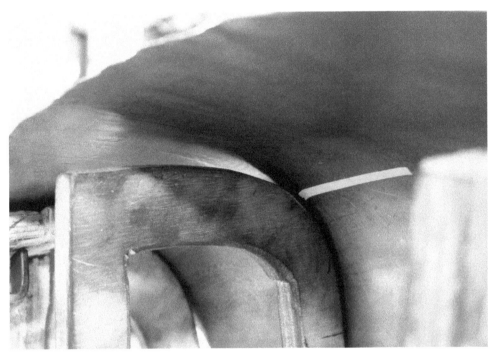

On a high crown panel, deep early shrinks should establish the fit of the metal along the highlight line. On the next round of shrinking, shrink to ½ inch above the point where the panel departs from the buck.

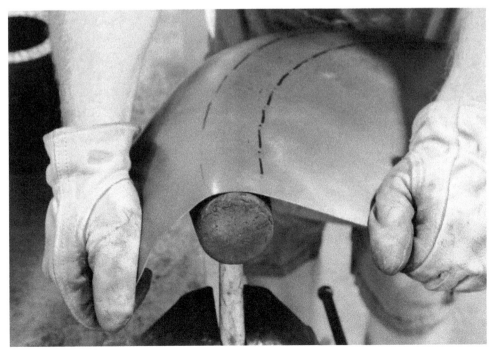

In your quest to find the right combination of shape and form, bend your piece over any object that plausibly matches the radius you need. A rubber or wood mallet held in a vise works well and won't leave marks.

ABOVE: After the first round of shrinking and smoothing, I checked the high crown panel on the buck and marked where additional shrinking was needed.

RIGHT: The high crown panel I shaped for the Plymouth had unresolved tension after my last round of shrinking and smoothing. I returned the form to normal and hammered the curved areas with a 6-inch-radius die. I hammered the flat area lightly with a 24-inch-radius die.

178

Eventually I was satisfied with the fit of my high crown panel on the Plymouth buck. Although an excellent panel would hold itself in place as if by magic rather than rely on a Vise-Grip, this panel is usable.

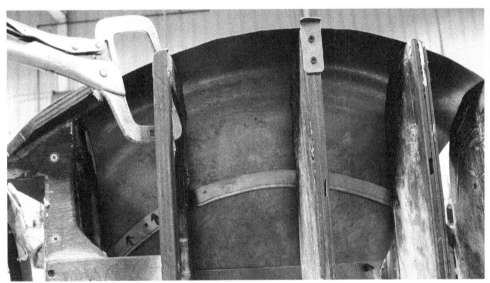

Viewed from behind, the utility of "The Buck of Happiness" is plain to see. Assessing one's work is easier when you have an unobstructed view.

If you have shaped accurately, a panel should fit the buck or original and it should pass the radius gauge test.

tended to twist under its own power as a result of residual tension. Misbehavior of this sort can be relieved by lightly working the entire panel evenly with the power hammer, wheeling machine, or planishing hammer. I lightly hammered the area between the highlight line and the panel edge with a 6-inch-radius die. I also hammered the 1-inch band below the highlight with the same die, then gently hammered the flattest part of the panel with a 24-inch-radius die. I did not hit the metal hard enough to create a crown, but the panel nevertheless relaxed as a result of the hammering.

PANEL PITFALLS

Sadly, the best way to become educated as to the many ways a high crown panel can go awry is to experience them personally. Here are some common pitfalls so you will know what is happening when you feel as if you are taking a beating.

If you have shrunk too much, the panel will touch the buck beyond the highlight line and leave a gap on or near the highlight line.

Uneven shrinking leaves lumps in the surface.

Shrinking too deeply creates a bump in the flat part of the panel that is very difficult to remove other than by heat shrinking.

Creating too much form for the amount of shrinking performed creates a deep bow in the flat area beyond the highlight.

If extra material appears out on the sides where the panel crosses the highlight, re-form the piece to relocate the extra material so that it can be shrunk perpendicular to the edge like all the other shrinking. I won't say that you will *never* shrink parallel to the highlight, but it can be a temporary fix that you will later regret. On more than one occasion when I have shrunk parallel to the highlight line, by the time the rest of the panel was shrunk adequately to fit the buck, the area near the highlight needed to be stretched back out. Other times, though much less often, a shrink parallel to the highlight is exactly what is needed. In this trade, there are just enough exceptions to every rule to both frustrate and fascinate the enthusiast for a lifetime.

If you shrink too much near the edge of the panel in comparison to the metal inboard, a tumor sitting high off the buck will be apparent.

The slight bulge near the hand at left in the image indicates that more material needs to be shrunk on the edge. If that length is turned into thickness through shrinking, the panel edge will hug the buck.

THE SECOND HIGH CROWN PANEL

The panel directly forward of the previous piece was a smaller version of the same panel. Because the construction process was exactly the same, I won't repeat myself unnecessarily. I laid out three trees and did two individual lines of shrinks between them.

Toward the front of the fender, the 6-inch radius below the highlight line tapered away to nothing. On the middle tree I somehow blundered past the highlight line and created a lump in the flat area below the highlight. I corrected my mistake with a couple of heat shrinks.

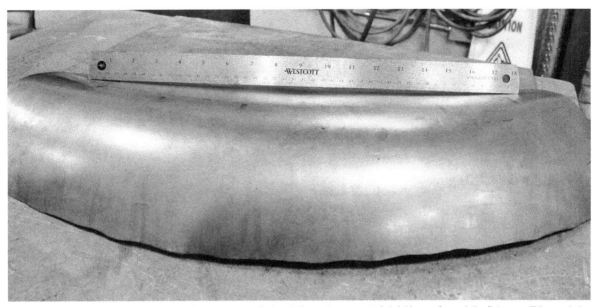

If the shrunken part of a high crown panel is formed over too far in relation to the amount of shrinking performed, the flat area will bow out at the ends. Change the form until the flat area sits flush and look for areas needing more shrinking.

If you find a bulge at the edge of a high crown panel right on the highlight line, re-form the metal to see if you can turn the blubber on the highlight into an appetizing wrinkle on the outer edge that will be easy to shrink. If not, shrink parallel to the highlight.

The panel ahead of the high crown panel I just demonstrated is largely a repeat of that panel. I executed three shrinking trees like the one drawn on the panel and two single lines of shrinks in between the trees to ensure that the panel changed direction at the right places.

I tried a new way of securing this panel to the buck during shaping that worked wonderfully well: I placed two spring-loaded Clecos through flat areas that I knew would not be shaped.

TACKLING THE REVERSE CURVE

Eager for a new challenge, I moved on to the reverse curve at the rear of the fender. I created a paper pattern by attaching a sheet of paper to the fender with magnets and cutting it as needed with a razor blade until it would lie flat. The gaps where the pattern spread apart suggested that stretching would be needed around the rear of the fender. In practice, I discovered that the pattern was a little deceiving, but I'll get to that in a moment. Disregarding the beaded area on the rear tip for a moment, the sharpest radius of this fender—the highlight line—passed through the center of the panel. I planned to treat the highlight area at the very center of the panel as an area that would not be shaped. Any thickness change taking place in the surrounding metal would generate shape in comparison to the very center of the panel. Looking at the center of the panel as a neutral point, the metal at the front and rear of the blank needed to be raised in comparison to the center, while the metal on either side—corresponding to the interior and exterior sides of the fender—needed to be lowered in comparison to the center.

This panel called for the transformation of metal thickness into length. Although any bashing tool could have done the job, the power hammer's linear dies perform this task like a knife spreading a lump of peanut butter. Wherever stretching was needed, I placed the panel perpendicular to the dies and passed it back and forth to add shape. When hammering, the tendency of the metal to go up or down is a question of form. Applying slight downward pressure on either side of the die causes the metal to rise. Curling the piece up on either side of the die during hammering sends the metal down. If you are unhappy with the direction the metal takes when you start hammering, stop and bend it where you want it. Once the panel has started curving either up or down, it will continue going in that direction during stretching unless you direct it otherwise.

Apart from the beaded area at the rear, there were no abrupt shape changes in the reverse curve panel, so smooth blending throughout was needed. Controlling the speed and thus the force of the hammer blows with the foot pedal, I stretched the metal smoothly as I moved the panel from side to side between the dies. At the same time, I worked my way from the panel edge to the deepest points and back out again. With linear stretching dies, the inboard metal will have nowhere to go if you do not continually spread it nearer the edge out of the way.

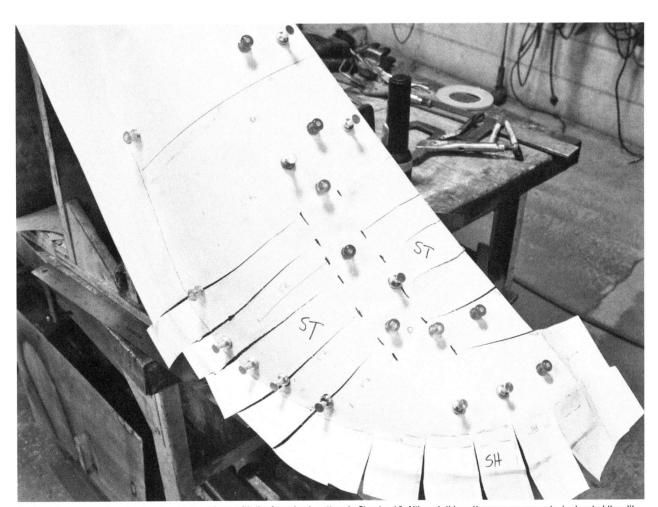

Contrast the paper pattern for the reverse curve here with the foam buck pattern in Chapter 16. Although this pattern seems accurate, I relocated the slits on the second pattern to conform with what I had experienced earlier while shaping this panel.

When I began shaping the reverse curve, the metal touched the buck only in a narrow line down the center. Stretching the sides and ends in relation to the middle raised and lowered the blank as needed to conform to the buck. One troubling phenomenon that comes into play on this panel is the need to be mindful of metal adjacent to the area where you are stretching with the linear dies. This sounds a little like being asked to discipline your neighbor's kids. On the Plymouth fender, stretching the metal at the forward and rear ends of the panel lengthens and raises those areas. As that metal rises, it pushes down the metal at the sides. The same scenario holds true when working the sides, of course. You must harness all your soothsaying skills to forecast how much the stretching in one area will move metal somewhere else. After overstretching a few panels, your soothsaying skills will improve along with your metal-shaping ones. My first paper pattern was misleading because of the neighbor's kids phenomenon. The paper unequivocally showed wider slits on the sides of the panel than the ends and yet, in practice, I stretched the ends much more than the sides. With the benefit of hindsight, I can forecast a more accurate pattern next time by placing more slits at the ends.

As with any panel you make, it might be necessary to re-form a reverse curve to average out the shape. Bend the panel as needed to get the best fit on the buck. Work the entire panel from time to time with light pressure on whatever shaping tool you have available to even out the tension in the panel. I have found that overall wheeling leaves a panel wonderfully floppy and evenly tensioned, which makes re-forming easier. Any direction of wheeling is okay with light pressure as long as the wheels don't dig into the metal and leave marks.

Until now I had disregarded the beaded area at the rear of the fender; the sharp downward bend there would have frustrated any other shaping efforts on the reverse curve. Once the main body of the reverse curve fit the buck, however, I placed my paper pattern back on the panel, transferred the highlight line along the

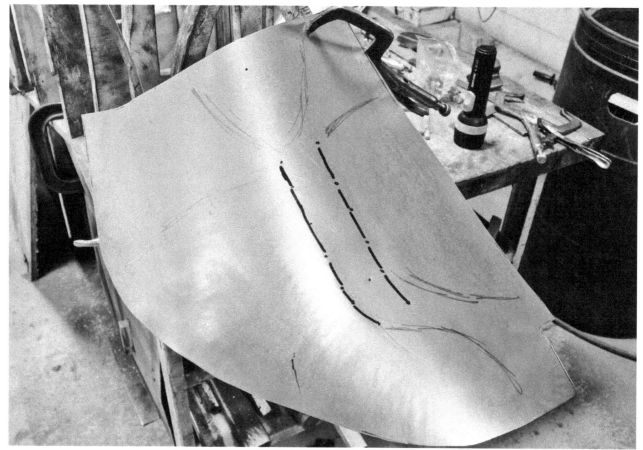

I stretched my blank according to the plan my paper pattern dictated. Early during shaping, however, I determined that I needed to concentrate stretching further toward the curve along the rear beneath the green marker line.

Stretching the metal with linear dies on the highlight marked by orange tape raised the metal there to create more buck clearance. Stretching the metal on the highlight also pushed the metal near my thumb and forefinger down into the saddle shape.

As long as you do not let a panel bind up between the wheels, any wheeling pattern is acceptable for averaging out the shape you have and achieving a nice, even finish. The panel will also be much easier to re-form if needed.

I shrank the rear of the panel more than necessary with thumbnail dies in the Pullmax so that I could stretch it back out to fit the buck with an acceptable finish.

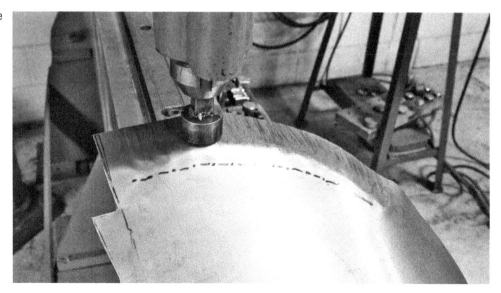

I selected a die for the planishing hammer that perfectly matched the radius of the small highlight line at the bottom rear edge of the fender and smoothed out the marks left by my shrinking.

If you do not have deep shrinking capabilities or you have trouble with a large panel, break it up into smaller pieces. This example is a different interpretation of the Plymouth fender.

rear of the fender to the blank, and began shrinking the end of the panel with small thumbnail shrinking dies in the Pullmax. With such a short flange, I did not bother staggering shrinks at different depths. To adjust the distance between the dies on the Pullmax, I start the machine with plenty of distance between the dies. I bring the lower die up while moving a panel in and out between the dies. As the gap closes between the dies, the shrink becomes more effective and the raised tuck becomes flatter. When the dies are too close, they make a growling sound and the metal looks as if it has been hammered. If you feel your pancreas jiggle, you have gotten the dies too close. Raise the top die immediately and readjust the machine. I tighten the gap, raising the lower die about a quarter to a half turn, until I am happy with the shrink. When the machine growls, back off about a half turn and tighten the lower die holder. I overshrank the rear of the panel to almost 90 degrees and stretched the area back out to "just right" with the planishing hammer. In the absence of shrinking dies,

the rear part of the panel carrying the bead can easily be made from a separate piece welded to the reverse curve panel.

JOINING THE PANELS AND FINISHING THE EDGE

After reaffirming that all the individual panels fit the buck, I clamped them in place two at a time and scribed lines where they overlapped. (Although one additional high crown panel is needed directly forward of the reverse curve panel, describing yet another high crown panel seems redundant.)

I trimmed and filed the panel edges as needed for a perfect fit and tack-welded the panels in pairs on the buck. I TIG welded the seams with 0.023-inch filler to leave small beads requiring very little if any grinding. I removed the hard blue oxide from the weld seams and stretched out the weld areas with the power hammer, though a planishing hammer, wheeling machine, or a hammer and dolly might better fit the area that needs stretching.

Working with pairs of shaped panels, I overlapped one over another, scribed a trim line, cut away the extra metal, and tack-welded them on the buck. Note the shrinking marks on the edge of one panel made to improve the fit. Panels must always be in the same plane for butt welds.

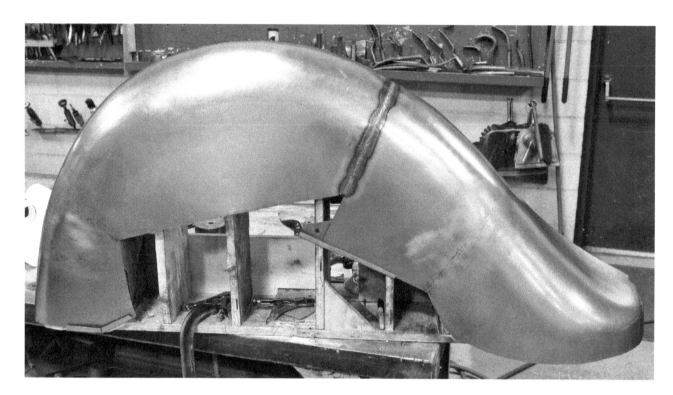

ABOVE: I made a third high crown panel to join the reverse curve to the rest of the fender. Note how the metal is low along the weld seam as a result of welding. Judicious stretching removed the low area.

RIGHT: An accessible weld is easy to stretch out and finish. Thanks to the large contact patch of the power hammer dies, this weld needed very little cleanup.

I was pleased to see that the fender fit the buck after welding. It also fit over the original fender. Even with the bead along the perimeter of the original fender, the new fender fit it so well that I decided to use the original fender rather than the buck to mark the new fender for trimming. I clamped the new fender on top of the original and scribed around the bottom edge with a divider set to ⅜ inch to allow for a wire-wrapped edge. I also marked the metal that makes up two 90-degree flanges along the fender's inner edge.

I used the original fender as a pattern for scribing the finished bottom edge on the new panel. I added ⅜ inch of metal before trimming to wrap a wire along the edge.

Next, I made a mold of the original fender bead out of plastic body filler. I used the mold to aid shaping a simple joggle die for the Pullmax out of ¾-inch hot-rolled square steel stock with a grinder. A bead roller could easily be used to make this sort of bead on a different fender if you have dies that match the original bead. One great benefit of the Pullmax is the ease and speed with which you can make custom dies. I decided to install a 90-degree bend along the fender's outer edge as a guide for the beading dies. I could have guided the panel off its raw edge against a guide on the die or a guide on the machine, or I could have wrapped the wire next and done the bead last. Because I previously demonstrated thinning the metal in the bead roller, this time I thinned the metal ⅜ inch from the edge in the Pullmax. I bent the flange to 90 degrees and shrunk or stretched the metal of the flange as needed until the flange formed a clean arc along the bottom edge of the panel.

For installing the shallow joggle bead, I dragged the flanged side of the panel through the Pullmax dies in one pass. The ⅜-inch 90-degree flange rode along the

Although a bead roller could have been used for this job, I chose this die set in the Pullmax to thin a line ⅜ inch from the edge of the new fender to start a flange for a wire edge.

I bent a ⅜-inch flange for a wavy but usable 90-degree flange along the outer edge of the fender.

Shrinking and stretching with a Lancaster-style tool corrected the flange's unevenness shown in the previous image.

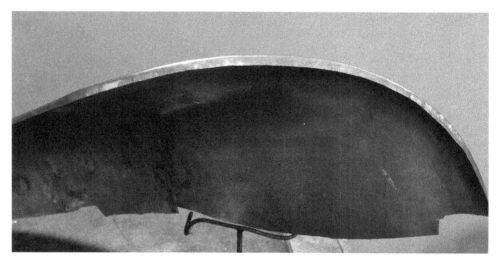

In one pass of the Pullmax I installed the short joggle bead along the edge of the Plymouth fender. I guided the piece against the dies. The long fender did not clear the floor easily, but I knew that bending the fender to fit was a reversible form problem.

The joggle bead along the edge of the fender added stiffness, which made the wire-wrapping process easier. I hammered the ⅜-inch flange into a U shape over a homemade tool.

After securing the wire in the panel edge by hand, I crimped the wire completely using dies I made for the Pullmax.

back of the lower die and made for an effective guide during beading. With the bead complete, I hammered the 90-degree flange to a U shape against a homemade steel dolly I fabricated for this purpose. Moving on to the wire edge, I trapped a length of ⅛-inch-diameter steel rod intermittently by hand with a homemade wire-crimping tool to keep it in place during wrapping. I finished wrapping the wire in the fender edge with a single pass through the Pullmax wire-wrapping dies.

The front of the original Plymouth fender has a strip of 18-gauge steel spot-welded behind the running-board mounting holes. I copied and welded in a facsimile with 3M Weld-Thru primer between the surfaces to prevent corrosion. I used a kick-shrinker to bend and shrink the two 90-degree flanges along the fender's inner edge and deemed the fender complete.

I welded a layer of 18-gauge steel behind the bottom forward end of the fender with 3M Weld-Thru primer between the layers. For best results with any weld-through primer, clamp the painted panels together and grind away with a wire brush the primer from the holes where welding will take place.

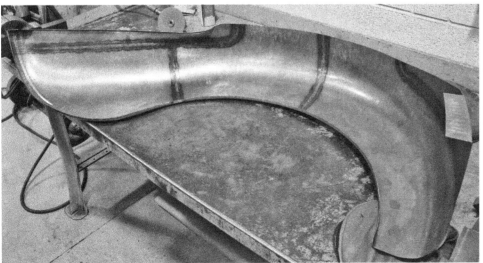

I used a kick-shrinker followed by a hammer and dolly to install the two 90-degree flanges along the inside of the fender. This view of Taylor Adams's fender shows how the 90-degree flanges could be made as separate pieces and welded on. This approach is especially helpful for reducing the depth of thumbnail shrinks needed on the forward-most panel.

Chapter 16
Pourable Foam Buck

When creating something from sheet metal, few of us can conjure anything accurate out of thin air. We need an original object on which to model our work. An *artiste* can claim that whatever they have made mirrors their intent and gives physical form to their inner angst, exhilaration, or ennui. Restorers of old cars, however, do not have this luxury—they must work to a much higher objective standard. Their new piece will look either fantastic—i.e., just like the original—or terrible.

If an original panel is available, one can often build directly on top of it. The duplicate piece ends up slightly larger than the original, but the difference is so small that it does not create any fitment problems. Depending on beads, creases, or other details, you must occasionally make the new panel out of more pieces than you'd like in order to assess the fit of the new panel over the old, but the time involved in welding and finishing weld seams is still far less than the time involved in building a wood station buck.

Building a wood station buck is tedious and often incredibly time-consuming. Although it can take longer than building the piece it fits, station bucks are a proven method of representing car shapes in a three-dimensional manner useful for metal shapers. The skeletal nature of station bucks makes them semitransparent, so you can check your progress during shaping.

A pourable two-part foam buck can be a valuable time-saver for your next metal-shaping project. I cut sections out of this 1934 Plymouth buck to allow viewing from the back during shaping.

For purposes of comparison, here under construction is a student's wood buck of the '34 Plymouth fender in the style of Fay Butler. When complete, the buck will be sturdy and great for viewing work.

In an effort to find an alternative to wood buck building, I tested a new technique using a pourable two-part foam. I credit Eddie Casas of Houston, Texas, for the brilliant idea of using the pourable foam taxidermists use to represent animals. I was describing my hopes and failed experiments one day during a summer class, when Eddie, a hobby taxidermist, quickly emailed me a link to a taxidermist supplier. Previously, I didn't know this two-part pourable foam (or hobby taxidermists) existed.

In retrospect, I am very pleased with the results. The foam effortlessly fills complex shapes that would otherwise be a huge hassle to represent with traditional wood stations. The cured foam is hard—comparable to a fresh apple—but lightweight and easy to sand. For a single use, the foam is fine as is. For greater durability in a classroom setting, I decided to paint this buck with two coats of fiberglass resin. I did not use any reinforcing cloth with the resin because I did not want to add too much thickness and throw off the fit of the fender. Nor did I want to introduce another step in a process that

I wanted to be simple. (In hindsight, however, the two layers of resin *did* interfere with the fit of the fender on the buck.)

BUILDING AN INNER STRUCTURE

I began my foam buck experiment by cutting out a base from ¾-inch plywood that perfectly represented the profile footprint of my '34 Plymouth fender as it sits when mounted on the car, perpendicular to the ground. I traced the wheel opening and cut two identical plywood sides to fill the void occupied by the wheel. Then I screwed a strip of sheet metal across the gap between the sides and checked the fit of the fender in place on the structure. Satisfied with the fit, I secured the fender to the plywood base with screws to prevent shifting during the process. I applied duct tape to all holes and gaps. The tape will not prevent the foam from extruding itself through any opening, but it will keep the uncured foam mix in place long enough to allow it to expand.

This simple wood structure provides a stable base for the foam buck and supports the strip of sheet metal I used to close the open side of the fender.

Mathematicians will delight in calculating the volume of a swoopy fender shape to estimate the amount of foam they will need to mix. Not a believer in math, I guessed how much foam to use by imagining how the size of my fender compared to a mounted deer head. In hindsight, I should've guessed a little closer to an elk, or perhaps a couple of deer heads plus a bobcat. Nevertheless, I was able to fill my buck in two stages. (Fortunately, mounted animal heads were recurring decorative motifs in my parents' house during my youth.)

Next, I laid the buck on its side and rubbed the inside of the fender with a handful of oily paper towels. I should have been more thorough with this step along the beaded edge and on the back of the 90-degree flange along the rear of the fender. After the foam cured, I had some difficulty separating the fender from the foam in these areas because they did not release cleanly along their entire lengths.

Following the supplier's directions, I poured the contents of part A and part B into a plastic bucket and mixed them for precisely 30 seconds with a standard paint-mixing tool chucked in a drill. At this stage, the mixed foam has the appearance and consistency of melted ice cream. I promptly poured the mix into my buck and watched with great interest as the foam expanded to three or four times its original volume. Because I failed to fill the buck completely on the first try, I finished the job a few days later when another batch of foam arrived. The foam takes about 30 minutes to cure.

Once I was sure the foam was hard, I unscrewed the fender from the plywood base and pried it free from the foam with two screwdrivers. The instructions said to use wax on the molds for taxidermy. I used oil because I thought it would be easier to remove from the fender than wax. Had I been more thorough in its application, I believe the oil would have made an effective release agent.

To make the foam buck more useful for metal shaping, I sawed out a few sections with a drywall saw. A hack saw blade with a duct tape handle would also work. Removing sections of the buck intermittently allowed me to assess the fit of the fender on the buck. Honestly, the fit seemed amazing. A few areas along the bead had minor gaps because my slipshod oiling had caused the foam to tear away in places where it had stuck to the fender. This was not a huge crisis, as I sanded away the bead anyhow, knowing it would get in the way during shaping.

I have assembled the pourable foam, a stirring tool to mount in a drill, a plastic bucket, and some rubber gloves. I laid the buck on its side for pouring.

Here is the freshly mixed liquid foam the moment it was poured into the buck.

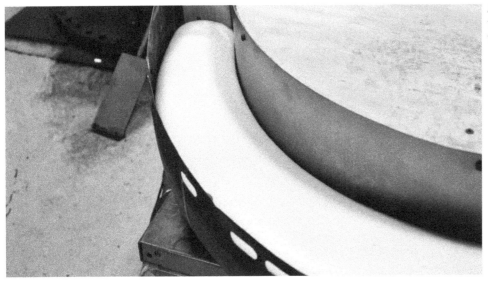

After a few minutes of curing, the foam expanded to three or four times its original volume.

One application of foam was insufficient for this fender. I poured a second batch into the voids left after the first application.

Duct tape provided a satisfactory seal over the various rust and bolt holes in the original fender. Foam still oozed from any available orifice, but the tape slowed the flow long enough that the liquid foam did not drain out excessively.

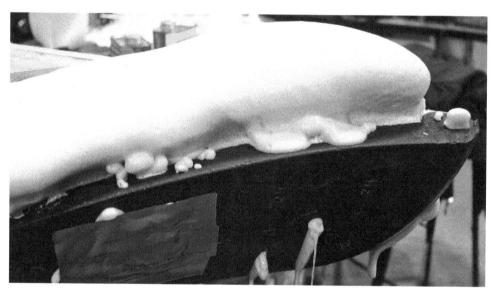

The variegated appearance of the buck reveals where the new foam occupied voids left after the first application of foam. Not surprisingly, the fresh foam adhered perfectly to the old foam.

For a single person, even for multiple builds, this foam buck would be fast to build and fantastic to use. Not knowing how rigorously it would be used in the classroom, I applied two coats of fiberglass resin. Afterward, I discovered that this added just enough thickness to throw off the fit. Carefully removing some of the fiberglass without chewing into the foam was a tedious chore, but I was able to get close to the pre-fiberglass fit eventually with careful spot sanding.

TESTING THE FOAM BUCK

I was especially eager to make this fender's reverse curve on the buck because locating the blank during shaping had proven such a hassle on the wood buck. To provide a method of securing and locating the metal during shaping, I had inset a short section of steel into the foam before I fiberglassed the buck. I drilled the steel strip with two ⅛-inch Cleco holes that corresponded to two holes in the original fender. I made a paper pattern on top of the fender, secured by the two Clecos, to identify shaping patterns and bead locations. I transferred the information from the paper pattern to a steel blank and began shaping. Using the same two Cleco holes, I was able to check the fit of my blank against the buck easily and know that it was in the same place each time. This location method worked beautifully, provided you use two Clecos placed close together in an area that will not see any shape change. Two Clecos are needed to prevent a panel from shifting.

I began stretching the reverse curve panel in the zones that I knew from previous experience would get me headed in the right direction. I was pleased by the

Adding fiberglass resin to the foam buck was a mistake because the extra thickness interfered with the fit of the fender on the buck. I sanded the resin away until I could get the fender to slide into place, but the fit was not as good as before.

ease with which I could view contact between the panel and the buck down low along the rear edge. The goal with this panel was to keep the central strip through which the Clecos pass untouched and stretch most of the surrounding areas in comparison to the untouched area. I was pleasantly surprised by the stiffness of the buck. I noticed between shaping sessions that I could apply pressure to the panel and check the form against the buck with the panel secured in place. By bending the panel against the buck, I assessed its tightness in

RIGHT: I pushed a U-shaped piece of steel into the foam in the middle of the reverse curve at the back of the fender and secured it with fiberglass resin. I used Clecos to attach my steel blank to the buck during shaping.

BELOW: Contrast this paper pattern for the reverse curve with the paper pattern for the same area in the previous chapter. This time around I placed more stretching toward the tail.

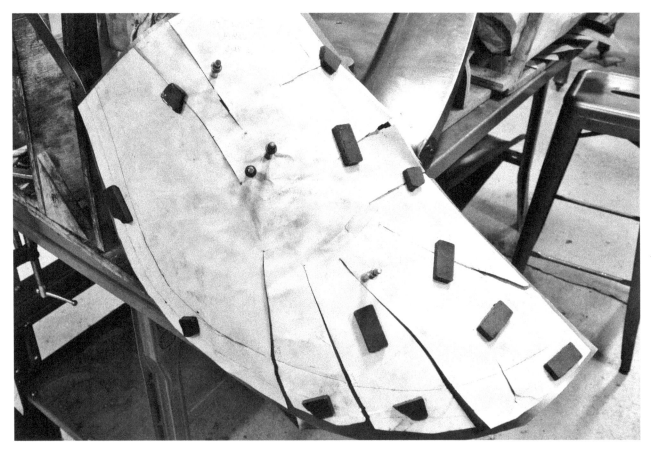

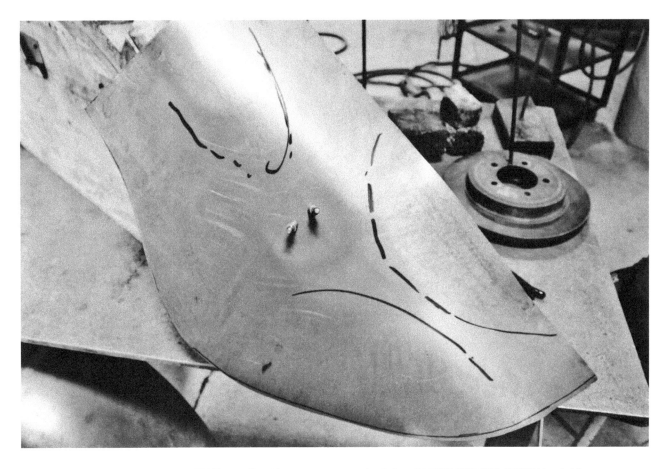

ABOVE: I located the reverse curve portion of the fender with Clecos inserted into a small piece of steel fiberglassed to the buck. This technique worked well. I have also used it on the fender without a buck at all, though one must rely quite a bit on intuition to assess fit without the buck.

LEFT: Visibility through the back of the buck in the troublesome reverse curve area was excellent with the foam buck.

the areas I had been stretching. Tightness indicated more stretching was needed. It is possible to become too overzealous in bending, however, as the small mounting point for my Clecos pulled out of the fiberglass. Luckily, it was easy to glue back in exactly the same place. To be fair to the material, I would never push as hard on a wood buck as I did on the foam one. Bucks are typically shape-checking tools only. In retrospect, the foam buck exceeded my expectations for the reverse curve.

ABOVE: With the foam buck complete, I attached sheet metal pockets to ensure that my paper pattern and the steel blank made from it would fit in only one place. I found the highlight line on the buck—the area with the tightest radius—and taped it off. As in the last chapter, I made a paper pattern to transfer my shrinking plan to my steel.

RIGHT: Partway through the shrinking process I placed the blank on the buck to assess my progress. Although I formed this piece over a little too far, large gaps between the metal and the buck showed up as large loose flaps of extra material when viewed from the outside.

MAKING A HIGH CROWN PANEL

I wanted to make a high crown panel against the foam buck so I could be satisfied I had put it through its paces. Following the example of my metal hero, Fay Butler, I fabricated two sheet metal pockets to locate my metal blank during shaping. Because I had left my foam stations reasonably wide, I was able to find the highlight line along the outside of the fender and mark it off with thin masking tape. With fiberglass still present on this part of the buck, the tape stuck well. Had I not fiberglassed this area, I would have made my paper pattern on the fender itself. Because the bead is fairly tall, patterning over it is mildly annoying; the paper wants to lift on the bead and is thus difficult to locate definitively along its bottom edge. I found that locating my paper pattern against the buck's flat surface was easier than on the fender. Having shaped this piece before, I had a good idea how much shrinking would be needed in the power hammer to make substantial progress quickly. The foam buck does not have the openness of a wood buck, but I did not notice any significant negative ramifications from this condition. If anything, wider stations make it easier to remain blissfully ignorant of small fitment issues that would be revealed in a wood buck. My hunch is that anyone building fenders to a buck will have, or will soon have, a kind of truth-seeking X-ray vision that swiftly identifies all the places he or she has fallen short.

For speed and accuracy, the foam buck is superb. Minus the fiberglass treatment I gave it, the buck took about four hours to construct and fill with two treatments of foam. Perhaps I am slower than most, but I believe an accurate wood buck for the same fender would take me four to five times that to build. As for cost, two applications of foam and the necessary plywood were about $100. A wood buck could be done for about $35. Also, a person would not be able to tack-weld panels together on the foam buck. An experienced metal shaper, who has learned to scribe trim lines and leave witness marks, would likely not consider this a huge obstacle. In addition, I wouldn't recommend attempting to build a foam buck from a nice painted original panel because protecting the paint would be next to impossible. A clean dry-cleaning bag might protect a painted surface without influencing the fit, but I'm only guessing. Because this is the first buck of this type I have built, I cannot speak to which shapes do not work as well as others.

I began shrinking about ½ inch from the origin of the 6-inch-radius band below the highlight line and worked my way out to the edge. I decided how deeply to shrink as I went along based on where the sheet metal rose up above the buck. With the foam buck it was not as easy to assess fit from the back compared to an airy wood buck.

Chapter 17
Louvered Hoods

Louvers are a proven way to enhance airflow. They also happen to be visually appealing. The techniques utilized for two very different louvered hoods—a custom steel hood for a Ford Model T speedster and a polished aluminum hood for a 1913 Cadillac—should prove useful for a number of custom and restoration projects.

LOW-BUCK MODEL T STEEL HOOD

Joe McCullough and Taylor Adams built the Ford hood with the simplest of tools. The only special tooling required was a set of Dave Williams's louver dies from Lowbuck Tools for the bead roller. For people on a tight budget, these dies are a great deal. They will not replicate the perfect quality of an expensive specialized louver press, but they do a fine job for their remarkably low price. My students and I agreed that the handmade look of louvers produced by the Lowbuck dies suited the Ford Model T perfectly.

The dies are made to shear and form the louvers by progressively tightening the rollers together as the panel is rolled back and forth between them. In practice, and with many untrained hands in the mix, we usually cut the slits for the louvers with a $\frac{1}{32}$-inch-wide cutoff wheel. The user must also come up with his or her own way of finishing off the ends of the louvers. I milled two cavities in an aluminum block with a Bridgeport mill to act as a form into which we could hammer the louver ends for a nice finish. Hardwood would have worked as well.

Sadly, the original aluminum hood for this 1913 Cadillac was severely corroded on its ends where steel supports had been riveted behind the aluminum. Luckily, the old hood was complete enough to use as a pattern for this shiny replacement.

The intake side of my students' Model T hood looks exactly like the exhaust side. All exposed edges have been doubled over to improve the rigidity and appearance of the panels. The louvers are a nice touch sure to intimidate the competition.

Dave Williams's Lowbuck louver dies work superbly. We had to add some shims to the shafts of this bead roller for the rollers to fit snugly, but the performance of the dies was not affected.

Joe made a poster board template for the hood blank, cut out the shape, and folded over an extra ⅜ inch of material around all the edges. The procedure for folding the edges involved thinning the metal in the bead roller along the bend line, folding the flange over in the wheeling machine, and running the doubled flange through the wheel again to flatten it. Joe formed the hood to match the curve of the car by pushing on the metal against a length of pipe. Because the engine in this Ford has been fitted with an overhead-valve Chevrolet head, the intake and exhaust sides require a custom hood treatment. The hood's top panel is one large liftoff piece extending about halfway down the engine bay on both sides. Matching oval cutouts reveal two carburetors on one side and a custom exhaust on the other. The bottom portion of the hood on both sides is a fixed louvered panel.

Once Joe formed the main hood panel to his satisfaction, he laid out the location of a half-round bead to correspond with the car's beltline. To minimize the distortion brought about by pressing a deep bead in a flat panel, Joe pre-stretched the bead area in the wheeling machine. To roll a straight bead despite the large oval cutout in the hood side, Joe tack-welded a strip of metal across the opening to run against the guide in the bead roller. He welded a stud in the center of both ends of the main panel to locate it on the car.

Doubling a raw edge over against itself looks professional. Thinning the metal on the bend line ensures that the flange will fold evenly and in the right place.

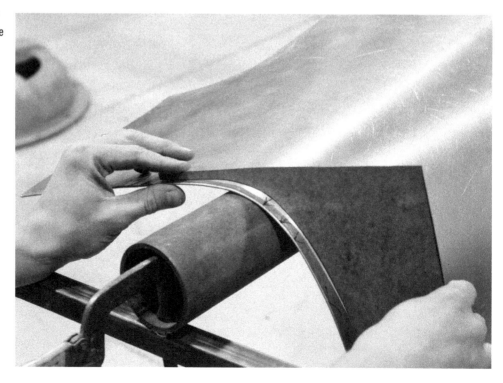

Because the radii at both ends of the hood were different, Joe made poster board templates to guide him as he bent the hood over a piece of pipe.

Joe adopted an unorthodox pose while pre-stretching the bead area of his hood because it would not fit any other way. He gleefully persevered and made a great hood.

Joe tack-welded a length of sheet metal across the half-oval cutouts of his hood panel to give him a continuous straight edge to run along the fence during beading.

Taylor laid out two rows of louvers in each of the two lower hood panels. Whether needed for cooling (as in this instance) or not, louvers greatly enhance the appearance of large expanses of flat metal. Taylor cut all the necessary slits and installed the louvers, counting the number of turns he tightened the dies on the bead roller so that each louver came out the same depth.

Taylor finished the louver ends by hammering them into the aluminum block I machined held in a vise. He finished his contribution to the hood project by fashioning a series of mild steel loops to secure the hood with leather straps. For a great-looking hood that is easy and inexpensive to build, this one is hard to beat.

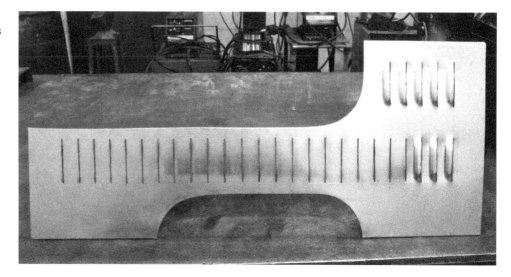

Taylor made hood sides similar to Joe's top panel with the edges folded over. He measured off the louver locations, cut slits, and installed the louvers. Fresh from the rollers, the louver ends are a little vague.

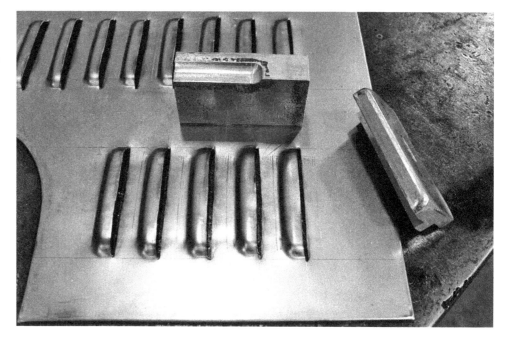

To add crisp symmetry to the louver ends, Taylor mounted the female block in a vise and defined each louver end with the male block.

POLISHING ALUMINUM
IN PREPARATION FOR LOUVERS

Like the T hood, the 1913 Cadillac hood has louvers, but three hinges, a zillion rivets, and a rectangular beaded detail add complexity. In addition, the finished piece is polished aluminum. In a perfect world, I would have started with polished aluminum sheet for this project, but because that material is not available where I buy metal, I had to polish each panel prior to putting in any louvers and details. When the car owner offered to lend me his Cyclo polisher, I looked forward to the project with relish. Since the early 1950s, the Cyclo polisher has been widely favored by anyone faced with

the prospect of enhancing vast expanses of aluminum sheet—namely, airplanes and travel trailers. The Cyclo is a magnificent tool, but it is a little costly for the occasional user. Because I am building an aluminum car body at home, I was eager to put the Cyclo through its paces and see whether I should acquire one for home use. In the end, polishing four hood panels was quite laborious but gratifying work. The beading, edge rolling, louvers, and riveting involved in the construction of this hood are likewise details that recur in the world of old cars.

I began this project by conducting several tests of the Cyclo polisher versus a conventional rotary polisher.

Leather hood straps are essential for a homespun hot rod. Taylor's side panels bolt to the car, but he made steel loops for attaching straps across the top of the hood.

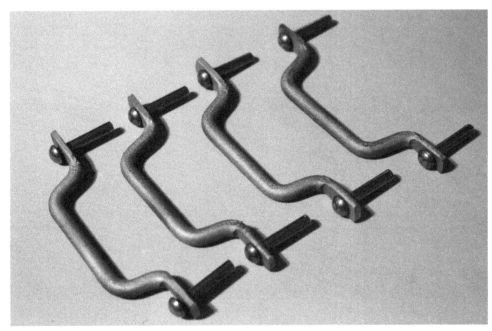

Taylor's finished hood strap buckles will be secured with hot rivets. As with cold rivets, make sure the shaft length past the hole does not exceed one and a half times the rivet shaft diameter. If they are too long, the rivet shafts will mushroom sideways and look terrible. You must heat the entire rivet and set it while it is red-hot.

What is so special about the Cyclo? It has two buffing heads that move simultaneously in random orbits, but its main strength is its ability to take a polished finish as far into the obsessive-compulsive stratosphere as any user will want to go, free of buffing marks. In addition, the Cyclo doesn't snag as easily on rivets or panel edges as a rotary buffer does unless it is held just right. In my opinion, the tool is well balanced, it does not vibrate objectionably, and it leaves the user with the impression that the Cyclo is impossible to misuse. I found the weight of the tool just right—enough to help the work along, but not so heavy that using the tool becomes tiring, unless of course you must work overhead. Its

owner loaned me several grades of polishing compound to use with the Cyclo.

I first tested the Cyclo on a sheet of new, unpolished aluminum with three different grades of Nuvite compound listed here from coarse to very coarse: G6, F7, and F9. As with any brand of compound, the trade-off among grades is always speed of material removal versus clarity of finish. For comparison, I tested a large Bosch handheld rotary buffer turning at 1,950 rpm, which is in the range specified by Nuvite. Not surprisingly, with either tool, two applications of a less aggressive compound seemed to be about equal to one application of the next aggressive compound for material removal.

The enormous diaper beneath the Cyclo is the method the manufacturer recommends for getting the most efficient use from your buffing cloths. They provide clear instructions for rolling up and securing the extra material during buffing.

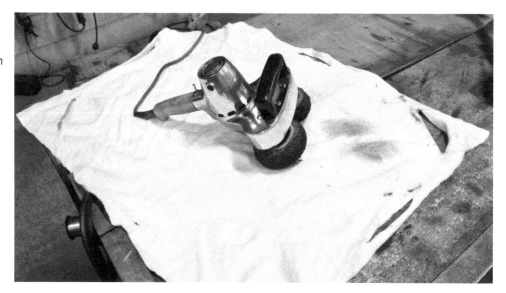

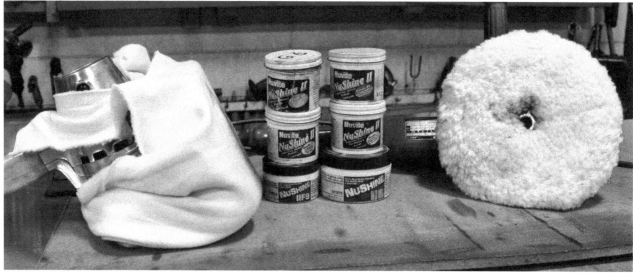

I approached the Cadillac hood determined to find the shortest path to shininess. Ready for use, the Cyclo, at left, looks like a bundle of rags, but works great. The Bosch rotary buffer is at right. A foam camping mat made a good buffing surface.

The rotary buffer, by virtue of its design, cut faster than the Cyclo, though both buffing tools achieved a shiny, supremely reflective surface. Sadly, the process forced me to come to terms with a latent fanaticism I had not previously acknowledged. Groaning audibly, I realized that the grain of the metal was perceptible. If I wanted a truly perfect finish, sanding would be necessary.

Over two days I conducted a series of sanding tests, the thoroughness of which the world has likely never seen. I experimented with combinations of wet sanding by hand and dry sanding with a dual-action sander using grits between 220 and 1,000. The shortest path to success involved sanding with a dual-action sander using 320 followed by 600. I estimated that sanding with the dual-action was about four times faster than sanding by hand. I thought wet sanding was going to be terrific and worth the extra work, but this assumption proved false. After sanding, I used the Bosch rotary buffer with two applications of Nuvite F9, followed by two applications of Nuvite C, followed by one or two applications of Nuvite S with the Cyclo. Some stages involved repetition in spots. When buffing, try to orient the tool so that the spinning head or heads rotate off the edge of panels, rather than into the edges of panels. Doing this once with the rotary buffer makes a lasting impression.

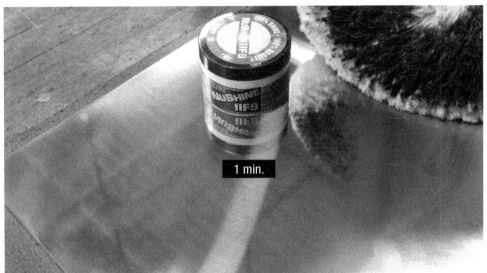

After sanding this panel using a dual-action sander with 320- and 600-grit sandpaper, I buffed for one minute with F9 Nuvite compound to provide some point of reference for the work done per minute of time. The haziness and swirl marks reveal that this compound would have to be followed by something finer, but F9 cuts very fast.

1 min.

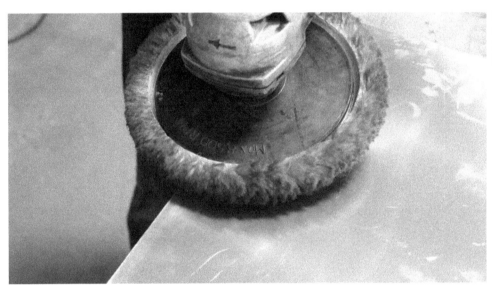

Note the arrow drawn on the top of the tool indicating its rotation. In this image, the buff is rotating harmlessly off the panel edge.

In this case, the buff is rotating into the panel edge, which it is sure to grab, usually with dramatic results. Avoid this scenario.

Forced to buy only one polisher, I would get a rotary tool because it seems able to cut more aggressively on metal that has never been polished, which is what I deal with most often. In addition, the rotary buffer can achieve a nice finish if the user segregates all buffing pads by compound. For surfaces with lots of places to snag a spinning buffing wheel, like this Cadillac hood, the Cyclo is a better choice.

PULLMAX LOUVERS

With my panels polished, I moved on to installing details and louvers. Knowing that I would want as much stiffness as possible before I did the louvers, I began with the rolled edges along the bottoms of the side panels to add stiffness. I used the sheet metal brake to put a ¾-inch-wide 90-degree flange along the bottom of the hood's side panels. Then I fabricated a custom apparatus to hammer the flange over against by welding a ¼-inch-diameter rod to a 3-inch-wide strip of ³⁄₁₆-inch-thick steel. I was careful not to let any of the welds end up proud of the surface, lest they maul the aluminum once I bent it over the ¼-inch rod. I put a thin piece of cardboard between the aluminum and the table and secured the die in place with C-clamps. I hammered the flange over the steel rod with a wood mallet and left no marks. This process gave me a

U-shaped roll along the bottom edge of each lower hood side panel. I still needed to close the U-shaped piece to enclose the roll.

I planned to close the U-shaped flange around a steel rod, but I needed to be able to withdraw the wire afterward, so I welded a bolt onto the end of a length of ¼-inch-diameter steel rod. I coated the wire with grease, crimped the ends by hand to make sure the rod didn't wander out of the U, and then ran the piece through the Pullmax machine using a set of dies I made to close the metal around the wire. The opening between the dies is wider on the insertion side and gets narrower as the metal is passed through the dies. As the panel moves from right to left, the U shape is crimped down around the wire. After crimping one of my panels, I could still rotate the wire by hand, but it was gripped too tightly to pull it out by hand, which I expected. I laid the panel down on a piece of cardboard and C-clamped a block of wood next to one end of the panel to act as an anchor. Next, I attached a slide hammer to the bolt welded to the end of the ¼-inch-diameter rod and smacked it until the rod came out. This worked well, but I was left with the impression that I could have probably done it just as easily by hand. On the second panel, I crimped the wire by hand, which worked even more smoothly than by machine.

I made a tool to assist the transformation of the 90-degree flange into a U shape along the bottom edges of the hood side panels. I hammered the flange against the tool with a wood mallet for a blemish-free finish.

I crimped a U shape around a ¼-inch rod with the Pullmax on one side panel using the wire-closing dies illustrated in Chapter 15. The upper die is wider on the entry side and thus folds the U shape around the wire as the piece is passed from right to left through the dies.

I crimped the second side panel around the wire by hand. I suspect I achieved better results by hand because the wrapped ¼-inch rod was a bit large for the Pullmax dies we use regularly for wrapping ⅛-inch rod, even with the lower die moved back as far as it would go.

Having welded a bolt to the ¼-inch rod before wrapping the aluminum around it, I had recourse to a slide hammer for removing the rod if necessary. I clamped a block of wood to the table for the panel to butt against and was careful to protect the polished surface from being scratched by the table.

Because of the proximity of the louvers to the rectangular beaded detail on the finished panel, I knew the bead had to be installed next or the beading dies would hit the louvers. The correct way to complete the intersecting beads at the corners would have been to make a separate die set with the intersection built into the dies. After conducting a few tests on some scrap pieces, however, I determined that I could run one bead over the end of another and then push out the flattened bead end by hand from the back of the panel with a shaped wooden tool. This technique worked beautifully and saved countless hours because it obviated the need for making another die set that would register perfectly with the beading dies.

I pressed the half-round beaded details in a little deeper than I needed to or should have, with the result that I created a little distortion. If you think about this, it makes perfect sense. Pressing the metal into a raised bead is asking that metal to occupy some plane about 1/8 inch higher than the flat metal. The conventional way to prevent distortion on beaded panels is to stretch the metal in the area of the bead before installing the detail.

Because I had already made a set of dies to match the Cadillac fenders, installing the beaded borders was simply a matter of careful measuring.

Intersecting one beaded detail with another inevitably smashes one bead. I was pleasantly surprised to discover that I could reverse the damage by hammering from the back with a finely crafted wood bonking tool. I supported the work with a shot bag.

I affixed a sheet metal border on both sides of the louver area and cut slits for the louvers with the Pullmax.

The metal seems to look out of shape momentarily, as if you have done something wrong and foolish, but once you install the detail, the extra surface area created by stretching is taken up by the detail and the panel looks perfect. The deeper the detail, the more of a concern pre-stretching becomes. Had I been conservative, I would not have pressed the detail quite so far into the metal and it would have been fine. Alternatively, I could have pre-stretched the areas that would receive the bead with a planishing hammer or wheeling machine. I did not pre-stretch the bead because I was afraid of mauling the surface finish. Because of my greed for bead height, the beaded area of my panels rose up like a low plateau in relation to the surrounding border. I fixed the problem by hammering a clean, flat piece of hardwood down against the border on top of a sturdy wood tabletop.

With the beaded rectangles complete on the side panels, I laid out my louvers with permanent marker in the same locations as on the original hood. I did all my measuring off a centerline rather than the edges. I clamped a length of sheet steel bent at 90 degrees down each long side to act as stops for my cutting die and sheared the slits for the louvers in the Pullmax.

I installed the louvers using a set of louver dies created by one of my students, Matt Goist. Matt made the male side out of trailer hitch ball. He cast the female side out of Kirksite, a hard zinc alloy with a relatively low melting point. He built a sheet metal border around the male die, coated the inside with acetylene soot as a release agent, and poured in the molten Kirksite. (An illustrated description of the process may be found in William Longyard's *Power Hammers*.)

The two hood top panels were very similar to the side panels minus the louvers. They did need to be formed to follow the curve of the radiator and cowl support, however, so, in a sheet metal brake I first bent a ¾-inch flange along the bottom edge of each panel as found on the original. The flange stiffened the panel and helped keep it straight during forming. I taped a large piece of thin cardboard to an empty argon cylinder to prevent scratching and bent the panels to the appropriate curve.

I trimmed the top center hinge to length and temporarily secured it to the top panels with four Clecos per side. Not surprisingly, as far as old cars are concerned, when I checked the fit of the hood on the car, I discovered that the left panel needed to be shifted slightly rearward in relation to the right panel. After correcting the alignment, I welded my incorrect holes and fitted the hood side panels. When I was satisfied with the overall fit, I marked the locations of the hood hold-downs near the frame and made the necessary support panels found on the back of the factory hood.

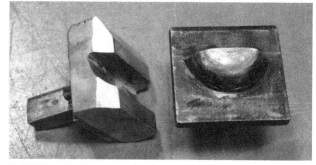

Matt Goist made these louver dies from a trailer hitch ball and cast Kirksite. This die design leaves a softer end than the factory-style Pullmax louver dies, which coin the louver ends.

Dalton Whitfield machined these factory-style louver dies from the dimensions found in Fay Butler's *Universal Sheet Metal Machine Handbook.*

With the slits cut beforehand, I formed the louvers by lowering the top die down over the bottom die while moving the panel laterally between the two.

Fortunately, the new hood side panel looks like a believable replacement for the original behind it.

Riveting together these large polished aluminum panels was a little unnerving. Because all the areas to be riveted were at least two layers thick, there was no way to hammer out serious goofs from the back of the panel without drilling out a lot of rivets. I must have whispered all the right incantations because I only had to drill and replace three rivets out of more than I can count. In those three cases, incantations were replaced by choice expletives that I won't repeat in print. Riveting mishaps occur when a buck slides off the back of a rivet or when a rivet set bounces on a rivet head during setting and leaves a nasty mark. To ensure your success, de-burr both sides of each hole, select the proper drill size for the rivet size, and make sure the shaft length of your rivets does not extend very far beyond one and a half times the rivet shaft diameter past the hole. If the shaft protrudes too far past your sandwich of material (grip length) or is not square on its end, the rivet will certainly be mauled during setting. My favorite resource for riveting is Nick Bonacci's *Aircraft Sheet Metal*. In the unlikely event that you do make a boo-boo setting a rivet, centerpunch the damaged rivet and drill it out. Gingerly separate the remnants of the rivet head from the shaft with a sharp cold chisel and any rivet shards will fall free.

I covered my bending station with poster board to protect the polished surfaces and formed the necessary bend in the hood top panels by hand.

This rivet layout tool from Yardstore in Wichita, Kansas, dramatically speeds the process of laying out rivet holes at measured distances. The tool is graduated so you can check your work at a glance.

A burr around a rivet hole is a recipe for disaster. The rivet will not sit flush and will likely launch either the set or the buck into pristine metal nearby. Punched holes are usually burr free and ready to go. Because I was drilling holes, I deburred both sides of each with a kiss from a countersinking bit.

Ideally, always match the rivet set—the tool in the gun—to the type of rivet head you are setting for maximum contact without mauling. I had to use a universal set on these round-head rivets, but the rivets turned out satisfactory. The rivet buck is the heavy handheld steel block that compresses the rivet from behind by transferring the energy of the rivet gun.

Spring-loaded Cleco fasteners are the only way to keep panels aligned during riveting. They must be matched to the size of the rivet. If you goof while setting a rivet, as I did here, center punch it and drill it out.

For removing tool marks from the tightest areas, such as around the ends of louvers, I mounted a buffing wheel on a 4½-inch electric grinder and was particularly careful of the direction of its rotation.

If you find yourself faced with a large riveting project like this, I encourage you to order a catalog from Yardstore in Wichita, Kansas (www.yardstore.com). Perusing the catalog will make you aware of the staggering array of specialized rivet bucks, rivet sets, and other tool treasures that can make your project go much more smoothly. Over the past seventy years, many crafty men and women have worked diligently to solve countless aircraft riveting problems. The perfect tool you have vaguely sketched out in your mind is probably already sold at Yardstore. You may even dream up new projects just to have an excuse to buy some of their specialized tools.

With my riveting complete, I revisited scratched areas with one of the buffers to recapture the previous luster. At this phase, the Cyclo displayed its forgiving nature on uneven surfaces. Although it is possible to snag a Cyclo buff if you poke it into a louver, in my experience of normal careful buffing, I did not. I polished the tightest areas around the louver ends with a buffing wheel mounted on a 4½-inch electric grinder. Wiping down the freshly buffed surface with a microfiber towel removed all traces of buffing compound and the hood was finished.

Flabbergasted that I did not suffer more riveting mishaps than I did, I polished away any lingering scratches and called the hood done. Although I have always avoided microfiber cloths because I cannot stand the feel of them against my skin, I learned that they are surely the best towel for removing buffing compound.

Chapter 18
MGB "Zagato"

In 1960 Aston Martin sought to improve the competitiveness of their DB4GT by commissioning the Italian coachbuilding firm Zagato to build an even lighter aluminum version. Approximately nineteen examples of the DB4GT Zagato were made between 1961 and 1963, each handmade and distinctive in appearance. These delectable vehicles are widely regarded as some of the most desirable sports cars in history. Although we don't happen to have a DB4GT Zagato for students to work on, the skills needed to build such a body are what we practice every day. In addition, Zagato bodied cars for other British automakers, such as Bristol, so it is conceivable that Zagato could have bodied a car for MG had that firm wanted to do something amazing.

Knowing that I had a pair of MGB front fenders and several hoods, I thought the students would enjoy building an aluminum MGB "Zagato" front clip.

PLANNING FOR WELD SEAMS

I divided the fenders into eight panels each. These could have been done in fewer panels, but I had to consider material costs in the event of mistakes. Because my primary aim was teaching the skills of patterning, shaping, welding, and finishing, practicing a little more of all those skills was a good thing, particularly because aluminum moves around quite a bit during welding. Managing all that distortion made for a rich pedagogical experience.

Don't tell my students, but in my opinion teaching sheet metal is partly transferring information, partly training people to think critically, and partly facilitating enlightenment. Most young whippersnappers today don't realize that amazing cars were once built by hand, often by teenagers.

Dalton began the three-bump hood scoop by kick-shrinking the leading edge of the piece. Shrinking stiffened the panel through work hardening and sped the shaping process. Shape relies on thickness change, so the greater the contrast, the greater the shape.

In hindsight, shaping on top of original panels rather than on a buck worked out spectacularly well and was very time efficient. Had we built a buck, no one would have had a chance to shape any metal that semester. This exercise was also beneficial for making shaping less intimidating. Other than a few flanges on some panel edges and a long reverse curve where the fenders meet the hood, the entire front clip is essentially a collection of low crown panels welded together. After finishing one project like this, students see every car as a series of doable shapes rather than one impossible shape. Because the "Zagato" was not the only project option for students in this class, each could do as many or as few panels as he or she desired.

Knowing that the classic three-bump Zagato hood could set the tone for the entire project, before the semester began I drew out a plausible design on a piece of paper and laid it on the stock MGB hood to determine the right size. By welding a fabricated scoop to the factory aluminum hood, we could avoid the tedious process of making an entire hood with all its understructure and thus get a huge head start on

the project. Dalton Whitfield traced the pattern onto a piece of aluminum and added ⅜ inch of material around the perimeter for butt-welding to the factory hood. He transferred the separations between the 8-inch-wide blisters onto the aluminum in permanent marker, including a 1-inch-wide "no touchy zone" between each blister. Knowing that Dalton has a good eye for shape, I felt a more elaborate buck was unnecessary. Besides, a little asymmetry would be expected on a handmade sports car built by Italian coachbuilders back in the day.

Dalton began shaping with a couple of passes around the leading edge of the scallops in the kick-shrinker. He made one pass about 1 inch deep followed by a second pass about ¾ inch deep. The kick-shrinker rapidly work hardens the metal, thus stiffening it along the front edge of the panel, which helps the panel keep its shape when the area back from the edge is stretched. Dalton did not hesitate to bend the middle bump back out of the way to gain access to the scallops on either side. You should always change the form if doing so gives you better tool access. After all, form is easy to change.

Exercising care to avoid the low areas that would be creases in the finished piece, Dalton used the power hammer to raise the three bumps in the scoop.

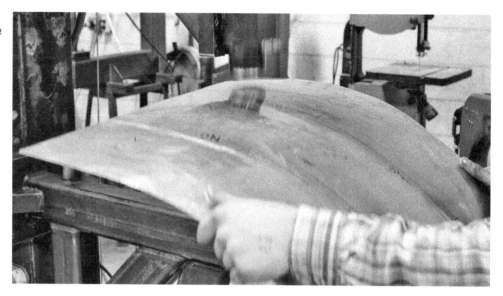

The scoop naturally curled up in response to the stretching just carried out, but Dalton, a burly gridiron star, pressed the scoop almost flat against a table.

Dalton accentuated the creases between the bumps with a custom die shaped like a small Vienna sausage in the power hammer. The rubber die opposite the sausage die formed the aluminum cleanly into a trough without leaving marks.

Dalton then raised the deepest part of each bump with a 4-inch-radius die in the power hammer over the forward-most third of the panel. Swapping the 4-inch die for a 12-inch-radius die, Dalton then raised the second third of the panel and blended it back to the rear edge with a 24-inch-radius die. After stretching, the panel curled up quite a bit from front to back. Knowing that forming the deep creases between the bumps would flatten the panel considerably, Dalton pressed the panel flat by hand as much as possible against a table before returning to the power hammer.

With a rubber bottom die, a custom top die made of a length of ⅜-inch-diameter steel rod, and a length of angle iron bolted to the power hammer as a fence,

Dalton installed the creases as evenly as he could. Because he had done a good job stretching symmetrically, the creases came out symmetrical. Dalton further flattened the panel against a table by pushing down on the creases with a homemade wood chisel. Next, he created a ⅜-inch flange around the perimeter with an old acetylene chuck key with a ⅜-inch cut in its end.

Dalton secured his panel to the original hood with Clecos, carefully scribed a trim line, and then cut a hole out of the hood in two stages. For the first stage, he cut to within about ¼ inch of his trim line with a cutoff wheel. In the second stage, he trimmed to his scribed line by hand with aviation snips. Dalton welded the seam and filed down the welds as needed.

By now the scoop looked good, but it curled too much from front to back. Pushing the creases down against a table with a homemade wooden tool removed the excessive curvature.

To give himself a flange on a flat surface for welding to the stock hood, Dalton folded back a ⅜-inch flange with a custom tool.

With Dalton's hood done, enthusiasts flocked to the front clip like kids around an ice cream truck. The tape lines indicate the panel separations I recommended for prospective volunteers.

Dalton's swank hood was exactly the inspiration his fellow students needed to jump into the project with both feet. Erik Wallace and Cody Beasom each selected the large low crown panel labeled "#1" just behind the front wheel. Their working methods were quite different from each other, yet both pieces turned out beautifully. Erik chose a 12-inch lower anvil wheel with a flat contact patch and added shape by wheeling vertically across the panel. Cody used an 8½-inch-radius anvil wheel and wheeled exclusively longitudinally with lighter pressure. As I like to remind students, shaping is, to a large extent, simply putting a hump in the right place by whatever means.

WORKING AROUND FACTORY DETAILS

Although the factory fender has a weld seam below the joggle detail that runs lengthwise down the side of the fender, we chose to move the weld seam slightly above the joggle. Moving the weld seam allowed the students

making the #1 panels to assess the fit of their work on top of the original piece. Once the fits were deemed correct, the detail could be added to drop the top edges of the panels down into place. Students making the #2 panels directly above them would not be affected. Had we left the weld seam in the factory location, the students making the #2 panels would not have been able to assess the fit of their panels on top of the original fender. The joggle would have interfered and kept their panels from sitting flat.

Once Erik and Cody's #1 panels had enough shape, they added the joggle detail along the top edge in the Pullmax. They could have used a bead roller, but both students wanted to get more experience on this, the most glorious of all Swedish pleasure-inducing appliances. Adding the joggle detail was a good decision at this point for another reason: the joggle helped further stiffen the panel for bending. Erik and Cody formed their panels over a trash can to match the top-to-bottom curvature of the MGB fender.

Erik vertically wheeled the necessary crown into his panel #1 with a 12-inch-radius die. He periodically checked the piece against the fender to avoid overstretching.

Erik attached a guide to his panel rather than using the guide on the machine. The guide rests against the upper die and the joggle happens beyond the guide. When guiding against the machine, the metal gets shorter as the joggle is installed, so accuracy can suffer.

Fortunately, we have several large round plastic bending dies around the metals lab. If a person doesn't mind emptying them in the dumpster, they are ready for use at a moment's notice. Cody put the necessary form into his panel #1 over this one.

Now delirious with metal-shaping fever, Dalton and Cody each executed a #2 panel with surprising speed. Again, their approaches were very different. Dalton smacked his panel a few times with a big mallet into a shot bag and wheeled vertically along the panel with a 12-inch-radius anvil wheel to smooth it out. Cody wheeled his panel longitudinally with the same 8½-inch-radius wheel he used on his previous panel.

REVERSE CURVE PANELS

Panels #3, shallow reverse curves, run along the inner edges of the front fenders where they meet the hood. Xander Lehn and Anthony Johnson tackled these panels.

The best approach to this ubiquitous fender shape is to treat the bottom of the trough that runs down the middle as your flat panel, which needs to be bent longitudinally to whatever degree the fender curves.

Cody shaped his panel #2 by wheeling longitudinally with an 8½-inch-radius die using light pressure. Cody averaged out the resulting shape by bending the piece against an empty gas cylinder.

Cody checked the fit of panel #2 by placing it on the fender and rocking it back and forth. He stretched areas that rubbed until the entire panel fit the fender like a refrigerator magnet.

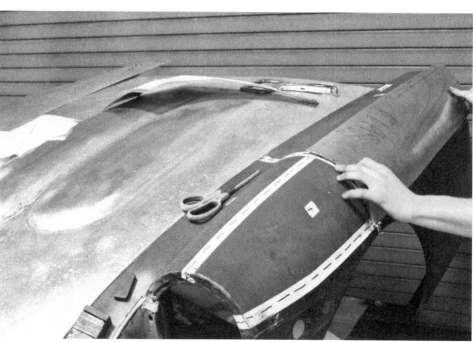

Panel #3, the long subtle reverse curve along the engine bay side at the rear of each fender, required a different treatment from panels #1 and #2. Xander wheeled its edges longitudinally but left the central trough alone.

Xander checked the fit of his panel #3 on the fender. The trough was a little sharp, but the shape looked good. Flipping the panel over and re-forming it against a pipe solved the problem.

Meanwhile, the metal on either side of the trough must be stretched to achieve the greater radius assumed by the higher metal on either side of the trough. Any number of stretching methods will achieve the desired result, but Xander and Anthony both chose to wheel the panels longitudinally along their edges.

While the sides of a long reverse curve need to be stretched, there is a balance to be struck between stretching the sides and forming the trough over a stake or piece of pipe. A common mistake on a long reverse curve panel like this is to crease the trough too sharply from front to back. If the crease is too sharp, the panel will be so stiff that new stretching manifests itself as lettuce along the sides. The longer sides don't generate enough force to bend the panel more lengthwise, so the extra material just becomes flabby excess. The

solution is to soften the crease (annealing may be necessary for aluminum panels) and re-form it over a cylindrical object, keeping in mind the need to bend the piece lengthwise. As the panel gets very close, you may be tempted to hammer into the trough. Resist this temptation or the panel will flatten out or even curve up like a banana. Hammering down into the trough is stretching, that is, adding length in the place where you least want to add length. Remember, shape is always a function of the metal's thickness in one area relative to its thickness somewhere else. The reverse curve demands thinner/longer metal along the edges than in the middle. Both Xander and Anthony learned these lessons on the #3 panels, but both survived to move on to install the flange along the innermost edge of the panel.

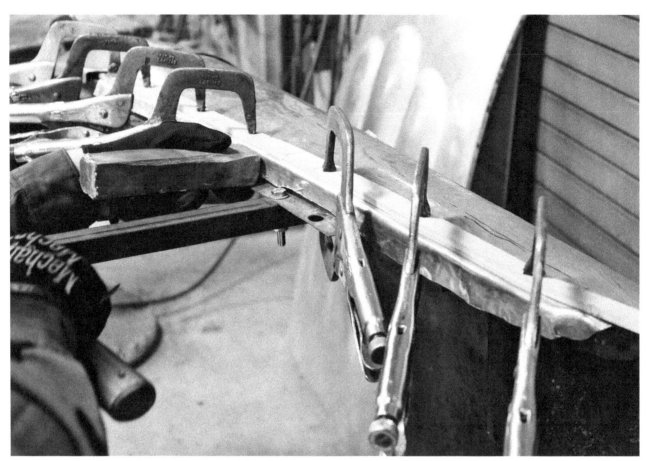

Once he had perfected the fit of panel #3, Xander annealed the flange area and clamped the panel against the fender under a piece of plywood. With the panel restrained, Xander hammered the flange along the fender's inner edge down to 90 degrees with a wooden tool.

If our main goal were strictly building aluminum fenders for this car, the best approach to installing the many flanges found would likely be to weld first and add flanges last. A 90-degree flange is easier to install cleanly across two welded panels if the weld is completed first and filed as needed. The metal will fold over as if it was never welded. Because our goal was to gain as much individual experience as possible, however, I told the students to fold their flanges if they desired so they'd have that learning opportunity. Both Xander and Anthony chose to install the innermost flange on their #3 panels even though this meant a slightly more difficult job of joining them to the adjacent panels.

READY-MADE HAMMER FORMS

One of the delightfully Italianate coachbuilding opportunities provided by the MGB Zagato was the chance to hammer-form panels over a buck. Although Italian coachbuilders commonly used flimsy wire bucks for one-offs and small runs, they used elaborate wood bucks when large production runs justified the labor involved in building them. On these sturdy, more thoroughly developed bucks, details around grilles, drip rails, and fender edges were solid wood or even wood reinforced with steel. As a result, the exterior sheet metal in those areas was literally shaped against the buck with mallets, aluminum-headed hammers, and spoons.

To give students the chance to work in the Italian mode, I suggested they hammer-form their flanges over the buck whenever possible. For Xander and Anthony on the #3 panels, this meant sandwiching the aluminum between a long piece of wood and the fender and hammering the flange over into the drip rail with a wood chisel. There is more to the technique of hammer-forming than one might suspect. Following John Glover's sage advice in *The Practical Sheet Metal Worker*, my students established the bends along the panel lengths by striking the edge of the flange first and then moving from the apex of the bend down with the chisel held at a 45-degree angle to the flange.

HEADLIGHT OPENINGS ON LOW CROWN PANELS

Moving forward on the fenders, the #4 panels reach from the headlight back and join the #2 panels just above the long joggle running down the side of each fender. Panels #4 are in fact a little deeper version of panels #2, with a 90-degree flange on the leading edge for the headlight opening. Dalton and Cody swiftly smacked out two #4 panels by stretching most of the shape into a shot bag with a hammer followed by some wheeling to smooth them out. The 90-degree flange along the headlight opening was installed with a combination of bending and shrinking in the Lancaster-style shrinker and hammering the flange over the fender with a wood mallet.

Panels #6, also low crown panels, join panels #4 along the latters' bottom edges. Brady Carroll and Erik Wallace made two fine examples by shrinking around the perimeter of their blanks with a Lancaster-style shrinker. They next installed the joggle bead along the top edges of the panels with the Pullmax. The flanges along the rear and bottom of the panels were installed by hammering the metal over the fender. We clamped thin plywood to the exterior and I held a steel dolly behind the fenders (a.k.a. hammer forms) during hammering so that the metal would fold over as desired. Without clamping or the extra weight of the dolly, metal will often seek out the path of least resistance, which in this case would mean a soft premature bend back slightly

Dalton made his #4 panel fit perfectly against the fender before moving on to the 90-degree flange at the headlight opening. Numerous small nibbles with the shrinking tool while bending gave him the flange he needed.

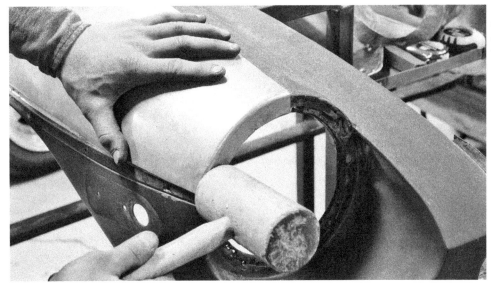

Dalton put the shape in his panel #4 before he installed the flange along the front. Had he put in the flange first, his access to the metal near the flange would have been very limited, making shaping nearly impossible.

from the intended edge, with extra metal manifesting itself in two wrinkles at the edges of the panel.

Inspired by their success on panels #6, Brady and Erik quickly moved on to panels #8, which house the turn lamps immediately beneath the headlights. To facilitate hammer-forming these small but interesting panels, I cut out two pieces of ⅛-inch-thick steel plate to sandwich the students' work in position over the turn lamp recesses. Using wood bonking tools, Brady and Erik worked the annealed aluminum down over the turn lamp features and hammered the necessary flanges into place along the bottom of the panels.

Panels #7, directly above panels #8, comprise the headlight openings. Dalton created one side by bending a 90-degree flange on the rear of the panel in a sheet metal brake and shrinking it to match a cardboard template he made of the headlight opening. After shrinking, the rear of the panel sat flush against the

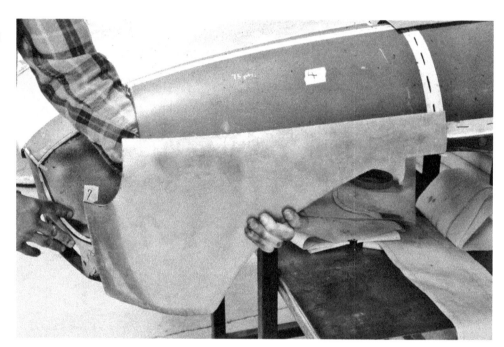

Brady did a lap of shrinking around the perimeter of his panel #6 to induce a low crown. A few passes across the middle with the wheeling machine raised the center of the panel just enough.

Although a bead roller could have done the job, Brady installed the joggle along the top edge of his panel #6 in the Pullmax. He stretched one flange of his "kustom" guide to curve it to fit the panel and earn the admiration of his instructor, as indicated by the red sparkly star sticker.

Erik and Brady hammer-formed the flange on the wheel opening side of panels #1 and #6. We supported the fender during hammering with a heavy dolly directly behind.

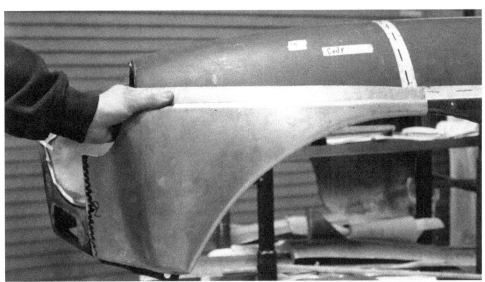

After installing the joggle on his panel #6, Brady placed two or three small shrinks along the curve to account for the reduced radius occupied by the metal on the topside of the joggle. With the wheel opening flange folded over, Brady's piece fit the fender like a decal.

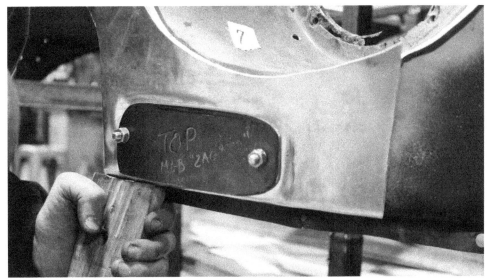

With his annealed sheet metal blank clamped firmly to the fender between two pieces of steel, Brady stretched the aluminum down over the turn lamp protrusion with a wood bonking tool.

If your shrinking tool seems to run out of steam when trying to install a curved flange at 90 degrees, vary the depth of your shrinks and change the angle at which the jaws bite the metal. Inserting the panel between the jaws at a few degrees off perpendicular will keep you moving forward. You can also anneal the flange partway through the job.

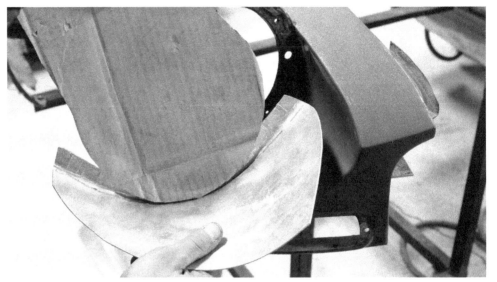

The gap between the aluminum and the headlight pocket indicates that more stretching is needed. The aluminum needs to become longer to occupy the greater radius of the curved opening.

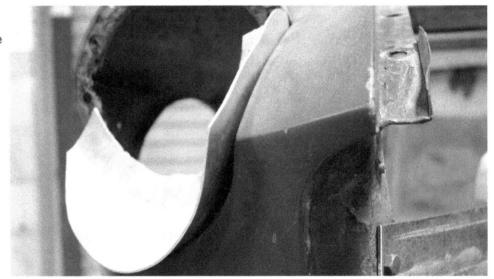

Dalton wheeled the edge of the headlight pocket panel to stretch it. With an almost flat anvil wheel, this motion is analogous to stretching with a linear die in the power hammer.

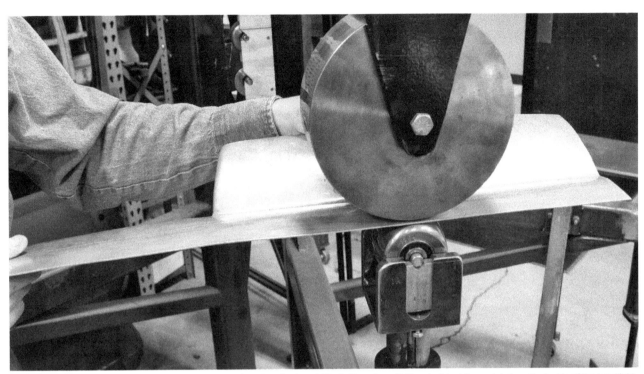

Dalton's thinking was spot-on, but as usual, the cruel taskmaster sheet metal had other plans. Dalton stretched the metal along the inside of the headlight opening to increase the curvature of the panel from front to back. The stiffness of the central crease in the panel frustrated his efforts, however.

fender, but the front edge still had a small gap, revealing that more stretching was needed toward the front. Dalton wheeled the problem area to stretch it and close the gap. Note that on his panel #4 at the top of the headlight opening, Dalton put the shape in the panel before installing the 90-degree flange. Here on #7, he started with the 90-degree flange and then added shape. The need for a crown near the flange bend line in #4 dictated the order of operations. Had he started with the 90-degree flange, Dalton would have been unable to raise the crown very easily so close to the bend.

The last panels, #5, are the reverse curve panels along the engine side of the headlight openings. As with their neighbors, reverse curve panels #3 discussed earlier, panels #5 require a small amount of stretching on either side of the bottom of the trough, or in this case, crease. Even more than panels #3, the crispness of the prominent central bend is a deceptive invitation to install it first. Doing so, however, stiffens the panel too much to realize the benefits of stretching the sides. Now it was Dalton's turn to learn the lesson Xander and Anthony learned on panels #3. Like his classmates, Dalton rebounded, annealed his panel, softened the crease, stretched the upper side of the panel especially, and emerged victorious.

The panels making up each headlight pocket assembly were welded and finished together as a unit. Placing the weld seams near, but not on, the panel edges left the edges pristine.

WELDING AND FINISHING

My students welded the various panels together with TIG, oxyacetylene, or oxyhydrogen torch welding. Because the students' potential employers may be insistent on one welding process or another, I encourage them to become as well versed in as many different forms of welding as they can.

After welding, the students used vixen files to remove any beads that were proud of the parent metal. With the bead flat, they planished the welds further with either the planishing hammer or the wheeling machine, using care not to stretch the weld seams to the point of creating high spots. In general, I remind students that there is no shame in frequently applying a guide coat during weld finishing to make it easier to assess the weld topography. A spray guide coat works, of course, but large-tip permanent markers are sometimes more convenient. Completely finishing the welds involved dual-action sanding with 80-, 150-, 320-, and 600-grit papers. Students interested in finishing their metal to a higher degree followed the rotary buffing ritual outlined for the 1913 Cadillac fenders in Chapter 14.

Erik planished the long weld joining panels #1 and #2 in the planishing hammer. The line of tape protected the metal along the edge of the joggle from being scuffed by the hammer die.

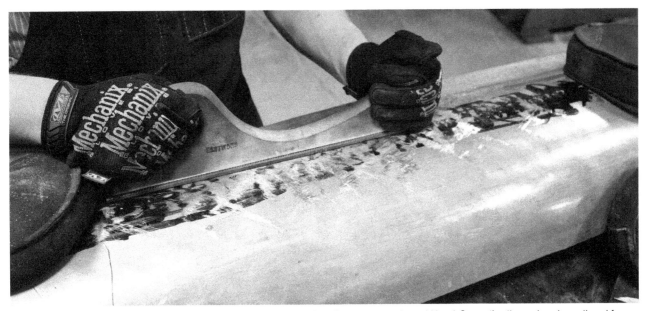

Xander filed the weld joining panels #2 and #3 for the right fender with a vixen file to remove extra weld bead. Supporting the work underneath and from above with lead shot bags held the work stable. The ink was a permanent marker guide coat.

Although panels #2 and #3 were not polished to a mirror finish, only a few minutes of buffing were needed to create a high shine. The weld along the top of this fender is the one Xander was filing in the previous image.

Resources

arc-zone.com. Sellers of fiberglass weld-backing tape.

austinharris.co.uk. Photographic repository of vintage race cars.

Barton, Timothy Paul. *Metalshaping: The Lost Sheet Metal Machines, # 1–4*. Burbank, CA: Autofuturist.org, 2010.

Bonacci, Nick. *Aircraft Sheet Metal*. Englewood, CO: Jeppesen Sanderson, Inc., 1987.

Butler, Fay. *Fender Shaping Book #1*. Wheelwright, MA: Fay Butler Fabrications/Metal Shaping, 2016.

——————. *The Universal Sheet Metal Handbook*. Wheelwright, MA: Fay Butler Fabrications/Metal Shaping, 2007.

Dees, Mark. *The Miller Dynasty: A Technical History of Harry A. Miller, His Associates, and His Successors, 2nd Revised and Expanded Edition*. Motorpark, CA: The Hippodrome Publishing Company, 1994.

Glover, John F. *Practical Sheet Metal Worker*. Marine City, MI: John F. Glover, 2006.

Hoadley, Frederick E. *Automobile Design Techniques and Design Modeling: The Men, the Methods, and the Materials*. Dearborn, MI: TAH Productions, 2002.

Longyard, William H. *Power Hammers: Using the Ultimate Sheet Metal Fabrication Tool*. Stillwater, MN: Wolfgang Publications Inc., 2015.

mckenziesp.com. McKenzie Taxidermy Supply. Source for pourable foam.

mittlerbros.com. Sheet metal tool source.

mtfca.com. Model T Ford forum.

Nawrocki, Casimir. *Any Impossibility in Shaping Metal* . Kearney, NE: Morris Publishing, 2011.

Sargent, Robert L. *Chilton's Mechanic's Handbook, Vol.3: Auto Body Sheet Metal Repair*. Radnor, PA: Chilton Book Company, 1981.

yardstore.com. Sheet metal tool source.

Index

About the Author

Since 2010, Ed Barr has taught sheet metal restoration and the history of automotive design at McPherson College in McPherson, Kansas. Included in *Sports Car Market* magazine's Top 20 Restorers in 2018, Barr has helped to inspire a number of young restoration professionals to find their place in the industry. Prior to joining the faculty at McPherson College, Barr restored British cars at Vintage Restoration Ltd. in Union Bridge, Maryland. Barr hails from Tyler, Texas.